SLAVE AGRICULTURE AND FINANCIAL MARKETS IN ANTEBELLUM AMERICA.

FINANCIAL HISTORY

Series Editor: Robert E. Wright

FORTHCOMING TITLES

SLAVE AGRICULTURE AND FINANCIAL MARKETS IN ANTEBELLUM AMERICA.

THE BANK OF THE UNITED STATES IN MISSISSIPPI, 1831–1852

BY

Richard Holcombe Kilbourne, Jr.

LONDON
PICKERING & CHATTO
2006

Published by Pickering & Chatto (Publishers) Limited
21 Bloomsbury Way, London WC1A 2TH

2252 Ridge Road, Brookfield, Vermont 05036-9704, USA

www.pickeringchatto.com

BRITISH LIBRARY CATALOGUING IN PUBLICATION DATA

Slave agriculture and financial markets in antebellum America : the Bank of the United
States in Mississippi, 1831-1852
   1. Bank of the United States (1816-1836) 2. Finance - Mississippi - History
- 19th century 3. Credit - Mississippi - History - 19th century 4. Banks and
banking - Mississippi - History - 19th century 5. Slavery - Economic aspects
- Mississippi - History - 19th century
   I. Kilbourne, Richard Holcombe
   332'.09762'09034

ISBN-10: 1-85196-890-3
ISBN-13: 978-1-85196-890-9

Typeset by Pickering & Chatto (Publishers) Limited
Printed in the United Kingdom at the University Press, Cambridge

CONTENTS

'I have read your speech about abolition with great pleasure. It is deplorable to see our people adopting with equal servility the latest English fashions of philanthrophy & dress.'

Nicholas Biddle to Charles J. Ingersoll, June 28, 1841

'I can hardly believe the "Union Meetings" can have the effect of quieting the excitement in the South-They are at most & at best, but an empty show and can have but little effect so long as the ballot Box tells a different tale.

So long as the free soil feeling was confined to the prevention of slavery in Territories now free-the South was divided in opinion & feeling. But now when there is too much ground to believe the intention is,-not only to interfere with slavery in the States, but to lock it up by all means-destroy the welfare of the whites, the whole South, is prepared to act, in resistance, to say nothing of the Harpers Ferry affair-of which-probably too much has already been said, there is that damning-& damnable-recommendation of the "Helper book."-signed by your governor, by an ex-supreme Judge of your courts-by eminent [?] by the uppity aristocracy, of all your cities & large towns-and by 67 members of Congress which by itself is calculated to make every man owning slave property-a true Souther in felling & action, and you may rest assured-the whole South will be united in opposition to the North, the whole North-Whenever mere abstract rights were threatened-there was no unanimity & sentiment, in action, in the South. But when our real tangible right: are not only threatened in the worst shape, but absolutely invaded-there will-be-can be-but one sentiment- I myself have always favored a conciliatory view, I can do so no longer- And unless I can see better evidence of a change of feeling in the North-than I can now see, I will say-farewell, a long farewell- to the North-I will never again visit it & never again hold commercial intercourse with it.'

Steven Duncan to C. P. Leverich, December 22, 1859

INTRODUCTION

This study began as a consequence of a number of fortuitous events. I had only recently completed a manuscript on the role of slave property in the antebellum credit system. A necessary condition for understanding that subject was gaining a knowledge of local and regional credit markets, and the instruments antebellum planters and their agents had used to hedge their exposure to various risks inherent in producing staples for very distant markets. At a time when the institution of credit seems to have become detached from the underlying economy because of the mammoth role government plays in underwriting our fiat monetary regime, as well as sponsoring credit subsidies for various activities which are deemed to be worthwhile pursuits by society, such as encouraging home ownership, it is easy to lose sight of the fact that the institution of credit initially evolved as a risk spreading mechanism. The institution of credit arose from the same economic environment which gave birth to the modern insurance industry.

I, like most financial historians, had focused initially on chartered banking corporations and like others had assumed that chartered banks played a role in the antebellum financial system which roughly corresponded to the role commercial banks play today. It was only after I began to unravel antebellum credit relations, a task greatly aided by the bankruptcy of antebellum slave agriculture and the consequent exposure of thousands of relationships in collection suit records, that I came to realize that chartered banks had functioned principally as 'amplifiers' in a complex network of slave planters and their commercial agents.

It was a disappointment to discover that nowhere had even a partial set of business records for one antebellum commercial agency survived into the late twentieth century. Indeed, nearly all of the evidence which documented that commercial agencies or factorage firms had ever existed was to be found in collections of plantation records. Law suit records provided an important supplement, especially estate proceedings wherein inventories often listed the assets and liabilities of a defunct factorage firm. None of these sources, however, came close to providing what I believed a set of business records would

1

no doubt yield as an aid for understanding how slave planters mediated their risks and extracted maximum concessions from buyers of their staples in faraway markets.

While searching inventories of manuscript collections in various locales, which might illuminate the precise technicalities of risk spreading among planters, factors and chartered banks, I found myself digging a very deep hole in a collection whose existence has been known about for many decades. The collection, which is located at the Louisiana and Lower Mississippi Valley Collections at Louisiana State University in Baton Rouge, is identified simply as the 'Bank of the United States, Natchez Branch'. A huge body of material which had come to the archive in the 1930s, its inventory had been prepared shortly after its arrival. In the midst of trying to understand how and for what purposes entries would have been made in various ledgers, discount books, and 'bill ticklers', it became necessary to assemble the entire collection in one room and prepare a new inventory. This undertaking would have been impossible without the committed support of the staff of the library. Over a period of days, it soon became clear that the collection was even larger than originally had been supposed. Not only were the records of Natchez Branch of the Second Bank of the United States present in the collection, but also the records of the commercial agency of the United States Bank of Pennsylvania which operated in Mississippi from 1836 to 1841. Perhaps the most important undiscovered treasure, though, were the records of the collection agent sent to Natchez in 1841 by the assignees of the failed United States Bank of Pennsylvania. These records span the critical period from 1841 to 1852 and include not only the usual account books, but also the agent's voluminous letter press books

The letter press books yielded information about the problems encountered by the United States Bank of Pennsylvania in the immediate aftermath of its being chartered by the Pennsylvania legislature to receive most of the assets and liabilities of the defunct Second Bank of the United States. As the agent set about collecting upwards of four million dollars in claims against debtors resident in the state of Mississippi, he wrote to his principals in Philadelphia several times a week. A number of very large claims could only be settled by receiving whole plantations, together with slaves. Before the close of the 1840s, the assignees of the failed United States Bank of Pennsylvania had emerged as one of the larger slaveholders in the state and their agent was remitting to them large sums realized from the sale of staples produced on those plantations. As fate would have it, one of the trustees was an opponent of slavery; so, the agent, along with the other principals, elected to keep him in the dark about the extent of their involvement in slave agriculture. Not only did the assignees receive income from slave agriculture, but their agent also trafficked in slaves, selling and hiring them out when prudent, responding to local market conditions.

The exertions of the agent and his lawyers to realize the claims against Mississippi planters and commercial agents, for the failed banks' assignees, bring into sharp focus the critical importance of slave agriculture in the formation of the United States' economy in the antebellum decades. Of all the assets assigned by the Board of Directors of the United States Bank to the trusts established for the benefit of the holders of the failed bank's circulation, none were as productive, or as sound, as the claims against slave agriculture in the lower Mississippi Valley. And without those claims, the failed bank's circulation would never have been redeemed.

It is perhaps ironic that virtually all of the funds realized at Philadelphia in the immediate aftermath of closing up of the Second Bank of the United States, had been deployed under Nicholas Biddle's not so able leadership in improvement companies for building canals and railroads. The stocks in these companies were also assigned to the trusts, and virtually all of those claims turned out to be worthless.

The Bank of the United States Collection presents us with a remarkably full picture of banking operations in the early decades of the nineteenth century. More important perhaps is the information it yields about the history of the Second Bank of the United States in the aftermath of Andrew Jackson's veto of its recharter in 1832. The Board of Directors of the Natchez Branch, following strict instructions from the Philadelphia parent, set about curtailing discount lines and purchasing only bills payable at short date in Eastern seaboard cities. Soon enough it became clear that the likelihood of realizing from a single growing season, even a portion of the bank's capital, which was deployed at Natchez, was an impossibility. The credit facilities available locally, at New Orleans, and elsewhere, simply were inadequate for permitting those who had discounted paper at the branch to move their loans to other banks or lenders.

The historiography has not fully appreciated the immense difficulties which accompanied a 'closing up' of the Second Banks' affairs at its many disparate locations across the United States. Those who had supported the bank's re-charter complained bitterly that its withdrawal from the nation's money markets opened the way for waves of speculation and the chartering of poorly capitalized state banks which expanded their portfolios and their circulation well beyond the limits of what prudence would have dictated. But in truth, chartering a plethora of new banks by state legislatures was the only rational response to the Second Bank's imminent cessation of operations. Private capitalists were few in number and possessed only a narrow means to facilitate locally, liquidations at branch locations. Closing the bank, under optimal conditions, would have required opening up large and highly liquid credit facilities at locations along the Eastern seaboard. The bank's operations in the country's money markets had simply dwarfed what remained after its final exit in 1836.

State legislatures chartered new banks, and some of these institutions were able to market their securities to investors in Philadelphia, New York and Europe. The sale of their stocks and bonds did provide a measure of liquidity for the local markets.   Conditions became so stringent in 1834 at some locations along the Mississippi River, that the only available paper suitable for remittance to points East were bills drawn by the newly chartered banks, checking on credit facilities which had been created at places where they had been able to market their stocks and bonds.

The empirical data, such as it is, suggests that overall more than enough new banking facilities had been opened in the country to fill the void left by the exit of the Bank of the United States. The combined authorized circulation of all of these institutions should have more than offset the withdrawal of the national bank from the money markets. But in truth, what we glean from the empirical data must lead us to the wrong conclusion; i.e. that state banks opened their discount lines with abandon and flooded the nation's marketplace with worthless paper. As will be seen, in the lower Mississippi Valley at least, the newly chartered state banks never obtained a 'circulation' in the parlance of the time. Their paper, for the most part, never obtained the negotiable character of what might be called money, or a money substitute. Their portfolios seemed to bulge with loans, but in truth many of those loans were nothing more than bills receivable taken in settlement of bills of exchange which had fallen under protest during their first months of operation. Their obligations were not suitable for remittance purposes to distant locations in settlement of claims.

It is perhaps a testament to the success of the Bank of the United States that nothing emerged to take its place in the immediate aftermath of Jackson's veto of its re-charter.. Indeed, over the course of the previous decade the national bank had shaped the course of exchanges within the country and dominated the traffic in foreign bills as well. It could and did press its paper on any and all locations in the country. If pressures developed at any location in its national system, it easily relieved those pressures by creating drawing facilities on another location, thus injecting instantaneous liquidity at a location where it was needed. No state bank, or group of state banks, would ever realize such remarkable powers for creating and sustaining a circulation, at least for the remainder of the antebellum decades.

Ultimate blame for the monetary chaos which followed in the wake of Andrew Jackson's veto must, however, be laid at the door of the parent bank in Chestnut Street. It is no coincidence that during the bank's last decade of life, the federal government suddenly found itself with the means to liquidate the entire national debt. The accumulated claims from the Revolutionary War, the War of 1812, the Louisiana Purchase, and sundry other huge expenditures by the government, under normal conditions, might have taken decades longer to retire. But thanks to the high powered money which sloshed around the national bank's network of branches, a speculation arose in western lands. The government sold vast amounts of land, thanks to the abundant credit provided by the bank and its branches. While the form of the loans being made caused them to appear to be highly liquid self-liquidating ones, in truth, by 1832, each branch had acquired a portfolio of permanent accommodation loans, guaranteed by nothing but endorsements.

The bank's enemies regarded it as a leviathan which made and unmade political fortunes and corrupted everyone it ever touched. There is scant evidence that the bank ever attempted to overwhelm the political process, though in the months preceding the Congressional re-charter, the discount lines did expand, ostensibly to facilitate the liquidation of the federal government's debt in Europe by marshaling the supply of foreign bills at points East to raise the needful. Thus, the bank was able to relieve the pressure on the domestic exchanges by offsetting its demand for foreign bills with an abundance of discounts at home.

In the decade preceding its 1832 Congressional re-charter, the Bank of the United States so enhanced liquidity levels around the nation, that it may be said to have unwittingly promoted an inflationary bias in the realm of monetary policy. Still, one is immediately struck by the relative rarity of specie either paid out or tendered at the branch in Natchez. How much that inflationary bias fed real economic growth and how much it stimulated the national propensity to leverage and speculate will probably never be known. Perhaps the best indicator, though, is the trade deficit which rose in most years preceding the 1837 Panic.

Whatever ambivalence many Americans may have felt for the Bank of the United States, Europeans invested a great deal of trust and money in the country because of the institution's reputation in the money markets of London and Paris. The willingness of foreigners to invest ever larger sums in American improvement companies, banks, and state government bonds, kept the insalubrious consequences of a rising trade deficit in check; at least temporarily.

It does seem clear that Nicholas Biddle and the directors of the parent bank at Philadelphia concluded sometime between Andrew Jackson's veto in 1832 and their application to the Pennsylvania legislature for a state bank charter in 1836, that liquidating the portfolios at the branches and realizing the proceeds in money which could then be distributed to the shareholders, was a complete impossibility. Initial attempts to shrink the more-or-less permanent discount lines at the branches with sight bills on locations in the east, resulted almost immediately in a great deal of domestic exchange falling under protest, and considerable embarrassment for drawees in cities up and down the eastern seaboard..

At Natchez at least, the branch sold the exchange which had fallen under protest, to the newly chartered Planters Bank of Mississippi. But the sale had to be made on a long credit which meant that little money was realized for the parent bank at Philadelphia. The initial reduction of the permanent discounts, then, had met with failure. And the national bank had been forced to increase its circulation because so many bills on the East had been dishonored and the bank was left without the means to retire even a portion of its circulation.

One can only imagine the consternation which must have prevailed as the board of the parent bank met to consider what options were available to prevent a fire sale of assets in order to raise the means to meet the bank's liabilities; namely its circulation, in the form of demands notes and checks. A good portion of the shareholders' capital would be lost if the bank had to continue meeting tenders of its circulation without its first having been provided with the means from the liquidation of its assets at the branches. Once the charter had expired, there would be no possibility of emitting any more circulation in order to buy time while the assets at the branches were being slowly liquidated.

So, it is highly probable that the inspiration for a state chartered bank, which could receive all the assets and liabilities of the old Second Bank of the United States, was born from necessity. Obtaining a new charter from the Pennsylvania state legislature turned out to be a very expensive proposition as will be seen; moreover, the federal government's stock in the bank had to be liquidated, no matter the sacrifices. From the beginning of its life, the United States Bank of Pennsylvania was crippled by heavy calls on its most liquid assets. Even though the new institution attempted to perpetuate the national character of the old bank by contracting agencies at the western branches which were contracted to buy exchange for its account on the East and on Europe, there was no possibility of continuing a circulation which would float throughout the nation. The new institution, then, was a pale imitation of its predecessor. The loss of a national circulation was also a huge blow because it meant that the new institution was little more than a localized state bank, although by far the biggest one in the country. It simply dwarfed every other banking company and was many times the size of all the other banks in Philadelphia and New York.

A national circulation had been one of the Bank of the United States' profit centers. A national circulation also had been its chief support, not only for profits but for dispersing risks throughout the country whenever pressures developed within the national system. During the life of the Bank of the United Sates, its paper was received by all offices of the federal government as legal tender, thus creating an instant demand for its obligations. Similarly, when a government agent drew a bill in favor of a payee, he drew it on an account at the Bank of the United States.

During the bank's lifetime, the nation had for all practical purposes, a national circulation; a condition which would not prevail again until the twentieth century. The bank had spawned the first true fiat monetary regime in the nation's history, and this in no small measure explains the difficulties which its management encountered when they tried to convert permanent accommodation lines at the branches into ready money. Once the bank disappeared from many disparate locations, credit conditions in each locale became localized. The capacity of a state bank in New Orleans, for example, to press its paper on markets far removed from it, simply wasn't there. And it is here that we can see immediately a vast difference between the note issues of a state bank or group of state banks and the notes emitted by the Bank of the United States.

Were one to aggregate the circulation of all the state banks in the nation in 1837, one would immediately see that the overall circulation had indeed increased dramatically from levels which had prevailed during the lifetime of the Bank of the United States. As previously noted, the reported amount of circulation at various locales around the country is misleading because so much domestic exchange had fallen under protest the previous year and as a consequence, the orderly retirement and reissue of bank notes had been interrupted. This, I believe, explains the monetary inflation which seems to have occurred in the two years preceding the Panic of 1837. But an examination of conditions at Natchez, which is possible because of the availability of the records of the United States Bank's agency there, together with a relatively complete collection of records for the Commercial Bank of Natchez, suggests that the credit system was already in liquidation mode, two years before the general bank suspension in the spring of 1837. The circulation was indeed augmenting, but it was augmenting because banks could not meet their own obligations timely when tendered.

Since so much of the currency of the nation's state banks in 1837 was already 'uncurrent', the seeming paradox of how the circulation could have expanded even as the credit system was contracting, is resolved. We may say, then, that the circulation of the Bank of the United States was simply more powerful as a money substitute than any circulation of a state bank or banks which obtained in the aftermath of Andrew Jackson's veto. All of which places a very different complexion on what people thought they were seeing after the Second Bank's charter expired, i.e. the proliferation of state chartered banks and the over issuance of notes, and what really was happening in various localized money markets around the country

The records of the Natchez branch and the commercial agency of the United States Bank in that city, indicate that credit facilities there were contracting from 1834 onwards. This fact has important implications for understanding the origins of the Panic in April of 1837 and whether events abroad, such as the Bank of England's raising its discount rate in 1836, contributed to the pressures which led to the national suspension. As more-or-less permanent credit facilities were closed in locales around the country, those in search of credit had to resort to short term bills on other locations to meet their borrowing needs.

Not only were debtors being required to liquidate their 'permanent' discounts, but there simply were no lenders in most marketplaces who could accommodate them with permanent lines of credit.

There is no doubt that the volume of bills offered for sale in the exchange markets nationally swelled considerably in the years after 1832. As permanent accommodations disappeared in places like Natchez, credit mediators necessarily sold bills on correspondents in other cities to meet their requirements. Initially the stress was greatest at points along the Mississippi River, places where the Bank of the United States had been especially important and more or less dominant in the local markets. The discount line at Natchez was larger than the branch's discount line at Boston, for example. But as commercial agents in Natchez and St. Louis and New Orleans tried to support their credit and that of their clients, they resorted to drawing on their correspondents in New York, Boston, Philadelphia, and even London. In such an environment, it was very easy for arrearages to begin accruing, as drawers in the West fell into debt to their correspondents in the East. Increasingly, bills from points west began to fall under protest and as they were returned to remitters in places like Natchez, the holders had no choice but to receive a highly illiquid long dated bill receivable in settlement. And so credit facilities in that locale became even more strained and paper suitable for remittance became unavailable.

The market for sterling exchange was turned upside down when the Bank of the United States stopped buying altogether in 1833. In prior years the bank had virtually made the market for sterling bills and foreign bills generally. It had been able to set the price and reduce the premium such bills commanded when little paper was offered for sale. For the first time ever, sterling bills fell to a discount in New Orleans and New York. The situation only reversed itself the following year when the Bank of the United States returned to the market as a big buyer.

By 1834, even the foreign exchanges were being called upon to shoulder some of the burden of liquifying the domestic exchange markets. So, eventually the pressure in the western cities was communicated to London. London might have supplied the needful, but already the money market there was spooked by events abroad. Even more troubling was the Bank of England's declining specie reserves; a clear indication of disquiet and distrust in the money market.. Financial historians have studied this phenomenon with much attention to the details of the Bank of England's specie crisis and the consequent raising of the discount rate in response to the drain. They have observed that specie was not being exported abroad as contemporaries had generally assumed was the case. But here the investigation of what happened to the specie, which was drawn for, has stopped. Several hypotheticals present themselves. The specie drain simply reflected the activities of speculators, betting that the Old Lady of Threadneedle Street would be forced to suspend. But the bulk of the specie drain probably resulted from the actions of commercial agents in the City, dutifully protecting their clients whose money they managed. Currency debasement didn't excuse them from returning to their depositors, an equivalent in specie if called upon to do so. And since London was an international money market, these same agents would have held large sums for foreign clients as well, clients who could [and no doubt did] demand that their own bills be honored in specie when presented for payment by a third party holder.

By 1836, the principal merchant banks which had financed the Anglo-American trade in preceding decades were in trouble. Four of the six largest firms failed outright and were liquidated for the benefit of the Bank of England. The liquidations continued for more than a decade. All the firms had conducted extensive underwriting operations for American securities which had been offered for sale in the London market. Purchasers of foreign bills in the United States, bills which had been drawn against sale proceeds from securities and staples, were overwhelmed with waves of protested bills, returned to them when the drawees were forced into liquidation.

Long before the general suspension in 1837, the credit system had already moved toward contraction. The anecdotal evidence indicates that specie redemption by the banks of their circulation, when tendered, was at best nominal. So, as long as a year before every bank in the country was forced to suspend, deterioration in the credit system was clearly observable. And once the banks everywhere suspended, liquidation of discount lines commenced in earnest. Suspension brought no relief. The banks saw their circulation become an object of speculation as debtors with the wherewithal paid their debts in depreciating bank notes. Only if a bank were able to start redeeming in specie, could it hope to preserve the value of its paper and its shareholders capital.

Most bank charters provided for a forfeiture of the charter in the event the bank suspended. State legislatures attempted to alleviate the hardships by authorizing temporary suspensions, but market forces overwhelmed such stopgap measures. As bank notes depreciated, assets in the form of loans also declined in value. So, it is little wonder that in the two years after 1837 banks pressed their clients to liquidate their debts and steadily reduced their discount lines. Most banks in the East resumed paying specie, at least nominally, in 1839. The banks of Mississippi never really did resume and resumption at New Orleans was tentative at best.

A second bank suspension commenced in 1841. The United States Bank of Pennsylvania was at the epicenter of the crisis. Its collapse took all of the banks of Philadelphia with it, and most of the banks in the South and West followed in its wake. One historian of the bank has said that its difficulties sprang from its heavy concentration of resources in places like Natchez, rather than diversifying its resources in manufacturing and enterprises closer to home. But in this instance, Nicholas Biddle's reasoning was sound and it made perfectly good sense. Southern staples provided most of the nation's foreign exchange earnings. As Peter Temin, and others have observed, the condition and size of the nation's money stocks in the antebellum decades depended heavily on sterling exchange; that is, a capability for realizing funds in sterling. With sterling bills in hand, the world's marketplace was accessible. And the nation's principal source of foreign exchange were the sterling bills drawn against consignments of staples like cotton and sugar, exported from southern ports. Slave plantations greatly enhanced the nation's monetary system as a whole, because they were the engines which generated most of the nation's foreign exchange earnings. No other economic enterprise of the time came close to them in importance.

Shortly before the Natchez branch of the Bank of the United States opened, Biddle had been questioned about the desirability and necessity of opening a branch and that city. He answered that no place in the world were there more rich proprietors so concentrated as in Mississippi. He might well have added that at no location in the United States was the potential greater for generating foreign exchange, the lifeblood of the American financial system. More than twenty years after his death, as the nation was plunged into civil war, realities had changed only slightly. Exports of southern staples still provided the bulk of the nation's foreign exchange earnings and sustained the underpinnings of its financial system. How important those earnings were, still, can be seen in the premium paid for sterling bills in the New York money market in 1863. It had risen from one or two percent in 1860 to nearly four hundred percent a few years later.

EXCHANGE AND MONEY MARKETS

The so-called 'Bank War' between Andrew Jackson and Nicholas Biddle, a contest in which both protagonists would have cast themselves as 'David' to the other's 'Goliath', is a central event in antebellum America's political historiography. Political and economic historians have scratched over the remains and rendered rather precisely the implications of that contest for the nation's political and economic fortunes in the nineteenth century. A picture has emerged of a powerful chief executive who for reasons that are less than clear made the bank's re-charter and his subsequent veto of the bill extending the life of the 'Monster bank' the pivotal issue in his reelection campaign in 1832. Depictions of the bank as a giant engine of political devilment were not, however, altogether absurd or unjustified.[1]

The bank met its fate at the hands of a strong-willed chief executive whose veto was sustained as much by party loyalty and discipline as any negative assessment of the bank's value to the country. Jackson's political opponents, Henry Clay and Daniel Webster, both had a hand in making the bank and its re-charter in 1832 a critical election issue, and both were no doubt delighted when the President handed them a veto message. In every way Nicholas Biddle was naïve for allowing the fate of the bank to become hopelessly linked to the fortunes of his mentors, Henry Clay and Daniel Webster. They as well as the incumbent President made the bank a campaign issue.[2]

The bank's friends and enemies did tend to divide along sectional lines, but this had as much to do with the geographical location of Democratic constituencies as any regional predisposition to favor or oppose the bank. True, southern delegations voted heavily against the re-charter but it is far from certain that 'Jackson's assault on the Second Bank of the United States...delighted the South' as one historian has written. In truth the bank had powerful constituencies in the south and if southern delegations voted overwhelmingly against the re-charter, some at least did so half-heartedly, motivated by their loyalty to Andrew Jackson.[3]

It is well to remember that proprietors in South Carolina held more shares of stock in the Second Bank of the United States as proprietors in Massachusetts by a ratio of almost 4.5 to 1. It would be difficult to argue that the bank monopolized the Charleston money market. The extent of its local discounts and exchange dealings there were relatively small in relation to the business transacted by South Carolina's other banks. The bank moreover concentrated more of its resources at the Natchez branch than at its branch at Boston.[4]

Senators and representatives from the southeastern Atlantic states did vote solidly against the bank, but only the Alabama and Georgia delegations were unanimous in their opposition to the re-charter. The senators from Virginia, North Carolina, Tennessee, and South Carolina voted in the negative, but at least some representatives from those states voted for re-charter. Virginia's representatives were nearly evenly split, while those from North Carolina were against the re-charter by a margin of two to one. Delegations from the western states tended to split, and only Louisiana's to a man voted for the re-charter. What perhaps is most important about the voting patterns is that they rather confirm the bank's limited influence in those areas where it had been least active in soliciting local business. How the Congressional delegations voted also indicates how important the bank's operations were along the Mississippi River. The New Orleans branch was the most important one in the system, and the bank accounted for a sizeable percentage of all the local discounts in that market. The bank was the dominant financial concern in Mississippi, Missouri, Kentucky, Illinois, Indiana and Ohio. The delegations from those states either supported the re-charter or divided evenly when the roll was called.[5]

While the Bank of the United States undoubtedly is important in the historiography of the early antebellum decades, little has been written about its actual operations, especially in the localities where it had branches. It should come as no surprise that a sizeable portion of its resources were concentrated at the western branches. Arguably, opening expansive credit facilities at points up and down the Mississippi River stemmed from a dearth of banks at those locations, but the conditions which shaped the formation of the nation's early money markets suggest a different attribution. The bank was first and foremost the national government's fiscal agent. Indeed, its very incorporation had proceeded from a recognized need to support the market for the national debt both at home and abroad. The act incorporating the Second Bank provided for tenders of federal securities at par to meet stock subscriptions. With the government's debt then at a discount, domestic and foreign investors converted their claims into stock in the new bank, a bank with monopolistic privileges that had a good possibility of increased earnings in the years to come. The bank's capital stock, then, was drawn principally from the nation's stock of public debt.[6]

Much of the federal debt was held by foreigners, and one of the bank's primary functions in the early years was to guarantee that the government would always have at its command the exchange to meet installments and interest payments on the debt to the foreigners. Governmental finances as well as the import trade were well served if the costs of foreign exchange were kept as low as possible. The bank pursued a policy that was in many respects similar to the one which central bankers in some third world countries have followed of artificially maintaining an overvalued currency. Staple producers who accounted for the nation's principal exports were adversely affected in two ways; first, an overvalued exchange increased the costs of their exports to foreign consumers, and second, producers experienced a corresponding decline in the value of their crops in local moneys. But the bank to some extent offset the disadvantages of its exchange policy to staple producers by providing them with generous credit facilities, especially in the West.[7]

While the value of the dollar was fixed by law in terms of gold and silver, market exchange rates changed frequently, but within fairly narrow transaction bands. That was because the currencies of America's major trading partners were also defined by law in terms of gold and silver. Basically, the entire world enjoyed the same money, though they expressed value in different nominal units. Those who needed to make payments in other countries could do so by purchasing a credit instrument, called a bill of exchange, denominated in the respective currencies of their creditors (sterling, francs, guilders, marks). The price of a bill of exchange, like the price of most things, was a function of supply and demand. *Ceteris paribus*, the price of bills increased (decreased) if supply decreased (increased) or demand increased (decreased). If bills became too expensive, debtors could instead remit a known quantity of gold or silver.

Comparisons of foreign and domestic exchange rates in various money markets across the country indicate that the nation's money markets were integrated in the antebellum decades.[8] This study, however, argues that the nation's principal money markets in the South and in the North were only nominally connected, that the flow of debits and credits between cities, while essential for the circulation of bank notes, reflected trade patterns rather than the movement of investment capital from afar. That is not to say that those in search of investment financing were not able to meet much of their need by resorting to the exchanges and floating their paper in commercial channels; rather, the incidence of large blocks of investment capital from foreign sources ready to be immobilized in illiquid investments was rare. Money markets, then, were to a large degree localized and their interconnectedness rather tenuous.[9] That should not be surprising given antebellum America's huge size, its recent origins, its slow and costly system of information transmission, and its increasingly intense sectional animosities.

The nation's principal money markets were largely influenced by local conditions; moreover, the relative value of local exchange media - bank notes and liabilities -- diverged significantly. Evidence of an integrated national market in the antebellum decades just as surely supports an assertion that the American and English money markets had converged by 1860. This study contends that nominal exchange rates could move significantly above the actual costs of shipping specie and that this was due primarily to the constitution of financial institutions, both public and private, and the way money markets mediated credit facilities in discrete locales. Specie availability and public willingness to give currency to paper substitutes for specie also influenced the constitution of early money markets.

The most obvious feature on the financial landscape were the chartered banks, and historians generally have focused on little else, erroneously assuming that banks performed functions analogous to today's commercial banks. But the traffic in exchange, that is the buying and selling of bills of exchange on points near and far, was the institution that was uppermost in the constitution of every money market in the country. Credit facilities were paper facilities, and without a continuous ebb and flow between banks and exchange dealers, and between money markets, the system that evolved in the early decades of the nineteenth century would soon have atrophied. A bank's primary function was gaining a circulation either with a deposit credit in bank or with bank checks on points where credits had accumulated. What was uppermost to an exchange dealer was supporting the credit of his clientele by obtaining discounts of their paper, whether from the banks or private 'capitalists', thus permitting them to anticipate future income immediately. Because future income was likely to be realized at some distant point, a bank had every incentive for purchasing that claim in order to meet any accumulation of its circulation at the point where the bills were to be paid.

By the 1830s an identifiable pattern of exchange transactions had emerged in the nation's money markets. Banks, both private and public, bought long bills and sold sight bills. Exchange dealers, on the other hand, sold long bills and bought sight checks. Exchange dealers, especially in the South, covered their drawing facilities at the North with remittances of sterling bills. With sight bills on the North frequently at a discount, they found it advantageous to postpone selling long dated sterling bills and instructed those to whom they remitted to hold the bills for the best possible market. The costs of borrowing short-term by drawing on commercial agents at New York and Philadelphia were less than the loss that was occasioned by selling long dated sterling bills in a glutted market which was usually the case in the spring. The bill market fluctuated according to the season, and the best time to sell sterling bills, either at New Orleans or New York, was during the summer months. The cost of purchasing bills on New York in southern markets also tended to rise in the summer, but not so much as to warrant a sale of sterling during the late winter and early spring when agents of every description were drawing bills on England.[10]

The term 'exchange dealer', for purposes of this study, applies to any commercial agent who dealt in exchange, either domestic or foreign, or both. A factor, for example, is generally understood to be a commercial agent whose specialty was marketing planters' crops and purchasing supplies for their plantations. But the primary function of a factor was financing his principal's ongoing planting operations, a feat that he accomplished in any number of ways. A factor was an exchange dealer; he lent his endorsement or guaranty to his principal's paper and secured discounts of the same 'in bank' or 'out-of-doors' in the commercial parlance of the day.

By the 1830s, the institution of factorage embraced a complex organization of interconnected syndicates whose primary function was to spread planting risks over a period of years. Syndicates were groups of commercial partnerships, each partnership having both general and limited partners. The partnerships were interlocking; that is, the firms shared their general partners. Each partnership was domiciled at a strategic location: Yazoo City, Natchez, Vicksburg, New Orleans, New York, and sometimes London and Liverpool. These networks could reach from the wilds of Mississippi's Delta all the way to London and Paris.

A continuous stream of commercial paper passed among the affiliates. A single syndicate brought together in one organization hundreds of planter clients spread across the Lower Mississippi valley. In every way the clients were limited partners, enjoying the excellent credit facilities garnered by the syndicate and in return lightening the responsibility borne by the general partners. They lent the syndicate their credit in the form of indorsements on individual bills and notes generated by the firms. Some clients were simply passive investors. Occasionally they required ready money and arranged for discounts of their paper through one of the partnerships. But many speculated on commodities, while others pledged their fortunes in order to capture a portion of the fees generated from acceptances and discounts of syndicate paper. Syndicates mediated the risks of planting by insuring that even in the most distressed market their clients could always find adequate credit.

A single syndicate brought under its control tens of thousands of bales of cotton and thousands of hogsheads of sugar. A vast accumulation of any commodity placed the syndicate in an excellent position to command extensive concessions from consumers of southern staples. Quantities of cotton and sugar arrived each year at New Orleans for shipment to the North and to Europe. It is generally assumed that most of the harvest was sold at transmission points in the South, such as New Orleans, Charleston, and Richmond. In fact, the bulk of the harvests were consigned by producers to partnerships at the major gathering points. Agents at New Orleans and elsewhere then filled the orders of their correspondents at New York, Liverpool, and Le Harve. Even at this stage the number of bales and hogsheads actually sold was low. The important statistic in the New Orleans *Price Current* for example was a comparison of shipments during the prior year with cumulative arrivals over the course of the new season. Consignments from agents in the country were then re-consigned in places where the commodities would eventually be sold.[11]

Bills were drawn at every stage in the transfer of commodities from producers to consumers. The local agent drew on the agent at New Orleans who then drew on consignee agents at New York or Liverpool. None of these bills were predicted on actual sales. They were advances on consignments yet to be delivered. Even agents of European firms who came to New Orleans during the shipping season rarely purchased for the accounts of their principals; rather they advanced a portion of the proceeds which might be reasonably anticipated when sales were finally consummated. In consequence, many of the bales shipped from New Orleans to New York and Liverpool were still owned by producers in the South, but subject to the claims of consignees who had advanced on forthcoming shipments. Even the great firms like Brown Brothers and Baring Brothers bought relatively little of any commodity for their own accounts, preferring instead to advance cash. Advancing on consignments was a risk spreading mechanism that brought producers and consumers of southern staples together in one giant enterprise.[12]

The Philadelphia merchant, May Humphreys, who managed the Liverpool end of the United States Bank's cotton operations in the late 1830s, explained clearly in a letter to his junior, Edward C. Biddle, the risk spreading mechanism at work in advancing on consignments.

> I could confine the limits to be given in most cases in *two-thirds*[13] of the value of the produce when shipped, and in consideration of this restriction *H [umphreys] & B[iddle]* will agree to hold on to the consignments in case of need as long as may seem for the interest of the shippers-generally speaking when advances are made in America to the full or near the cost of shipments, the consignees here [in Liverpool] avail themselves of the first opportunity to realize their money and make good the account, and as harsh as this course may appear to the interest of the party on the other side, it is also more than fair to the one here, as in most cases when extravagant advances are taken and the property comes to a good Market, the shippers gain the advantage & on the other hand if the proceeds unfortunately fall short the consignee suffers the loss, or at any rate is a long while in getting back the balance due him-hence it is our plan to confine our operations to such Houses who will be content to furnish me one third of the required capital on the spot, and draw on H[umphreys] & B[iddle] for the other *two* thirds, and with these conditions you may stipulate that the House will hold on to the cotton to the end of the season, if required by the owners.

In this case the owners were Mississippi planters who had consigned cotton to Liverpool through various commercial agencies for the accounts of the Commercial and Rail Road Bank of Vicksburg and the Mississippi and

Alabama Rail Road and Banking Company. The risk of sudden declines in the price of the commodity over the course of the shipping season remained with the producers. Because Humphreys and Biddle were long in the market and were able to support the credit of those who had consigned to them, the planters profited when their consignments were sold almost one year after this instruction was given.[14]

The system that had evolved by the 1830s was indeed remarkable, but it rested primarily on the ability of southern planters to combine in huge syndicates, concentrating their yearly production in large masses and thus constitute a powerful institution that contributed to a stable market. Advancing on the consignments was as much an accommodation loan as any other credit facility mediated through the channels of commerce. This system differed decisively from the one that evolved to take its place after the emancipation of the slaves. The facilities for concentrating production for the benefit of producers were gone. In consequence, the power of planters to command the best terms from an international credit market evaporated. The system that prevailed before the Civil War was one of the Old South's great achievements.

Identifying exchange as the central institution in the development of the nation's early money markets is important for a number of reasons. It shifts the focus from public and private banks, whose operations appear to have supplied a need very different from what their modern counterparts answer for today, to an institution whose configurations are still rather vague. Nevertheless, the evidence that is available indicates that through the exchange markets antebellum planters were able to decisively influence the market for their crops, and it is perhaps not an exaggeration to say that the market for southern staples was made in the South, not in Liverpool or New York. Gavin Wright has suggested that planters' concerns over glutting the market for their staples figured in their political strategies, which tended to retard the opening of western lands for cultivation. Similarly, planters were unanimous in their opposition to reopening the Atlantic slave trade, which they perceived would have depressed the market value of their slaves. They were equally sophisticated in their strategies for commanding maximum concessions from the marketplace. Their participation in the exchange markets, either directly or through their agents, tends to confirm Robert William Fogel and Stanley Engerman's assessment that before the war the supply of cotton was elastic, that production was responsive to overall market conditions. The drive for profit took many forms, not just squeezing more production from land and slaves. Exchange strategies were integral to long and short term financing of plantations and provided a crucial mechanism for borrowing against future income and insuring that those streams would be predictable, regular, and stable. Participation in the exchange market could also be a source of handsome profits.[15]

The Structure of Local Credits

Who garnered the consignment business and the fees it generated when sales finally were made, as well as the exchange business, was contingent upon the general commercial partners' ability to arrange more-or-less permanent accommodation loans for their planter clients. Similarly, a bank's access to a lucrative exchange business depended on its capacity to support a large portfolio of local accommodation loans. A bank's local discounts and exchange dealings gave tone to the local market, but the relations among banks, exchange dealers and their customers were symbiotic ones. Banks were not monetary arbiters if we assume a modern usage for that term, although their notes were an important yardstick for settling the value of local monies of account; rather, they were commercial agencies that eased the movement of paper between America's cities.

The General Depositors' Ledger of the Natchez Branch of the Bank of the United States shows transactions in upwards of two thousand accounts for a period between March 1831 and the summer of 1833. Some accounts show only two or three transactions, a credit by exchange or discount and a debit by a single check for the proceeds. All of the individual items were for large sums of money, ranging from a few hundred dollars to thousands. (A very rough estimate of an equivalency in today's dollars can be obtained by multiplying an 1831 dollar by 21.16.)[16]

The most important accounts at the branch were those of the exchange dealers, eight or ten commercial partnerships resident at Natchez with correspondents up and down the Mississippi River. Hoopes and Moore was one of the smaller concerns, a firm composed of Passmore Hoopes and Joseph H. Moore. Their syndicate would figure prominently in the first indications of trouble in the branch's exchange account in 1836, shortly before its closure at Natchez in consequence of the expiration of the federal charter. While Hoopes and Moore was a small concern in 1831 and 1832, during the months from 2 April 1831 to 20 January 1832, the firm's account showed credits of $96,960.04. During all of 1832 credits aggregating to $250,000 were registered in the account, mostly from discounts afforded by the branch and bills of exchange purchased by the same. Over the course of 1833 the firm's account showed an equally impressive volume of business. The exchange purchases consisted primarily of bills drawn on correspondents at New Orleans, whereas the local discounts were simple orders to pay a named payee or promises to pay someone at Natchez. Local discounts, as well as the New Orleans bills, were all guaranteed by indorsements, either the clients of Hoopes and Moore or affiliated firms in localities near Natchez. The indorsers were guarantors, not bona fide holders who had received the paper as transferees independent of the underlying transaction. The form the paper took, then, mattered very little:

whether bills or promissory notes these instruments were finance mechanisms. Only the Bank of the United States could claim to be a bona fide holder when it either discounted local accommodation paper or purchased bills on New Orleans.[17]

Indorsers were compensated in a variety of ways. Clients of a firm who had accommodation loans through its agency were expected to guarantee a proportional share of the firm's paper. Some indorsers were commercial sureties and were paid the customary fee for a commercial indorsement, which was 2.5 percent of the amount of the loan. When the Philadelphia branch of Jackson, Todd & Co. suspended in August 1839, Stephen Duncan, the Natchez planter and financier, confided his fears to William J. Minor, another large planter, about the 'disastrous' consequences that would follow if the Liverpool branch suspended as well. His concern stemmed from the fact that he was 'an endorser for large amts'. of the firm's paper. He then observed: 'I must really quit the business of endorsing'. A few days later he expressed his opinion that Todd, Jackson & Co. of Liverpool would never be able to cover all the advances it had authorized at the rate of $20 dollars a bale on 20,000 bales. They would he thought continue to cash the paper 'so long as they had pounds of cotton to pay with'. He then reveled that he had 'tried to make provision for [his bills]-but h[ad] not yet succeeded' in arranging loans at Philadelphia to meet the protested bills. He seemed more optimistic when he wrote to Minor in September that Washington Jackson's Liverpool house would 'hold out' and that Jackson himself was making strenuous exertions at Philadelphia to restore his credit.[18]

Steven Duncan became increasingly circumspect about indorsing paper for others as the 1839 Depression took hold and ravaged Mississippi's banks. He declined Minor's request to release him as an indorser on the notes of Samuel Gustin, Minor's father-in-law and a former president of the Planters Bank of Mississippi, in return for a mortgage on most of Gustin's land and slaves. Duncan assured Minor that he did not doubt the adequacy of the property proposed to be pledged to stand as security for the loan, but believed that 'without the guiding influence of an endorser, ... [he] could not rely on the punctual payt. of the debts-nor the ultimate payt. without trouble and difficulty'. Minor was so anxious to obtain a release that he offered to pay Duncan $5,000 in specie as an additional incentive. Duncan, however, declined to grant the release, preferring Minor's indorsement as the best security for insuring the eventual payment of Gustin's debt.[19]

Indorsers could of course lessen their risks by taking mortgages to secure themselves in the event of a default by the obligor or any other party to the transaction, and they could also contract to rank behind other indorsers on a note. In the event of a default on the underlying transaction payment could be demanded from the indorsers according to the order of their indorsements on the back of the note or bill. Generally, the last indorser was the party to whom the loan proceeds were paid. Demand could next be made on the party whose name appeared above his on the back of the note or bill. But, it was always possible that even the best indorsers could fail to pay when demand was made on them. When the general partners in the partnerships which comprised the syndicate of Buckner, Stanton & Co. filed for bankruptcy in 1842, Duncan again expressed his apprehensions to Minor. 'Tis true', he wrote, 'I have Col. Wilkins & Col. Bengaman before me on 3/4ths of the amt. [of the paper which they had together indorsed]-But neither of them redoubted knights-are very walamen-or chinamen-in the way of meeting endorsements. In truth, if their will-was good-their means-are the reverse, and I must shoulder the burden'.[20]

Joseph L. Roberts, a collections agent sent to Mississippi in 1841 by the trustees of the failed United States Bank of Pennsylvania, quickly arranged for local agents at various localities around the state to assist him with his work. He seems to have been particularly attached to Fielding Davis, a Woodville planter, and even arranged some of Davis' outstanding paper. On 5 April 1842, Roberts wrote to Davis that he had been chagrined to learn that morning that two of Davis' notes remained to be settled at the Planters Bank. 'I thought I was paying all your debts for you & relieving you in every way to make you easy &-comfortable-Now let these at once be arranged for, & keep yourself under promise neither to endorse or sign notes for the future for any one'.[21]

Some indorsers, at least, drew a clear distinction between their own debts and those they had guaranteed for others, and the excuses and defenses they proffered were similar to those urged today by 'names' in various Lloyd's syndicates who also seek to escape liability. However, none ever pleaded simple ignorance of their legal responsibility. Joseph H. Moore, for example, a general partner in the Natchez firm of Joseph H. Moore & Co. proposed to the United States Bank to transfer property in settlement of all claims for which he was directly liable, but expected to be absolved of all responsibility for bills which he had indorsed.[22]

Historians, perhaps relying on the claims of some contemporaries, draw a clear distinction between the creditworthiness of merchants and planters. The judge of New Orleans' second District Court, writing after the Civil War, presented one of the best articulations of this viewpoint in the case of *Shiff vs. Shiff*:

> The value of paper, in commercial communities, is very greatly governed by the promptness with which the drawer or endorser usually pays. A single protest is ruinous to a merchant while the character of the careless planter is almost entirely unaffected by it. At the time the investments were made the endorsement of a well known commercial house of this city gave, on the market, greater value to paper than that of any planter in the State, however secured in addition by mortgage on his plantation. Very soon however after these investments were made the

'great war' came and merchant princes became bankrupts, and in the language of one of the witnesses 'mortgages became good things to fall back on'.

That assessment reflects contemporary prejudices and a degree of envy as well, but it is far from accurate. A commercial agent's credit depended as much on the credit of his clientele as his clientele's reliance on him for optimal credit facilities.[23]

Many planters scrupulously met the terms of their credit facilities, often at great sacrifice, lest even one note or bill should fall under protest. Steven Duncan was justifiably enraged when the president of the Agricultural Bank of Natchez negotiated his drafts which had without his knowledge been altered so that payment of them had to be in specie and not bank notes. In consequence his banker had declined accepting the bills and all had been duly protested, thus besmirching Duncan's reputation. Duncan ordered his banker to pay the bills according to their tenor, even 'if it cost [him] ... all [he was] ... worth in th[e] world to do it'. He continued: 'I cannot bring myself to view the transaction in any other light than as one, marked with extreme unkindness towards me & I cannot persuade myself, that such a course would have been pursued, ...' with anyone else connected with the Agricultural Bank. The year before he had had the option of checking on the bank for $50,000 in specie but 'instead of doing so, at a profit of 2 to 5 percent', had drawn his checks payable in notes. The protests had placed him 'in a condition in which [he] ... never was placed before & never expected to be placed-to wit, <u>dishonored on a bill of [his] own ... drawing.</u>'[24]

John Perkins, one of the richest planters in the Lower Mississippi Valley, continued to make heavy investments in his plantations in Louisiana and Mississippi throughout the Depression Years. In 1839 alone he estimated that he 'paid out in the best currency Fifty five thousand $ for lands and Negroes besides current expenses for Plantations & ... family, which [was] ... not less than Ten Thousand more'. He proposed opening a credit facility which Washington Jackson at Philadelphia conditioned on his having the privilege 'of always anticipating ... [Washington Jackson] Honoring [his] ... Dfts. for small sums for <u>current</u> expenses & <u>Short bills</u> as ... formerly ... on [his] commission <u>Houses</u> in New Orleans'. Additionally he expected to draw on Jackson at long dates for any amount he 'deemed prudent payable by the sale of other bills on ... [Jackson's] Liverpool house founded on the shipment of cotton and all without commission for <u>accepting</u>'. On no account, however, was Jackson ever to 'allow ... [any of his] Bills [to be] returned dishonored'.[25]

The day to day operations of exchange dealers are clearly represented in the individual depositors' accounts at the Natchez branch of the Second Bank of the United States. Aggregate net credits in Hoopes & Moore's account from 1 April 1831 to 9 August 1833 exceeded $600,000. The richest Natchez dealer,

Reynolds, Marshall & Co. showed credits of $1,252,781.66 in the period from 3 July 1832 to 12 August 1833. A. Fisk, Burke & Co'.s account showed net credits of $2,450,575.17 in the months from 2 July 1831 to 3 April 1833. While these are staggering sums, it should be remembered that local accommodation facilities ranged from 90 to 180 days; moreover, the limit for exchange purchases was 120 days or less. This meant that the firms had to always have at their command the means to settle their accommodations as well as those of their clients, whether twice yearly or more often. Frequently the needful came from clients who checked on their own accounts at the branch. Similarly when a client required credits to cover his account, checks on the firm's account sufficed. Debits and credits flowed back and forth between the firm account and clients' accounts. The practical effect of this system was to even out the peaks and troughs in income streams over a period of years.[26]

What is perhaps most startling about this accounting system is the incidence of checks drawn by member firms on each other. In most accounts, the bulk of the credits were by discounts and exchange purchased. Most debits were for checks paid, drafts forwarded to Natchez for collection by the same correspondents who provided acceptance facilities for bills drawn at Natchez on New Orleans and elsewhere. During the 1840s, critics of this system complained that it was nothing more than check kiting. But the reality was more complicated. The whole system was predicated on giving currency to debt instruments, whether bank notes, checks, drafts, or bills of exchange. The nominal role of specie in the actual process of making prearranged settlements clearly is evident.[27]

That specie was nominal in these relations should come as no surprise. The New Orleans branch yielded large quantities of sterling exchange, i.e., bills payable in English money. Maintaining large specie reserves, which earned no income, was rather redundant when sterling bills could always be sold to the Bank of the United States and thus facilitate settlements between regions.

Activity in firm accounts was voluminous, but most of the credits can be traced to either discounts or exchange purchases. Each deposited item represented a bill or note discounted for the firm and passed to its credit. But an exchange dealer stood guaranty on innumerable other pieces of paper passed to the credit of firm clients. B. Hughes was deeply involved with Hoopes and Moore, and the firm was indorser on dozens of bills and notes. Hughes likewise indorsed his share of paper offered by the firm to the branch for discount. A. Fisk, Burke & Co., Reynolds, Ferriday & Co. and H. Carpenter & Co. indorsed or accepted paper for Hughes, sometimes the same notes and bills guaranteed by Hoopes and Moore. In a 2-year period, $144,653.57 of credits passed into Hughes' account. Much of that flowed back out again in the form of checks passed to the credit of his indorsers. Thus it can be seen that an exchange dealer was to some extent involved with every other dealer in a locality through the medium of co-indorsements on individual bills and notes.[28]

The system that evolved was intended to reduce risks by spreading them far and wide to numerous individuals in the locality and others far away. Vast networks are evident in individual depositor's accounts, a confirmation of the old adage that 'the devil is in the details'. Indeed, far-flung correspondences rather tend to undermine the concept of patriarchy in wealth accumulation strategies, a concept which some historians claim is an essential construct for understanding antebellum plantation households. Some assert that the patriarchal organization of extended families was pervasive in the formation of plantation agriculture, a condition that accounts for the distinctiveness of the South's economic and social development. The argument here is not that patriarchy is irrelevant for gaining insights about social relations in a set of related households. The family is, after all, the most elementary organization for spreading risks among those who claim kinship to one another. Rather, when grappling with that most illusive of institutions, the organization of financial relations, we must conclude that successful antebellum planters looked far and wide for help in mediating their risks. Their financial relationships extended well beyond the so-called web of patriarchy.[29]

A credit facility, in theory, was predicated on shipments of staples soon to be sold, thus providing the means for liquidating the claim, but in reality the ebb and flow of paper had a life if its own that reached beyond several planting seasons. Quickly reducing that flow to a trickle of specie was infeasible without precipitating a collapse of ongoing credit facilities. The syndicates and their clienteles who regularly discounted 'in bank' had every incentive for giving currency to notes and checks rather than demanding specie.

The literature on the Panic of 1837 and subsequent Depression tend to obscure the Bank of the United States as an active agent in the unfolding of that crisis. As will be seen, the bank's course in the wake of Andrew Jackson's veto of its re-charter was a major factor in the derangement of the domestic and foreign exchanges in the years after 1833. The bank's concentration of resources in the West played havoc at those locations as it sought to liquidate its claims and repatriate the proceeds to the commercial centers of the East. The bank was integral to the system of commercial exchange that took shape in the 1820s. Its departure placed an intolerable burden on financial institutions in the region, a burden that proved to be highly disruptive to the national and international exchanges. The void created by the disappearance of so vast a commercial exchange mediator was not immediately filled by an equally viable network of relationships. As will be seen, the disruption was especially evident in Mississippi, although the state legislature chartered a plethora of banks in the years after 1832.[30]

THE BANK OF THE UNITED STATES IN MISSISSIPPI, 1831–1836

Few threads of the story of money markets in the Lower Mississippi Valley derive from any other provenance than the dominating presence of the Second Bank of the United States and its New Orleans branch; more so even in the case of Mississippi in the 1830s and 1840s. From 1814 to 1831 one bank alone, at Natchez, was the extent of state chartered banking in the state. The Bank of the State of Mississippi had, however, by the late 1820s fallen into the orbit of the Bank of the United States, and whatever course the leviathan in Chestnut Street adopted, the much smaller Natchez bank soon found itself moving in the same direction. If the New Orleans branch of the Bank of the United States reduced its discounts of accommodation paper, the Natchez bank quickly did likewise.[31]

By 1827, the relations between the Bank of the United States and the Bank of the State of Mississippi were precisely formalized. The relationship was predicated primarily on supporting the circulating medium emanating from the two institutions. The checks and demand notes of the Bank of the United States and its branches circulated throughout the Union, some of which found their way to Natchez where they were tendered by holders to the Bank of the State of Mississippi in settlement of claims to that institution. Moreover, the Natchez bank performed various agencies for the federal institution and its branches such as collecting bills made payable at Natchez and making disbursements for the federal government in the state of Mississippi.[32]

The circulation of the Natchez bank tended to move toward New Orleans. Holders could tender Natchez banknotes at the branch and receive immediate credit for their deposits. They could withdraw those deposits in New Orleans branch notes or obtain checks on other branches in the system. If the course of exchange was against Natchez, the branch debited their deposits by the amount of the market discount. If the course of exchange was in favor of Philadelphia and against New Orleans the depositors paid the market premium for a check on the City of Brotherly Love.[33]

Neither bank paid out each other's circulation as it accumulated at Natchez and New Orleans. There was no profit in giving currency to the obligations of another bank however amicable the relations in such reciprocal agencies. Settlements of bank note accumulations were monthly, the New Orleans branch simply forwarding the notes of the Mississippi bank to Natchez and debiting its account. There can be little doubt, however, that the facilities afforded the Mississippi bank by the New Orleans branch were of immeasurable value to it in supporting its circulation and insuring that holders could readily tender Natchez notes in the marketplace.

The Natchez bank covered its account in a variety of ways. It remitted the obligations of the Bank of the United States and its branches and the obligations of the state chartered New Orleans banks collected at Natchez. Generally the Bank of the State would receive immediate credit for such remittances even though the obligations of distant branches of the Bank of the United States could not be immediately converted into the New Orleans branch's demand notes. Checks drawn on distant branches generally were always available.

The Bank of the State usually covered its account with the New Orleans branch by regular remittances of bills of exchange drawn at Natchez on New Orleans. These bills were either payable at sight, thirty days from sight, sixty days from sight, ninety days from sight, four months, and even six months after presentment. Generally, longer maturities commenced running from the date of the instrument, not from the date of presentment to the drawee for acceptance. These bills constituted the Natchez bank's exchange operations, the primary medium for supporting its circulation, and as a rule the discounting of such bills was predicated on the movement of cotton from Natchez to New Orleans and thence to New York, Liverpool, and LeHarve. Bills were remitted to the branch for collection, and until paid by the drawee/acceptors at New Orleans, functioned as collateral security for any deficit in account.[34]

The Bank of the State, however, had other options. Even in the 1820s the cotton trade at Natchez was large enough to support direct shipments to Liverpool by area producers. Large planters frequently found it advantageous to consign the cotton under their control to a Liverpool house and obtain advances from the consignee on the eventual sale of the consignments. These transactions generated sterling bills, first when the consignors drew for any advances authorized by the consignees in Liverpool, and then after the consignments were sold, more bills were drawn to collect any balances remaining in favor of the consignors. Holders of sterling bills, whether drawers or transferees, could cash their bills at the Bank of the State and receive Natchez money and thus capture the sterling premium which prevailed during most of the antebellum period throughout the United States. Until the decade of the 1830s the sterling premium at Natchez and New Orleans ruled about 2 percentage points below the prevailing premium at New York and Philadelphia. The Bank of the State could make a profit simply by remitting sterling bills to New York or Philadelphia for sale, but as a general rule the opportunities for arbitrage of rate differences of this kind would have been relatively few because the bank's own exchange dealers could have just as easily sent their bills to those cities for sale. Of course, some exchange dealers were induced to discount their sterling bills at the Bank of the State, and thus permit the bank to capture a portion of the premium, in consideration of the accommodation facilities the bank afforded them. Even if the bank failed to profit from an arbitrage of rate differences between Natchez and New York or Philadelphia, there were still other incentives for purchasing sterling exchange. Remittances of sterling to Philadelphia created a drawing facility at that location which the Bank of the State could employ to settle its balances at the New Orleans branch. The Bank of the State could also use its Philadelphia funds to cover the checks it sold on the North to its local customers who needed funds suitable for remittance. Bank checks on Philadelphia generally commanded a 1 percent premium at Natchez.[35]

The Bank of the State's traffic in sterling was rather neatly summed up by its cashier in an 1831 letter to the cashier of a bank in New York. George Tichnor began by apprising his correspondent that 'several of our Planters who ship their cotton crops to Liverpool [had requested him] to ascertain the terms on which their bills could be negotiated thro your Institution, being guaranteed by the endorsement of this Bank and the amount when sold subject to the order of this Bank by checks to individuals having occasion for remittances to N. York or elsewhere'. Clearly it was important for the Natchez bank to create drawing facilities elsewhere in the country even if it received only a fraction of 1 percent for negotiating and guaranteeing the sterling bills it sent to New York for sale.[36]

The Philadelphia parent of the Bank of the United States generally purchased all of the sterling bills remitted to that market by the Bank of the State. It paid the Mississippi bank the prevailing premium which was 1.25 percent below what the Bank of the United States sold sterling exchange for in the Philadelphia and New York markets. Even a fraction of 1 percent figured importantly in the calculations that comprised ongoing relationships based on mutual confidence. In 1827 Samuel Jaudon, then an assistant cashier at the Bank of the United States in Philadelphia, thought it necessary to remind the cashier at the Natchez bank that their arrangement was predicated on remittances of 'Sterling Bills payable in London'. A previous remittance had contained two bills for £1,190 payable in *Liverpool*, which, had they been thrown into the money market, would have 'command[ed] less than if made payable in London, by 1/8 to ¼ of one p. cent'. Jaudon credited the Bank of the State's account at the more favorable London rate, but he nevertheless thought it necessary to mention the difference 'under the belief that the Drawers of the Bills with you are not aware of this difference'.[37]

The relationship between the Bank of the State and the Bank of the United States was at times strained. The drawers of sterling bills at Natchez, who negotiated them through the Bank of the State, expressed dissatisfaction over the 1.25 percent point spread between the buy and sell rates for sterling maintained by the Bank of the United States. William McIlvaine, the cashier of the Bank of the United States at Philadelphia, wrote to Stephen Duncan, the eminent planter, financier and President of the Bank of the State, that the 'percent which the Bank [of the United States] c[ould] generally sell its bills …[was] at least ½ p. Cent higher than that which other bills, not excepting those endorsed by distant Banks [including the Bank of the State] command[ed] in … [the Philadelphia] market, that … [his bank] pay[ed] ½ p. Cent in Commission to … [its] Agents abroad on all … remittances, for which [the Bank of the United States] … [should] have an equivalent …' In taking an additional quarter percent from the Bank of the State in lieu of customary brokerages, which were substantially more, the Bank of the State was receiving the most favorable rate commensurate with prevailing conditions in the Philadelphia money market. McIlvaine further informed Duncan that the Bank of the United States declined paying a higher premium for the bills remitted from Natchez. The bank was then buying bills at its southern branches at lower rates than had been allowed to the Bank of the State.[38]

But the greatest source of friction was the commencement of operations in the spring of 1831 of the Natchez branch of the Bank of the United States. Thus began a period that would span nearly two decades when the physical presence of the Philadelphia institution in the state of Mississippi would be of paramount importance in shaping the financial institutions of that state. It may seem paradoxical in light of the vast literature which has accumulated on the comparative retrograde character of economic development in the antebellum South that the country's preeminent banking institution in the nineteenth century should have become so deeply immersed in the economy of one southern state, but such nevertheless is the case. During the remainder of its lifetime the Bank of the United States concentrated as much as 10 percent of its resources at Natchez. But that was only the beginning of the Bank's involvement in the state of Mississippi.[39]

The establishment of the Natchez branch had an immediate effect on the Bank of the State. Instead of monthly settlements, which amounted to an interest free loan of any balance up to $30,000 against the Natchez bank at the New Orleans branch, the new branch now required almost daily settlements, thus circumscribing the capacity of the Natchez bank to inflate its circulation. Formerly the New Orleans branch had charged no interest on a balance in its favor unless it reached $30,000. Interest then accrued at the rate of 5 percent per annum, but only if the branch was without remittances from the Bank of the State which could be discounted to cover overdrafts in excess of that limit. The Bank of the United States afforded such generous facilities to the Natchez bank for a variety of reasons: first, and foremost, the relationship channeled much of the exchange business between Natchez and New Orleans in the direction of the New Orleans branch. That gave the branch a competitive advantage in purchases of exchange on the North and Europe when the cargoes against which the Natchez bills had been drawn were either sold or reconsigned at New Orleans. Second, because the Bank of the United States had a monopoly on the federal government's deposits, and paid no interest on those deposits, it diffused the envy and opposition of the state banks to run deficits in account for periods of time interest free.[40]

The Bank of the State had enjoyed similar uncovered drawing facilities with its correspondent in Philadelphia prior to the formalization of a facility with the Bank of the United States in 1827. The Farmers & Mechanics Bank had permitted the accrual of balances of up to $20,000 without interest beginning in 1824 and honored drafts against remittances of bills set to mature at some future date. The Bank of the State could command such generous facilities from its Philadelphia correspondents because it largely influenced exchange dealings in the Natchez region. Banks elsewhere that trafficked in foreign exchange necessarily afforded the Bank of the State, and other banks similarly situated in the South, considerable latitude, honoring overdrafts and supporting their circulation by accepting tenders of their notes.[41]

But the branch at Natchez rather changed things. No longer was the Bank of the State in a position to dominate the exchange business in Natchez. The branch began discounting accommodation paper for area planters and their merchants almost at once, steadily increasing its portfolio to something in excess of $1,500,000 by February 1832, a mere twelve months after opening the discount line. Such an expansive portfolio of accommodation loans perforce assumed a large volume of New Orleans exchange was drawn to the branch and away from the Bank of the State.[42]

In a balanced portfolio discounts from bills of exchange and discounts from local accommodations should have yielded about the same amount of income. But identifying the sources of bank income doesn't begin to estimate the true significance of exchange dealings and their impact on the local and regional financial systems. Accommodations were for the most part simply renewals of short term paper -- up to six months in maturity in the case of the Bank of the United States. Bills drawn on New Orleans or the North and payable in thirty, sixty, ninety and sometimes one hundred and twenty days were simply orders drawn at Natchez on agents elsewhere. The bank 'purchased' those orders and sent them on for collection. The aggregate value then of bills drawn at Natchez on other points was in fact three or four times the amount of permanent accommodations due to mature at approximately the same dates as the bills. But settlement of the bills at maturity, whether at New Orleans, Philadelphia or London, was largely outside the bank's sphere of operations. The bank might make itself responsible for the payment of a bill negotiated to a third party or remitted to an agent for collection, but a bank was quite powerless to arrange a settlement by simply renewing the bill once it had been dispatched to the place where it was to be paid. The overall condition of a bank's exchange portfolio was far more important than the relative illiquidity of its local accommodation loans. Bills remitted elsewhere for collection created credit facilities in places where a bank's circulation might accumulate, facilities which were essential for sustaining that circulation at home and afar, insuring that paper emitted in the course of business remained current. The system that had evolved by the 1830s was first and foremost a risk spreading mechanism, a way of immediately liquidating paper claims on future income streams.[43]

By the end of the 1820s the system envisioned by Nicholas Biddle of a national bank with branches in every important locality was largely in place; indeed the Natchez branch was the last to open before Andrew Jackson's veto of the re-charter. That system greatly accelerated the circulation of paper currency but more importantly opened up the possibility of expanding circulation well beyond the usual constraints imposed by the domestic exchanges, that is leveraging well beyond the foreseeable and reliable level of national income. Bills drawn at Natchez on New Orleans could be met by drawees obtaining accommodations from the New Orleans branch and afterwards keeping their accounts current by cashing sterling bills or bills on the North; which might themselves be drawn against uncovered credits. A national system greatly expanded the opportunity for producers of commodities to speculate on future price levels for those same commodities in Europe and the United States. Many of the cotton bales unloaded at Liverpool were owned by the same southern planters who had produced them, but subject to the claims of consignees for advances, through whose hands the bales had passed in route to Liverpool. The longer a sale of a bale of cotton could be postponed, by borrowing against its eventual sale, the greater the opportunity for influencing prices and extracting the greatest concessions from the marketplace. The national bank, on the other hand, could always rely on its role as fiscal agent of the government to shore up its circulation: the obligations of the Bank of the United States and its branches were acceptable tenders for claims owed to the government.[44]

The national bank contributed to market liquidity in other ways. It organized the flow of domestic exchange within the United States and more-or-less set the price of foreign exchange. The extent of its influence on foreign exchanges can be estimated from the havoc it wrought when it refrained from purchases of sterling and franc denominated bills from the autumn of 1833 to the early summer of 1834. Its absence from the market resulted in a collapse in the price of sterling: the premium disappeared and bills fell to a discount of as much as 3 percent at New Orleans. But the Bank's influence on domestic exchanges was in many respects far more profound. Every part of the system was predicated on an accounting mechanism of debits and credits. The western branches ran a deficit with the eastern branches, the branches in the Lower Mississippi Valley generally ran deficits with the Nashville, Louisville, St. Louis, and Cincinnati branches; Natchez ran a large credit with the New Orleans branch which in turn ran a credit with the New York and Philadelphia offices. The Bank thus created an optimal environment for influencing the pace of economic expansion throughout the country. It was rather more difficult, if not impossible, for a state bank in Mississippi, for example, which operated in the New Orleans market through an agent, i.e., a Louisiana bank or even a merchant in that city, to support its circulation by pressing its obligations on distant localities throughout the United States. The Bank of the United States had not only a seemingly limitless potential to rationalize relations between disparate and regional money markets, but also to pursue a monetary policy largely divorced from the usual market regulators which determined the course of domestic exchanges.[45]

More often the commercial agents of the Natchez exchange dealers at New Orleans simply redrew on them and negotiated those bills to meet the acceptances coming due at the New Orleans branch. Traffic in exchange certainly was subject to more regular and more frequent settlements than local accommodation loans, but such expansive domestic exchange dealings among the branches of the Second Bank afforded a splendid opportunity for extending those facilities well beyond the anticipated proceeds of the next year's planting.

The Bank of the State began experiencing difficulties from the onset of the branch at Natchez. Weeks after the branch opened its discount line, George Tichnor, the cashier of the Bank of the State, advised the branch cashiers at Woodville and Port Gibson that '[t]he pressure occasioned by the actual and the expected transfer of large balances due the Bank of the U. States' offices [elsewhere in the United States] and the government, from our Bank to the office at this place …' prevented them from engaging in any new business and 'no deviation from this course c[ould] be allowed'. Tichnor wrote to one loan applicant that his bank's 'means of granting facilities are greatly diminished at this time, no discounts even for short periods can be made' on account of the introduction of the new branch.[46]

In some respects the problem affecting the Bank of the State's circulation was localized. Notes accumulating at New Orleans were not subject to immediate calls for redemption, but those which remained in the area of Natchez, according to Tichnor, usually found their way to the government's land office 'in large masses and as the government money … [would be] deposited in the United States Bank, [his bank] … was liable to be called on to redeem … paper in very short periods'. The new branch 'materially interfer[ed] with … [the Bank of the State's] circulation, requiring all the precaution in … [their] power, until experience [could] show ...' how far they might operate commensurate with the activities of the branch.[47]

A less immediate concern weighing on the Bank of the State was the Mississippi legislature's chartering of a new bank, an action the directors and officers believed was in violation of their charter rights. They contended that their charter had given the stockholders an exclusive franchise to conduct banking in Mississippi, and they proceeded to engage some of the most eminent lawyers in the land to support their pretension, namely Horace Binney of Philadelphia and Daniel Webster of Boston. The legislature had not only chartered a rival bank, but had reserved two-thirds of the stock to the state, which amounted to a direct subsidy of $2 million to the new bank. The state's initial subscription of $1 million was to be funded by the issuance of state bonds payable in installments of from 10 to 25 years. Tichnor dispatched letters to bankers in the North cautioning them not to subscribe to the bonds. The new bank had been got up 'by persons of no experience or sober calculation, in violation of the charter rights of our Institution'. Horace Binney had given his opinion that the new bank was unconstitutional and 'its operations c[ould] be suppressed by an injunction'. These facts, he continued, ought to be made known in New York, and he requested his correspondents to circulate the information, but without attribution.[48]

Efforts to check the progress of the new bank aside, the officers and directors of the Bank of the State soon determined that the best course for their stockholders was to surrender the charter and begin liquidation proceedings. The presence of the new branch, rather than the chartering of the Planters Bank of Mississippi, was probably decisive in their reaching this decision. The Planters Bank had not yet even commenced operating when the stockholders of the Bank of the State resolved to petition the legislature to accept a surrender of their charter and authorize a six-year long liquidation. The branch, however, had already severely circumscribed the bank's regular course of business. A persistent difficulty was that the Bank of the State's portfolio of accommodation loans had rather longer maturities than what the Bank of the United States granted; which rather tended to reduce the Bank of the State's exchange purchases. This in turn created short-term difficulties in settling the bank's demand liabilities. Finally the paper in the exchange portfolio generally bore longer maturities than the paper purchased at the branch, some bills running for as long as six months, which meant that the Bank of the State would fall rapidly in debt to the branch. The bank ceased its purchases of bills with long maturities, requiring its customers to settle their accounts at more frequent intervals. The new branch was forcing the Bank of the State into a de facto liquidating posture.[49]

By the summer of 1831 relations were so strained that the Bank of the State's officers were contemplating moving their New Orleans agency from the branch to a state bank, and even made overtures to the Bank of Louisiana. Stephen Duncan estimated that the bank's exchange business from the Natchez area would be 'diminished fully one half or more' in consequence of the new branch having already made heavy purchases. He hoped that exchange operations at the bank's Vicksburg and Port Gibson offices, locations where competition from the branch was inconsequential, would offset the lost business. Tichnor cautioned one stockholder that while a reduction in the dividend was not contemplated, the likelihood of an increase was indeed remote in consequence of '[t]he interference of the Branch of the Bk. U. States in our city …'[50]

The Natchez branch created a host of other difficulties. At settlement time it declined tenders of Louisiana state bank notes which meant that the Bank of the State likewise had to refuse its customers the convenience of paying those notes over at its counter to keep their own accounts current. But this policy did provide some short-term relief to the Bank of the State by increasing the demand for its circulation. In a letter to the cashier of the Woodville branch, Tichnor precisely articulated the necessities pressing on all banks to obtain and sustain a circulation.

> A part of the policy of every Bank is to gain a circulation of its own notes and drive out of circulation the notes of other Banks. The effect of the course you suggest [of paying out the notes of other banks] will tend to defeat this measure- If the notes of other Banks are recd. they should be returned to the Bank where issued, and not paid at your counter, because they in fact will then occupy the place of your own.

Because there was no safe means at Woodville for returning Louisiana bank notes to their issuers, Tichnor advised rejecting all tenders of such paper.[51]

In November 1831 Tichnor wrote to William McIlvaine, the cashier of the Bank of the United States at Philadelphia, that the stockholders of his institution would likely vote to place the bank in liquidation, in which case 'the field w[ould] be open for the employment of a much larger amount of capital by [the Natchez branch] … than c[ould] … [then] be profitably used'. The newly chartered Planters Bank would, he believed, 'afford but little interference', and the branch's discount line might safely be increased to $3 million; 'more especially if discounts were made for 9 and 12 months'. Balances were rapidly augmenting against the Bank of the State in favor of the Bank of the United States in consequence of the former bank being saddled with portfolios of paper with rather long maturities. By the late fall of 1831 the balance in favor of the Natchez branch exceeded $100,000, and there were comparable deficits at the New Orleans branch and the Philadelphia parent of the Bank of the United States. The Bank of the State began accruing interest charges on its accounts and was forced to make calls on its debtors with curtailments in its discount line.[52]

The stockholders voted to liquidate the Bank of the State, and the cashiers of the several branches were directed to renew two-thirds of their bills receivable, but with twelve month notes payable only at Natchez and not at any of the locations where such bills had formerly been made payable. The remaining one-third of their discount lines were to be discharged 'by acceptances on New Orleans at from 60 days to 6 months'. This meant that one-third of the bank's accommodation portfolio of $1,500,000 was thrown into the exchange market, thus creating a demand for credit facilities at those points outside of Mississippi where the bills were to be paid. Moreover, the bank would soon cease its purchases of bills drawn at Natchez on New Orleans, thus depressing the value of Natchez exchange in New Orleans and elsewhere. The officers soon found it necessary to extend a portion of the curtailment with six-month bills payable at Natchez.[53]

The difficulties experienced by the Bank of the State in the conduct of its liquidation are an indication of the localized character of money markets in the antebellum era. True, a portion of the portfolio could be pressed on money centers elsewhere in the country, but only because the Natchez area was a prime producer of cotton, the primary source of foreign exchange. The Natchez branch did expand its discount line by 40 percent and more than doubled its purchases of bills of exchange in the first half of 1832. Those measures relieved the pressure but by no means filled the void left by the withdrawal of the Bank of the State. The Natchez branch transacted scant business with the newly chartered Planters Bank until 1833, a strong indication that the branch was a towering presence in the market in subsequent years.[54]

Stephen Duncan certainly had second thoughts about a rapid curtailment of discounts and recommended to Samuel Gustin, the president of the Planters Bank, the wisdom of seeking authorization from the legislature to allow the Bank of the State to renew all its accommodations rather than just two-thirds of the whole.

> Fears have been expressed that the present capital of the Planters Bank will be considered too limited for the wants of the community and now especially if our discounts are reduced $350,000; and although I have doubts whether we can renew with safety for more than $1,200,000 and at the same time reserve a fund sufficient to redeem our circulation, yet I regret, we did not stipulate for the renewal of the full amount of our permanent loans; .... I feel fully persuaded that if we could renew for two millions instead of for $1,200,000, your institution would not suffer .... There cannot be a doubt that you will have applications for double that amt. that you can safely loan in permanent accommodations.

The Bank of the State would soon cease altogether dealing in exchange on points inside and outside of Mississippi in consequence of which the Planters Bank might expect 'profits in exchange operations alone ... equal to 1 ½ percent of the … [Bank's] entire capital'. Duncan meant exchange profits in addition to the interest gained when the bank purchased a bill for its portfolio.[55]

Even with six years to complete the liquidation, important substantive changes were made in the terms on which the remaining portfolio was to be renewed. At most, debtors might expect to renew a portion of their debts every six months, rather than yearly, and in the form of acceptances and notes payable at Natchez. Tichnor advised one branch cashier that the bills he took in renewals were not however to be confined to Natchez drawees alone, 'but extended to residents in your County and elsewhere, provided the person ha[d] a fair character of stability and punctuality-men who me[t] their engagements and provide[d] in due season for what ever they undert[ook]'. The acceptor was first and foremost a guarantor, so too the endorser, and Tichnor's instruction is a fair indication of how far the regular traffic in paper had fundamentally changed ancient formulations about bills and notes.[56]

Function, not form, mattered most, and drawing a clear distinction between bills and notes was an anachronistic formulation. Contemporary practices demonstrated the power of commerce to radically alter traditional perceptions respecting those instruments. The reason behind converting accommodation paper into bills and notes payable at Natchez was simple and highly practical: any subsequent collection proceedings could be brought in that venue, not in sundry other inconvenient localities around the state. Some of the loans were placed in the posture of trade acceptances, but the understanding among the parties was that they in fact represented nothing more than renewals of old loans. Duncan wrote to the cashiers that he hoped all the branches would 'by all means endeavor to have undoubted security for all renewals made payable at …' the Natchez office.[57]

As previously mentioned the directors and officers found it necessary to provide additional relief to their customers by allowing them to extend a portion of the original curtailment of one-third of their accommodations with bills of exchange drawn payable at Natchez, six months from date. They hoped this would provide some relief until the Planters Bank could offset the curtailment with new discounts. But there was no provision in the enabling legislation for liquidating the bank to continue those loans after they fell due. In the meantime the Natchez branch of the Bank of the United States had begun curtailing its discounts of bills drawn and made payable in state. Tichnor ordered the branch cashiers to cease their purchases altogether, 'apprehending that balances w[ould] soon be greatly increased against … [the Bank of the State], for the payment of which these bills … [had been] mainly relied on'. He urged the cashiers to purchase exchange on New Orleans to the extent of its availability. Stephen Duncan, however, cautioned the cashiers not to purchase exchange 'at longer sight than 60 days'.[58]

The Bank of the State continued to remit its New Orleans exchange to the branch in that city for collection. Because the branch discounted these bills as the need arose in order to keep down cash balances against the Bank of the State, the Bank of the State soon found it necessary to tap this facility in order to settle balances against it at the Natchez branch. The circulation that accumulated in New Orleans was now returned not to the Bank of the State but to the Natchez branch for settlement. Duncan complained to the assistant cashier at New Orleans that the circulation might have been returned directly to his bank instead of to the local branch, and Samuel Jaudon, now the cashier at New Orleans, agreed that in the future settlements would be made as they had been before, by a direct exchange.[59]

Duncan had few reasons to complain about the facilities afforded his bank at New Orleans. Weeks after Duncan lodged his complaint, Jaudon confided his concerns about the future course of the Bank of the State to William McIlvaine at Philadelphia

> I am quite dissatisfied with the A/C of the Bank, State of Miss.-at the time when it has been professing to wind up its concerns and when I had expected to see its accounts with us closed entirely, it has run ahead until the balance due us exceeds 400 M$ - We have on hand, it is true, Bills remitted to us for collection which we might discount, to cover the greater part of this sum, but under present circumstances we are unwilling to take this course-I have already had correspondence enough with Mr. Duncan to let him understand that we could not continue to discount for the Bank of the State of Miss., and I have written to him again to day, requesting that his A/C may be reduced.

Jaudon, indeed, had written to Duncan and tactfully urged a reduction of the Bank of the State's balance with the New Orleans branch.[60]

In 1831 the Bank of the United States had expanded its discount lines throughout the country, primarily to accommodate a partial retirement of the federal government's debt in Europe. Portfolios at the branches and at the parent had increased by as much as one third, and now the branch cashiers were under strict instructions from Philadelphia to bring down their discounts. Considering the highly localized condition of money markets and the limited facilities for absorbing paper rejected for renewal, it is not surprising that the Bank of the United States encountered difficulties when expelling even recently acquired loans from its discount lines. Indeed, that experience was full of important lessons in the event the Bank of the United States ever embarked on a course of liquidation.[61]

The Bank of the State faced even greater problems after it entered liquidation. Having curtailed its circulation and surrendered the power to deal in exchange, its only source of income were the discounts it continued to earn from renewals of accommodation loans and the yearly curtailments every debtor was supposed to make, the latter being the actual return of capital to the shareholders. Its liabilities tended to accumulate more rapidly than the payments from its debtors; consequently the balances against it ballooned at other banks. Jaudon explained to Duncan that '[a]t a time ... when [his institution] felt the necessity of restricting discounts for ... [their] own merchants, [he] ... c[ould] not refrain from requesting correspondents [like the Bank of the State] to abstain as far as possible from calling upon ... [the branch] for advances ... [on remittances of exchange'. Jaudon noted that the balance against the Natchez bank and its branches at Woodville, Port Gibson and Vicksburg, at the New Orleans branch was $442,000, exclusive of $18,000 of notes also on hand. The directors of the branch had directed him to convey to Duncan their sincere desire to reduce their bank's investments and particularly the large balance against the Bank of the State. Jaudon admitted that the branch then held exchange yet to mature, remitted by the Bank of the State, which could be discounted and thus reduce the cash balance 'to less than one fourth its amount'. But the branch directors were unwilling at present to increase the portfolio of bills discounted, and Jaudon could not persuade them to change their resolve. The only solution was for the Bank of the State to cease any business that might further increase the balance against it and wait for its bills on New Orleans to mature and liquidate the balance. It may seem paradoxical, but for a bank to successfully liquidate it needed generous credit facilities from the money market that could be drawn on to meet its demand liabilities until such time as the optimal return from assets could be realized.[62]

Given the history of banking in Mississippi in the years after 1832, the plethora of new banks and improvement companies with banking powers chartered by the legislature, it must seem ironic that that year seems to have marked the zenith of what may be described as a time of easy and abundant credit. That year there were three banks operating at Natchez: the Bank of the State in liquidation, the branch bank of the Bank of the United States, and the Planters Bank. Their aggregate discounts of accommodation paper approached $5 million and perhaps exceeded that sum. Their exchange portfolios contained another five or six million dollars of paper. At no time in the succeeding decade would the quality and size of those facilities ever be equaled. A check on virtually any place in the United States could be purchased for at most a 1 percent premium.[63]

At the end of 1836 Mississippi's banks are reported to have had portfolios which aggregated to almost $20 million, but a sizable portion of this may have consisted of exchange purchased and exchange under protest. Circulation appears to have been about $5 million at the end of 1836, roughly the same as in 1832, but the notes of all the Mississippi banks were then trading at a substantial discount, and little of that circulation could be called anything but uncurrent money. On the eve of the Panic of 1837, obtaining paper suitable for remittance to points elsewhere in the United States was next to impossible, and when it was available dealers could command premiums as high as 10 percent.[64]

The Natchez Branch of the Bank of the United States

The senior officers and directors of the Natchez branch were all prominent planters and merchants from the locality. The first president, James C. Wilkins, was a large planter with interests in Mississippi and Louisiana. In November 1832 he resigned his office and assumed the presidency of the Planters Bank, a position he held until his financial embarrassments in the latter part of the decade led to his resignation. All the directors were planters and most were either active or passive partners in commercial firms with affiliates in New Orleans, Vicksburg, and sundry points along the Mississippi River. They were well acquainted with local conditions and no doubt knew most of the people who offered paper for discount.[65]

In the Mississippi community domestic bills were bills drawn and made payable within the state. Domestic bills were deemed to be accommodation paper because of their local character. The accommodation portfolio also included promissory notes discounted by the bank. It seems probable that the latter description of paper was used primarily to evidence loans wherein all of the parties, i.e., makers, endorsers, and payees, were residents of Natchez or its environs. Domestic bills were used when one of the parties resided elsewhere in the state. At its second organizational meeting the board resolved that the discount line would be limited to 'business paper, or paper in business form, not having more than six months to run maturity; it being understood that payment in full w[ould] be required at maturity, either in cash, or an approved Bill of Exchange not having more than four months to run'. Settlement by a bill of exchange clearly contemplated a foreign bill, that is a bill payable at New Orleans, New York, or Philadelphia.[66]

The Board took the unusual step of dispensing with the requirement that in cases where a bill was drawn in state, an indorser at least had to be a resident of Natchez. '[T]he Security usually offered by the names of Planters & others, residing in the interior of th[e] state ... [was] at least equal to that usually offered by the names of residents ... [of Natchez], and the means of coercing payment in cases of default equally summary', as those where one of the parties was domiciled locally.[67]

The inclination of the board clearly was to afford the same convenient terms to bank customers as they formerly had enjoyed doing business with the Bank of the State. Ten months, however, was the maximum accommodation a borrower would expect without having to arrange for a liquidation of his loans through facilities outside of the bank, either a merchant in New Orleans who would advance him the needful or a local lender who could lend at a substantially higher interest rate than the bank. The Bank of the State had afforded its customers terms which extended for as long as eighteen months; first, discounting a local bill or note with twelve months to run, and then receiving a six month bill on New Orleans in payment of the same.[68]

On 20 December 1831, the Board petitioned the parent bank for authority to discount nine and twelve month accommodation paper. Longer maturities would permit the bank's customers to more easily settle their loans at a time when the crops were being shipped to market. They could then draw on their merchants at New Orleans at thirty, sixty and ninety days, and thus avoid the 2.5 percent commission 'always enforced by the Merchant in New Orleans on long bills'. The existing policy forced their customers to settle their loans in the summer, a most inconvenient season of the year for everyone, and inevitably they were forced to draw bills on New Orleans at four months or borrow from other sources. The Board attempted to refute any suggestion that discounting for longer periods would materially interfere with the exchange operations. Extending maturities would attract more business to the bank and thus over time swell the offerings of exchange. 'The effect w[ould] be, that short Bills w[ould] be taken which … [would] not [be] chargeable with commission but the same profit … [would] accrue to the institution'. The directors noted that the Bank of the State had pursued a policy of permanent accommodation, curtailing only one-quarter of their loans annually, and on an accommodation portfolio of $1,500,000, had posted upwards of $2,000,000 a year in the exchange account. The Board also noted that the new branch had attracted local opposition 'growing out of the Political feeling and the interests of rival State Institutions;' moreover the new Planters Bank had the power to discount twelve month paper and with an authorized capital of $3,000,000 would soon attract all of the best business to its doors. The parent bank, however, refused their application on 20 January 1832.[69]

Less than a year after the new branch opened the crisis began over the re-chartering of the Bank of the United States. Nicholas Biddle wrote to James Wilkins on 16 January 1832, recommending to him that he solicit the state banks in his area to memorialize Congress to re-charter the national institution. He penned a similar request to Samuel Jaudon at New Orleans the same day. Considering the adverse impact the new branch had had on the fortunes of the Bank of the State, and that bank's strong identification with individuals who were devotees of Henry Clay, it seems remarkable that Mississippi's congressional delegation was split on the re-charter question. Indeed, one of the national bank's most ardent defenders in Congress was Mississippi Senator George Poindexter.[70]

The relationship between the branch and the Mississippi community might best be described as an ambivalent one. The branch did provide a large measure of short-term liquidity to local exchange dealers and their clients, and with the Bank of the State's resolution to voluntarily liquidate, even accommodations with six months to run certainly were welcome. The branch's strong identification with local interests was, however, both a strength and a weakness. Its officers and directors were among the most eminent businessmen in the state, but there was a strong public perception, too, that the branch was a closed club. In the case of the state banks, public perception was much closer to the truth. The national bank's strong influence over the course of exchange within the United States and its seeming power to set the price of foreign exchange were factors which weighed heavily against it when officers and directors at the state banks began calculating the relative value of that institution to themselves. The national bank greatly reduced their profits from arbitrage. Finally, the national bank tended to retard the circulation of the state institutions in places where it had branches. Nicholas Biddle would later describe the effect as one that produced very positive results because it discouraged the state banks from over-trading. This might well have been true had the national bank's circulation been the only currency in the United States. But gaining a circulation was thought to be essential for any bank's profitability, and the national bank rather shortened the time notes emanating from a state bank could float in the channels of commerce. The Natchez branch had certainly caused the Bank of the State's circulation to wither. At the same time, the national bank was in a unique position to press its circulation on all parts of the country, and its notes enjoyed currency because debts owed to the federal government could be discharged with them.[71]

On 10 July 1832, Andrew Jackson vetoed the re-charter of the Bank of the United States. On 31 July Nicholas Biddle wrote to William Shipp, president pro tem of the Natchez branch, to 'forbear making advances for the purchases of domestic bills', that is in-state bills drawn on Natchez, a significant component of the accommodation portfolio. He instructed the other branches to make the same reductions. His policy had less to do with Jackson's veto than the slow progress made at the branches in reducing their discount lines in conformity with his orders of the previous year. Edward Shippen, the cashier of the Louisville office, was told to 'confine your purchases to bills on New Orleans and the Atlantic cities whenever you can avoid purchase on other places. Indeed a general diminution of your loans appears necessary in order to bring the business of your office into proper proportion with the other parts of the establishment, and reduce your debt to the Bank and the Atlantic offices …' Biddle advised one correspondent that his 'policy [was] … in a few words to bring down gently and quietly in the first instance the amount of the local discounts in the West and South and gradually to put the loans as much as possible into Domestic bills of Exchange which [would be] ... paid off at maturity'. To a director of the New York branch he confided that '[t]he Bank d[id] not mean to commence any systematic reduction of its loans with a view to winding up its affairs-It d[id] not mean to begin to close its concerns. [The Bank] ... mean[t] to go on in its general business, just as if no such event as the President's negation had ever happened'. The only change was 'rather in the form than in the amount of [the Bank's] ... loans-and [that was] ... to give gently and gradually the loans of the Bank the direction of domestic bills, converting where it c[ould] be done the line of notes discounted, into domestic bills of exchange, ... payable at maturity ...'[72]

The national bank increased its purchases of bills of exchange by 35 percent in the first half of 1832, well before Jackson's veto, and had by the end of that year reduced its accommodation portfolio by 12 percent. At the same time the bank began to accumulate specie, a faint indication perhaps that the curtailment had succeeded in raising the value of its circulation above the specie premium which was typically a fraction of 1 percent.[73]

Acting on instructions from Philadelphia Samuel Jaudon wrote to the Natchez branch on 13 November 1832, to further curtail its discount line, shortening maturities of accommodation paper from six months to a maximum of four months, and accepting in satisfaction of those debts only cash or drafts payable in ninety days or less. The volume of discounts continued their steady decline, and the exchange portfolio concomitantly expanded. By May 1833 the pressure at Natchez was so great that the branch directors felt themselves compelled to resume purchases of six-month bills on New Orleans. But more instructions arrived from Philadelphia in September reaffirming the previous resolution not to purchase exchange having more than ninety days to run. By November the branch board was rejecting so much of the paper being offered for discount that it began meeting only one day a week instead of two.[74]

The extent of the reduction at Natchez is immediately apparent from an examination of the Profit and Loss Account in the branch ledger. In 1831 income from discounts of accommodation paper and purchases of exchange were roughly the same. By the second half of 1832 exchange purchases accounted for almost two-thirds of gross income. By March 1834, income from exchange exceeded income from discounts received by a margin of three to one. The branch portfolio had been completely transformed in the previous two years.[75]

Even in the best of environments a bank's supporting the credit of its customers by maintaining the convertibility of its circulation required a great deal of manipulation, if not artful finesse. In the case of the Bank of the United States maintaining enough liquidity at every point in the system was immeasurably simplified through the mechanism of branch notes and drafts. The subject of branch notes and drafts has been much discussed in the literature on the Bank of the United States, in part because the Jacksonians grounded part of their argument against the bank in the alleged illegality of this species of paper. No doubt bank notes and drafts were an important part of the total circulation, but they also were one of those items which created inter-branch credits and liabilities. Natchez branch liabilities, for example, accumulated at the Louisville and Lexington branches; the Mississippi branch throughout its lifetime ran an unfavorable balance with the Kentucky branches.[76]

On the other hand, the Natchez branch enjoyed a favorable balance with the New York branch of almost $1 million at the beginning of 1834. During the previous year the Natchez branch had negotiated over $1 million of checks drawn by the Planters Bank on the Phoenix Bank of New York City, payment for a portion of the bonds sold by the state of Mississippi to fund its capital subscription to the new state bank. The Planters Bank soon drew down its balance at the Natchez branch, providing a large measure of relief to customers of the branch whose accommodation loans were being heavily curtailed. The balance against New York, however, was only slowly liquidated, and then by the cashier at Natchez checking on New York in favor of sundry western branches where his balances were unfavorable.[77]

Had the bank's enemies been more knowledgeable about its accounting methods they could have sustained a much stronger argument against its re-charter on economic grounds rather than political ones. Inter-branch accounting lent immeasurably to the currency of the bank's liabilities, lengthening the float time beyond anything a state institution could possibly sustain. No other institution had the facilities at its disposal to so completely rationalize the huge masses of debits and credits, or borrow so much with only the public's confidences as collateral. The bank's capacity to inflate the money supply went well beyond simple measures of its outstanding circulation.[78]

No doubt the system which Nicholas Biddle had created had much to recommend it, but even the great architect himself betrayed some rather quaint notions about the overall impact of his national system of highly leveraged branch banks. Offsetting deficits at one location with credits at another was more art than science, an exercise of good judgment tempered with imagination. Samuel Jaudon's frustration with his mentor's questioning the continued purchases at the New Orleans branch of domestic bills, particularly those on western cities, after instructions to purchase bills only on the Atlantic seaboard cities, was clearly evident in his letter to Biddle on 16 May 1832. Jaudon wondered how the wizard of Chestnut Street could even consider those purchases as being roughly comparable to discounts of local accommodation paper.

> [Y]ou speak of our Dom. Bills as if they were notes Discounted, and thus shew an enormous increase in our local business. We consider them so totally distinct from our Bills discounted that we have regarded the increase in the former, as the

best possible mode of decreasing the latter permanently. The money that is paid at New York, Philada. & Boston, for produce shipped to those points is applied here directly to the payment of Notes Discounted-We hear nothing more of these Bills, we are not called upon to renew them, either in whole or in part.

The purchase of bills drawn at New Orleans on the North was absolutely essential to keep the whole system in balance. The New Orleans branch was the agent for all the western branches. The branch not only collected the exchange remitted by the western branches, but was required to place the whole of those heavy collections at points in the North so those branches could discharge the balances against them at New York, Philadelphia, and Boston. This could only be accomplished by 'buying bills on the North, at a profit, or by remitting specie at a loss'. The branch had already shipped all the readily available specie in the local money market, and attempts to extract more could only result in the state banks falling heavily in debt to the Bank of the United States. During the previous year the branch had collected $4 million for the Nashville, Louisville, Lexington, Cincinnati, and Pittsburgh branches and paid nearly $5 million of checks drawn by those branches in favor of the northern branches. '[T]he difficulty [was] … find[ing] enough <u>Northern</u> funds, to meet [the] … checks of the Western offices besides putting the Bank & northern offices in the inconvenience of heavy cash advances [to the New Orleans branch] … until the Bills …' remitted to cover the checks matured. In addition to collections for the western branches, the New Orleans office was a large issuer of branch notes in consequence of the heavy demand from western traders who came to the city and sold their produce directly in the local market. The branch notes were the only tender these people would accept in payment, and they carried them back to Tennessee and Kentucky thus increasing the balances against New Orleans in favor of the branches in those states. Shipments of produce from New Orleans to points up the Mississippi River generated bills payable at Nashville and Louisville, and the branch always purchased to the extent of their availability in the money market. 'The Planter who sen[t] his sugar to Louisville for sale ha[d] as fair a claim upon … [the Bank] for accommodation in the purchase of his bill upon Louisville, as the one who prefer[red] shipping in his sugar to New York, ha[d] for the sale of his Bill on New York'. In prior years upwards of $2 million of branch notes had accumulated annually at the western branches, and this liability had in part been discharged by purchasing exchange on western cities.[79]

The day after he wrote to Biddle, Jaudon wrote to William McIlvaine and thanked him for acquiescing to the continued purchases of western bills at the New Orleans branch. He could not, however, 'cease to regret that Mr. Biddle ha[d] never been able to extend his tours of inspection as far as New Orleans - His theoretical views … [were] very sound, but … [the management] want[ed] him to see the realities of ... [their] position that he m[ight] sympathize more fully [with them] ...'[80]

In the weeks before the veto Jaudon confided much information to his superiors in Philadelphia about the new Union Bank lately chartered by the Louisiana legislature. The new bank had an authorized capital of $8 million dollars, $7 million of which would be funded by the state of Louisiana issuing 5 percent bonds. Jaudon genuinely believed that the Bank of the United States could and ought to capture the underwriting contract for the issue. The bank would profit handsomely from the sterling exchange facilities that a sale of the bonds in England would create. He clearly saw substantial advantages in the transaction for the bank; namely, gaining access to a large supply of sterling exchange which would answer for many purposes. More importantly, the new bank 'would at once take one half of [the branch's] ... Bills Discounted as they st[ood] and send ... Bonds to a large amount at a fixed rate [of exchange] or far negotiation'.[81]

A close look at the operations of the branches suggests that local conditions were more decisive in shaping the course each adopted, irrespective of directions from the parent bank. Indeed, money markets in the country were highly localized and even nominal levels of business in each locality influenced perceptions, at least short term; the amount of specie shipped to and from New Orleans during the week, or fractional changes in the price of exchange from day to day. For example, in May 1832 the New Orleans branch ceased selling checks on the North in order to curb the growing balances against it in Philadelphia and New York. According to Jaudon, this course should have resulted in a reduction in the exchange offered to the branch for purchase, but there had been no diminution 'owing to the installments paid at New York & Philada. on the stock of the Canal Bank, for which ...' that Bank was then drawing. The Canal Bank thus filled the void left by the branch's temporary retirement from this line of business. By answering the need for checks on the north, the Canal Bank added liquidity to the local market, and those who had accommodations at the branch could meet the curtailments with their exchange rather than having to remit bills directly to New York for collection to answer for bank checks. In each locality where the Bank of the United States had a branch it found itself having to adapt and accommodate.[82]

The legality of branch note issues, something opponents of re-charter continued to raise as a primary objection, was closely related to another concern, that notes issued at one branch needed only to be received at other branches of the system for collection and not for immediate credit. Tenders of New Orleans branch notes, for example, would be received at the New York branch for collection, and very often the holder did receive immediate credit if it was convenient for the New York branch to accept a tender. But no branch was under any obligation to receive tenders of other branch banks' notes. Branch checks obviated some of the difficulty; a check issued by one branch on another branch had to be paid immediately upon presentment to the drawee. If the check was a time draft, the drawee was obliged to pay it according to its tenor. But the subject of branch notes continued to inflame those opposed to re-charter.[83]

The re-charter legislation actually contained a provision which required every branch to receive all the notes of the Bank and its branches 'when tendered in payment by a state Bank'. Biddle strongly objected to the provision and gave his reasons in a letter to Thomas Ewing:

> It will afford me great pleasure to cooperate with you in any measure to prevent injustice to the banks of your State, but I am afraid that this general provision would operate injuriously in other parts of the Union-For instance in the seaports where the course of trade and the demands of the revenue create an accumulation of the notes of the distant branches, if a branch is obliged to receive in payment of debts due from a neighboring state Bank not merely the notes issued by the Branch and for which alone it is responsible but also the notes of all the other Branches there could not help to result from it great embarrassment and even risk to the Branch from its liabilities for the issues of other Branches.

The legislation, moreover, contained a provision that Biddle thought would obviate most difficulties. In future, branch notes could only be issued when made payable at the branch where issued. No third party to whom such notes were tendered could be under any misapprehension if he expected to antici-pate an immediate credit for notes issued by a branch in some far off city. The subject, however, does underscore those disparate elements which made the bank appear at times to be something more than a loose association of localized credit agencies, but certainly not a great national bank whose circulation was the nation's legal tender.[84]

At the very moment Jackson's veto of the re-charter legislation was being announced, the officers of the bank were in the midst of providing the means for retiring upwards of $15 million of the government's debt in the last quarter of 1832. Much of the debt was held in Europe, so the bank would have to make large purchases of foreign exchange. On 30 June 1832, Biddle apprised Thomas Cadwalader of the course to be pursued at the branches. Local dis-counts would have to be further curtailed, purchases of domestic bills would have to be restricted to those drawn on 'the Northern Atlantic frontiers and those at very short dates, certainly within 90 days', and every available dollar would be needed to invest in advances on the bonds set for redemption and purchases of foreign exchange. Advancing on the bonds would thus extend the redemption period into 1833 and diffuse some of the pressure in the nation's money markets.[85]

From the spring of 1832 until the expiration of the charter in 1836 the Bank of the United States pursued a policy of relentless curtailments of local discounts at the branches and the conversion of those claims into short bills on Philadelphia, New York, Boston, Baltimore, Charleston, Savannah, and New Orleans. The effect was to convert what were essentially long term loans into short term ones, and the natural tendency should have been to increase liquidity and move commodity prices higher. But the actions of the Bank of the United States tended to suppress, at least temporarily, the effects of increased liquidity in the system. To the extent that the bank could realize its western and southern funds at points east, it did so in specie. That, of course, caused the entire financial system to contract.[86]

Peter Temin and others have ascribed a somewhat neutral effect to the conduct of the national bank in the last four years of its life. It sharply curtailed discount lines in the last quarter of 1833, but by the last quarter of 1834 the portfolio was again expanding, and in the third quarter of 1835 it was as large as it had been on the eve of the re-charter crisis. Temin writes that 'the pressure was not as great as it had been in 1819 or as it would be in 1837. There was comparatively little panic, and banks did not refuse to redeem their notes in specie. As a result, we may assume -- although we do not have the data to confirm our expectations -- that the effects on the rest of the economy were not strong'.[87]

Local discounts tended to be localized in their effects, i.e., somewhat self-contained. Expansive exchange purchases sloshed about from point to point. The proceeds of maturing bills had to be invested, and generally the collecting agents were instructed to buy more exchange at the point of collection or allow the remitting branch to draw for the proceeds in order to purchase exchange at the locality or remit the proceeds from curtailments to the parent bank. The overall effect was to increase the pressure in the nation's commercial centers such as New York and New Orleans. The Natchez branch bought bills on New Orleans from local exchange dealers and applied the proceeds to the curtailments of local discounts. The acceptors at New Orleans met the bills by drawing bills on New York or London, and so the effect of the curtailments at Natchez were communicated elsewhere in the country and even abroad. At various points in the chain, which stretched from Natchez to London, acceptors borrowed to the extent of their abilities from sources in their localities and discharged some of their liabilities in that way. But eventually even those credit facilities had to be kept current, and to do so they checked for the balances owed to them by the drawers at Natchez. They, in turn, met the checks by negotiating more bills at the Natchez branch which were remitted to New Orleans for collection. The world of commercial credit suddenly had become a far more risky environment.

The situation was especially acute in the Lower Mississippi Valley at the beginning of 1833. Discount lines and exchange purchases at the New Orleans, Natchez, and Mobile branches aggregated to at least 22 percent of the bank's entire portfolio of $60 million. Local loans at those branches actually exceeded those at the Ohio, Kentucky, Indiana, Illinois, Missouri, and Tennessee branches. A large proportion of the loans at the western branches were in fact purchases of domestic bills, the bulk of which were payable at New Orleans.[88]

Although conditions had already begun to deteriorate at Natchez and New Orleans in the first quarter of 1833, Biddle manifested complete confidence in the portfolios at those locations. 'With regard to Natchez and New Orleans', he wrote, 'the loans are remarkably safe and in fact of a commercial character'. He meant, of course, that these locations yielded large volumes of high quality exchange, both foreign and domestic, which was so essential for the preservation of monetary stability throughout the Union.[89]

Biddle drew only the most limited distinction between exchange and the circulation of the notes of the national bank, its branches, and the state banks.

I think that we can show that taking into consideration the bills purchased by the Bank - those collected by it - the drafts drawn by it - and the Branch notes and state bank paper received - all of which is in fact exchange, the Bank is the channel of commercial exchanges thro' different sections of the country, to the amount of about <u>two hundred millions of dollars a year</u>. Yet this commercial railroad these miserable people are striving to break up.

It can certainly be inferred from his remarks that he regarded exchange as the primary circulating medium of the country, and if indeed they accurately reflect the true condition of the nation's monetary system, then some reappraisal of the contribution of excessive bank note issues to the nation's financial woes during the remainder the 1830s must be undertaken.[90]

For reasons not altogether clear the bank sharply curtailed its purchases of foreign exchange in the fall of 1833 and did not return to the market until the summer of 1834. The result was a collapse in the exchange premium, so that sterling bills gave up 10 percent of their value during the course of the bank's absence from the money markets. At the same time, the domestic exchanges underwent a rapid deterioration. The bank had also ceased its purchases of bills on the west and south. In January 1834, exchange on the western cities at Philadelphia was at 2.5 percent discount, and exchange on points south was at a 1.25 percent discount. The discounts reflected pure exchange and represented a five-fold increase in the cost of realizing western funds in the east.[91]

It is reasonable to suppose that the surfeit of western and southern bills drawn on eastern cities would have created some pressure in the east in consequence of the rapid curtailments of local accommodations at the remitting branches. But the situation was somewhat more complicated. Under normal conditions a large volume of bills drawn at the western and southern branches on eastern cities would have moved the exchanges decisively in favor of those localities where the bills had been drawn, especially with the curtailments of local discounts. But the bank had ceased largely to purchase bills on the west and south. The result was that drawers on points west and south found a limited market in which to cash their bills; in consequence an abnormally high discount arose on those bills. The actions of the Bank of the United States in 1834, then, more than offset the rise in liquidity.

It seems remarkable that Biddle expected the state banks to fill the void created by the absence of the Bank of the United States from the exchanges. If state banks in the east had become aggressive purchasers of bills on the west and south they would have immediately fallen deeper into debt to the branches of the national bank in their respective cities. Much of the paper then had to be done 'out of doors' and the rate of discount rose appreciably. The pressure created by the bank's withdrawal from domestic exchanges produced consequences similar to those encountered when it ceased its purchases of foreign exchange. The most apparent and measurable consequence was the withdrawal of specie from circulation and its rapid accumulation in the vaults of the parent bank and its branches. From the first quarter of 1832 to the first quarter of 1833 the bank's holdings of specie rose from $7,038,823 to $8,951,847. By the third quarter of 1834 specie stood at $12,823,997, and in November of that year it reached $16 million. During the same period bank notes outstanding contracted 25 percent.[92]

Historians have been particularly harsh in their criticism of Jackson and his subordinates over the removal of federal deposits from the national bank in the last quarter of 1833. Assuming for the sake of argument the withdrawals were unconstitutional, the overall impact was limited, an assessment reached by Temin on the basis of the relative size of the withdrawals. Indeed, the withdrawals probably provided some small relief, albeit temporary, from the pressure on the exchanges by allowing the depository banks to purchase domestic and foreign exchange without immediately expanding the balances against themselves at the national bank.[93]

The curtailments of local accommodations in the west and south and the repatriation of the proceeds with bills on the east had commenced in earnest even before the administration made known its intention to withdraw the federal deposits. The Bank of the United States withdrew from the active mass of commercial credits in the nation's financial system a sum approaching $50 million, as is evidenced by the rapid accumulation of specie in its vaults.[94]

Biddle took particular pleasure in personally arranging the financial transactions of eminent personages. On 20 January 1834, he apprised Henry Clay of the net proceeds passed to his credit from two items of Kentucky paper cashed for him at the Washington branch. An examination of the account revealed 'an unfortunate practical illustration of the difficulties which [were] ... coming upon the intercourse between the States in consequence of the disorder of the currency'. A few months before 'the exchange [had been] ... ½ to ¾ per cent'. The exchange for realizing Clay's Kentucky money at Washington had risen to 2.5 percent since that time, and what formerly would have cost $8 now cost $40.[95]

By the spring of 1834 the board of the Natchez branch had determined that unless some immediate relief was provided to that community, hundreds of thousands of dollars of New Orleans bills would likely be returned under protest. During the previous fall and winter the branch had purchased huge quantities of bills, anticipating a bountiful harvest and high prices for the great staple. But declining cotton prices and the curtailments of local discounts had 'put it out of the power of the Planters generally to place in the hands of the Commission Merchants of New Orleans and [Natchez] ... the funds necessary to meet the payment of Bills on them which had been drawn in anticipation of the continuation of high prices obtained in the early part of the season ...' The board decided to authorize the Bill committee to purchase bills on New Orleans at not more than ninety days, the proceeds of which would be applied to the payment of the bills then maturing at New Orleans.[96]

Arranging for the payment of bills in the manner directed by the board's resolution was without precedent. As a practical matter the board was simply allowing the exchange dealers an additional ninety days to marshal the resources with which to meet the bills. The only options open to the bill dealers was to endeavor to borrow from the state banks or out of doors from capitalists, either at Natchez or elsewhere. Many no doubt did so by selling sterling bills on their agents in England at substantial losses. Sterling remained at very depressed levels well into the summer of 1834, putting downward pressure on staple prices. The disappearance of the sterling premium had severely curtailed the circulation of every medium of exchange, and specie steadily accumulated in the banks.

At the end of April the board found it necessary to authorize the purchase of bills on New Orleans at six months, rather than three, and it began charging exchange at the rate of 1 percent on bills having more than four months to run. Even so the board still was rejecting most of the local paper offered for discount. A charge for exchange for bills drawn on New Orleans and negotiated at the branch had rarely if ever been exacted. The course of exchange at the moment probably was against Natchez in consequence of the device previously resorted to for extending the bills then coming due at New Orleans. One percent for exchange, however, effectively raised borrowing costs 50 percent on an annual basis.[97]

Damages arising from bills under protest became an increasingly important item in the Profit and Loss Account. In May 1833 the Bank of the United States' account with the branch was credited for $102,536.62. The items that comprised that sum were: discounts, $50,339.10; exchange, $53,561.07; interest, $4,654.48, and damages $1,410.32. A year later the parent was credited with $132,786.62. Discounts were $31,674.66, a clear indication of the extent of the previous year's curtailments. Income from exchange was $88,736.86, and damages, $17,977.60. During the next six months damages accounted for $13,595.86 of the $113,991.92 credited to the parent. Income from damages was far less significant in 1835, declining to about $3,000 for the entire year. But it is quite clear too that much of the paper under protest from 1834 had either not been settled or had been met by the debtors' negotiation of more bills on New Orleans.[98]

Suspended debt rose from $60,471.29 in January 1834 to $348,108.41 in June of that year. Over the summer and fall the balances were gradually reduced, but by March 1835 the suspended debt had risen again to $405,777.18. The branch effectively settled all of the balances in the Protested Exchange Account and the Account for Bills and Notes Under Protest with the sale of the portfolios to the Planters Bank on 7 November 1835. The branch, however, continued its heavy purchases of domestic exchange, only ceasing in March 1836, at which time the exchange account showed a deficit of nearly $4 million. During the course of the spring and summer of 1836, upwards of $500,000 of these bills were returned from New Orleans under protest. When the United States Bank of Pennsylvania commenced liquidating in June 1841, $212,048.09 of debts from bills that had been drawn in the fall of 1835 still remained unsettled.[99]

From August 1833 to August 1834 the branch contracted its portfolio of local loans 43 percent, from $1,526,459.12 to $837,974.37. Over the course of that year purchases of domestic exchange continued at a high level, only dropping below $2,000,000 in the first quarter of 1834. Instructions arrived from Philadelphia in August 1834 to cease the curtailment of discounts, which the local board sincerely welcomed, but they had no authority to increase the local portfolio. Local accommodations hovered between $800,000 and $900,000 for the remainder of 1834 and all of 1835. Purchases of domestic bills steadily increased in the summer and fall of 1835 and on 11 November stood at $2,948,235.33.[100]

Temin notes that the Bank of the United States ceased its curtailments in 1834 and expanded its portfolio thereafter. Available data do indicate that such was the case, but converting local loans into domestic bills was not an operation with neutral consequences. One probable result was an increased demand in the Atlantic seaboard cities, as well as New Orleans, for local discounts to meet the bills coming due at those locations. But anecdotal evidence suggests that the pressure continued unabated in the western cities during the remainder of the bank's life.[101]

The Bank of the United States reinvested much of the proceeds from maturing bills by advancing heavily on the stocks of improvement companies, a measure that practically transformed it from a commercial bank into an investment bank. These advances no doubt expanded the liquidity in the financial system, and may in some measure account for the inflationary pressures noticed in the years from 1835 to 1837. The bank converted millions from its discount lines of local paper into domestic exchange, a medium that Biddle equated with the currency of the country. That measure alone would have expanded the money supply, but its full effects would only have been realized when the Bank of the United States began re-deploying its funds. The bank's portfolio was increasingly outside the mainstream of income flows from agriculture and industry. Much of the stocks that collateralized the portfolio were in improvement companies which would be many years in realizing their income potential, something Biddle and the management of the bank failed to anticipate.[102]

In retrospect Biddle showed remarkable naivete about the disruptions that would result from a liquidation of a bank whose magnitude simply dwarfed every other financial institution in the United States. On 5 June 1835, he wrote to Charles A. Davis at New York that the most satisfactory result of the course he and the direction of the bank had pursued in the previous two- and-a-half years was that while 'the aggregate loans … [had] increased-the increase … [was] exclusively in that Atlantic and commercial cities-while the diminution … [was] going rapidly on in the most distant & unmanageable points'. The great object had been to concentrate the 'funds of the Bank in large masses of disposable capital'. The circulation and purchases of domestic bills had never been higher, but the whole debt was 'in a form very flexible and manageable', consisting principally of domestic bills payable at maturity.[103]

By the end of that summer Biddle had come to the realization that a complete withdrawal from those distant branches would be nearly impossible without continuous and heavy purchases of domestic bills drawn at those locations on the east. His immediate problem was that a complete liquidation of the accommodation portfolios at the branches was infeasible. The Planters Bank purchased the Natchez branch's local loans and protested paper on a four-year credit. The Gas Bank bought what was left of the portfolio at New Orleans on the same terms. Upwards of $4,000,000 remained to be repatriated from the Lower Mississippi Valley when the bank's charter expired in March 1836.[104]

Local arrangements were far from satisfactory. The first effect was, in Biddle's own words, 'to throw upon the Bank the circulation & deposits of the branches closed without any remittances from those branches'. The liabilities flowed back to Philadelphia, and having failed to fully recover its capital from the west, the bank now found that its means of meeting those demands were exceedingly stretched. In March 1835, the bank's hoard of specie stood at $16.5 million; its circulation, $19.5 million. By August specie in the bank declined to $12,883,968, and the circulation had risen to $24,329,222. In March 1836, the date set for the expiration of the charter, specie stood at $6,244,197, but circulation still exceeded $20 million. By December the bank possessed only $3,275,292 of specie, 60 percent of its loans were predicated on stocks of various concerns. Purchases of domestic bills accounted for only 20 percent of the portfolio.[105]

The difficulties experienced by the Bank of the United States as it moved from a contractile posture in 1833 and 1834 to a liquidation mode during the remainder of its life were very similar to the ones which befell the Bank of the State of Mississippi after it voluntarily surrendered its charter to the state. At the most basic level there was simply a mismatch between the bank's demand liabilities and its relatively illiquid assets. So long as a bank had a reliable ongoing supply of domestic bills with which to retrieve its circulation from the marketplace, that circulation would remain vital and desirable as a means of realizing value. When a bank entered liquidation, its first hurdle was retrieving its circulation and paying out any remaining deposits. After that, its stockholders simply had to wait until the bank's borrowers could either liquidate their bills receivable over a period of years or find another lender to take up their loans. Liquidations rarely were profitable for shareholders, and often enough other creditors too found their means locked up.

Conclusion

Temin has suggested that the impact of the contraction, which commenced in the fall of 1833 and lasted into the summer of 1834, may have varied from region to region, depending on the extent of the operations of the Bank of the United States in each area of the country. New England, for example, appears to have experienced only limited inconvenience. The Bank of the United States' operations there were relatively small. It may seem anomalous, but the bank's operations at Natchez were larger than its discount lines and exchange purchases at Boston. Boston, like New York, and even New Orleans, was well supplied with commercial banks that dealt extensively in domestic and foreign exchange. Expanding on Temin's assessment, it can be said that the curtailments at Natchez in 1833 and 1834 took a severe toll on the commercial community; suspended debts increased six-fold and remained at very high levels for the remainder of the branch's existence.[106]

In 1835 the branch expanded its exchange purchases, but ceased purchasing local paper altogether in July. Three months later, the entire portfolio of local accommodations and suspended debt was sold to the Planters Bank. In the second half of that year the parent derived only $7,567.89 of income from discounts. Exchange purchases, however, netted $100,000 in the last six months of 1835 and $105,000 in the first five months of 1836.[107]

At its highest point the branch's authorized circulation of notes and drafts was $2,717,420. Notes and drafts actually in circulation hovered between $1,250,000 and $1,500,000 prior to 1834, then declined precipitously during the summer of that year to 55 percent of their former level. Branch circulation climbed dramatically in 1835 and actually exceeded $2,000,000 by the spring. During the remainder of the year the entire authorization of notes and drafts appears to have passed into circulation, no doubt to fund the expansive purchases of domestic exchange which account stood at $3,857,275.46 on 1 March 1836. This operation, which no doubt was repeated elsewhere in the system, was the source of subsequent complaints against the United States Bank of Pennsylvania, that its predecessor had flooded the market with its notes on the eve of the expiration of the federal charter.[108]

In July 1835 notes and deposits of the Bank of the United States totaled $34,891,577. In March 1836 those liabilities stood at $25,000,000, but specie in the bank had declined from $13,429,328 to $6,224,197 over the same period. In June 1835 discounts and exchange purchases exceeded $65 million, a level only exceeded in the fall of 1831 and winter of 1832 when the loan portfolio bulged with $67 million of accommodations and bills.[109]

It seems unlikely that the branch could have arranged such heavy exchange purchases in 1835 without the other Natchez banks affording the mercantile community expansive accommodations. Initially, at least, the expansive purchases of exchange swelled the branch's circulation, much of which would have been tendered at the two state banks in Natchez, the Planters Bank and the Agricultural Bank. Branch notes and drafts were optimal for remittances to points east, and the state banks no doubt responded by expanding their discount lines. By expanding their local discounts, the state banks enabled the branch to continue its heavy purchases of ninety-day bills over the course of 1835. The state banks had every incentive for converting the branch's exchange purchases into local discounts for their own portfolios. They effectively absorbed the branch's notes and bills and replaced them with their own. The state banks merely reacted to the excessive monetary stimulus coming from the Natchez branch.[110]

Temin argues that the inflation which preceded the Panic of 1837 in part had its origins in an expansion of the nation's monetary stock, which in turn was predicated on a rise in the stock of specie. There can be little doubt that the collapse of the exchange premium in 1833 and 1834 encouraged imports of specie, or stated another way, the collapse curtailed exports. Why the stock of specie rose in 1832 and 1833 is less clear. The Bank of the United States was a heavy purchaser of foreign exchange in 1831 and 1832; as it accumulated balances in England it may have found it expedient to draw them down by selling six-month bills, payable in London, to merchants engaged in the China trade. Those engaged in the trade could have used these orders to make purchases and thus avoided the expense of shipping Mexican silver to the Far East.[111]

The sale of American securities to a large extent in England likewise would have encouraged the accumulation of specie in the United States. Seven million dollars of Louisiana state bonds were sold in England in 1832 and 1833 to capitalize the Union Bank at New Orleans. This one transaction affected the price of sterling at New Orleans as the bank sold bills to realize the proceeds. It is less clear whether the rise in the stock of specie caused the banks to expand their note issues by increasing their discount lines, and whether these actions led to the inflation in 1835 and 1836. It seems improbable that the state banks would have rapidly increased their assets in 1835 without some stimulus to do so from the Bank of the United States. The Bank of the United States' rather awkward conversion of its huge portfolio of local loans into short bills in 1834 and 1835 added substantially to the liquidity in what might rather be crudely described as the nation's banking system.[112]

Money markets were highly localized in 1836. The role of sundry discrete banks loosely spread over the land in bringing on the Panic seemed all too clear to contemporaries, and subsequently has seemed so to many historians. But while state banks could and did cause havoc in their localities, no single state bank or group of state banks could have created the financial climate that followed in the wake of Jackson's veto of the re-charter bill. The Panic of 1837 was first and foremost a belated recognition by the banks in sundry disparate localities that the domestic exchanges had fallen into chaos. Aggregating the banks' circulation and attempting to infer something about their operations from the flow of specie out of their vaults and their falling reserve ratios rather misses the point. Even in a single locality the condition of the banks *vis a vis* each other varied considerably; whether as to exchange and accommodation portfolios or the quality of demand liabilities in the form of circulation and deposits.

One particularly useful indicator of the rapidity with which balances against the branch were settled and its loans contracted or expanded is the level of activity in the Cash Account. A purchase of a domestic bill, for example, created a debit in the Exchange Account. The proceeds were credited to the Individual Deposits Account, and that account debited and the credit passed to the Cash

Account as the checks drawn by the depositors were paid. The Cash Account was debited for collections made for depositors as well as for branch notes and checks remitted by other branches and banks. The obligations of other branches and the state banks tendered at the Natchez branch created credits in the Cash Account and debits in the accounts of those institutions.[113]

Levels of activity in the Cash Account ranged between $2 and $5 million every month prior to 1833. During 1833 the monthly average was $3.5 million. From January to August 1834 activity steadily declined from a peak of $4 million to a low of $1 million. The Cash Account was always in deficit between $500,000 and $1 million in the years prior to 1834. The deficit in account grew steadily in 1834 and exceeded $2 million in the summer and fall of that year. The growth in the deficit no doubt reflects not only the declining levels of activity at the branch, i.e., the sharp curtailments of local discounts, but also the large number of bills under protest and the extension of many bills set to mature in the summer of 1834 at New Orleans. The deficit in the Cash Account fell to $1 million in January 1835, but primarily in consequence of the repatriation of $500,000 to the parent in Philadelphia. That sum reflected the curtailment of local discounts in 1834 and represented means no longer available to the branch and the Natchez community. Exchange purchases expanded rapidly thereafter, but the ratio of exchange to accommodation paper also rose dramatically. By November 1835, the ratio stood at $3 of exchange for every $1 of accommodation paper.

The available data on Mississippi's state banks in 1834 is of course exclusive of the branch and its circulation. Larry Schweikart indicates that notes in circulation and deposits were $4 million in 1834 and $5 million in 1835. By 1836 demand liabilities stood at $10 million, but that sum represented the combined deposits and notes in circulation of nine reporting banks. The sums reported in 1834 and 1835 were for the two state banks in Natchez and their branches then doing business in the state. Inclusion of the liabilities of the Bank of the United States' Natchez branch during those years raises the monetary stock in Mississippi anywhere from $1 million to $2.5 million. Much of the increase in demand liabilities, then, in 1836, may be attributable to the branch's exchange purchases in the fall of 1835 and the state banks' response to this stimulus by largely increasing their local discounts.[114]

PENNSYLVANIA AND MISSISSIPPI: THE UNITED STATES BANK, 1836-1841

[T]here is a strong jealousy of New York rising in the South. You know the schemes of the Southerners for getting their own trade into their own hands. What support they have given to the Sub-Treasury, has been to promote this view - The mass of them have been sincere. Mr. Calhoun has used it only to cloak his ambition. They are now alarmed at the prospect of a new union of the money power with the political power, by means of the free banking law of New York. The question is whether in their jealousy, (the present predominant feeling, whether well or ill founded) there is not a ground for an union of the Bank U. S. with the south. If you can make friends there, you will soon have Pennsa., for she always goes with the south.[115] -- John Sergeant to Nicholas Biddle, 28 April 1838.

The incorporation of the United States Bank of Pennsylvania in 1836 is a familiar story, and historians of the Bank have correctly pointed out that the costs of the state charter were a serious drain on the bank's resources. Over the twenty-year life of the charter the bank was obliged to pay $4,400,000 to Pennsylvania and its political subdivisions, advance on permanent loan up to $6 million on that state's bonds, and loan the state an additional $1 million on an emergency basis for up to twelve months. The bank was also required to subscribe to $675,000 of stock in various railroad and canal companies incorporated by the Pennsylvania legislature.[116]

There remained to be settled the federal government's stock in the Bank of the United States, which with the prorate of the accumulated surplus was $7,946,356.16. The Bank's agents reached an agreement with the Treasury in March 1837 which allowed for the liquidation of this claim with interest over four years, the first installment being due 1 November 1837. The government's fiscal embarrassments in the wake of the Panic of 1837 resulted in Biddle's agreeing to advance all of the second and third installments in 1838, an accommodation which no doubt flattered his vanity buy severely weakened the bank's balance sheet.[117] When the last installment became due in 1840, the bank was once again in a state of suspension. In consequence, there was a default and the government responded by suing the bank in the Commercial Court of New Orleans. The United States Attorney for the Eastern District of Louisiana proceeded to garnishee $2.5 million of claims in that city which had been assigned in 1841 by the stockholders to the John Bacon et. al. Trustees to secure the payment of the bank's notes.[118]

After the expiration of the federal charter and the incorporation in Pennsylvania the new institution attempted to reclaim its national identification, and to this end contracted agencies at various locations around the United States. Where state laws permitted, the new bank actually purchased banks, or subscribed to stock in well-situated institutions. The bank purchased the Insurance Bank of Columbus, Georgia, and the Merchants Bank of New Orleans, but in both instances all of the stock was subscribed to in the name of Nicholas Biddle and his nominees, not the United States Bank of Pennsylvania.

Joseph L. Roberts, a native Philadelphian and formerly cashier of the Norfolk branch of the old bank, assumed the management of the Georgia institution, and almost from the beginning clashed with the directors and officers, all of whom were well connected financially and politically in the Columbus community. In order to form a Board of Directors Biddle transferred small parcels of stock to these local eminences, a transaction which caused considerable difficulty for those responsible for liquidating the failed United States Bank in the 1840s. In 1846 Roberts recounted to the residuary trustees of the United States Bank that he had been

> aware that the Insurance Bank of Columbus, Georgia was bought by Mr. Biddle as President of the Bank of the United States & for its use as an agency but to guard against difficulties & *opposition* in Georgia under the circumstances of the times & the influence in the legislature of the dominant party then in Georgia, it was thought best to have the Ince. Bank of Columbus to appear as owned by Mr. Biddle individually; together with the necessary ownership of a few of the shares put in the names of certain individuals to render them eligible as Directors.

Each of those individuals executed promissory notes for the value of their shares and agreed to return the shares to Biddle when called upon to do so. Those elaborate arrangements were intended to 'give the concern the appearance of not being so exclusive or belonging to Mr. Biddle, or to the Bank of the United States'.[119]

The purchase and operation of the Merchants Bank of New Orleans involved a similar arrangement with locally important men which was negotiated by Biddle's personal agent in that city, a shadowy figure named James Erwin. Erwin epitomized the frontier speculator, a deal maker equally comfortable trafficking in land, slaves, commodities, stocks, and bonds. His relationship with Nicholas Biddle certainly predated the Merchants Bank speculation, and it seems likely that he had worked a number of real estate speculations in the west in which the wizard of Chestnut Street had participated. Nor did their relationship end with the purchase of the Merchants Bank; in 1842 and 1843 Erwin appears to have assisted Biddle in at least two ill-fated attempts to mount proxy fights at the stockholders' meetings in order to regain control of the management of the failed United States Bank and revoke the assignments made in 1841. Erwin was also instrumental in thwarting the collection of valuable Louisiana claims that the stockholders had assigned to the Bacon trustees to secure the late bank's notes. He showed a great deal of sophistication in his complex legal maneuverings. During the remainder of the antebellum period he operated largely at Nashville and New Orleans, and in a post Civil War decision of the Louisiana Supreme Court was described as a 'capitalist'. It is perhaps ironic that his brother was the cashier of the Bank of Yeatman, Wood, a banking partnership at Nashville in which Andrew Jackson was rumored to be deeply involved.[120]

The management of the United States Bank examined various options for obtaining a corporate charter to bank in Mobile, but confined their operations in that city to a local agent with close ties to Philadelphia.[121] Natchez and Mississippi were much too important to be omitted from the new national bank then taking shape in Philadelphia, and in 1836 the United States Bank made a direct investment of $400,000 in the newly chartered Commercial Bank at Natchez. The stock purchase represented only 20 percent of the Commercial Bank's outstanding shares, but the Philadelphia institution did secure for itself a corporate agent in Mississippi well positioned to deal in local and regional exchange. By virtue of the many rich local notables with ties to the Commercial Bank, that institution had the potential for becoming one of the best banks in the Lower Mississippi Valley, but its agency for the United States Bank would prove to be its undoing.[122]

At no time during the troubled life of the United States Bank did the scope of its operations ever approach those of its illustrious predecessor. Its presence in the important New York money market was merely nominal and its agency there was little more than a facility for collecting and remitting paper from business operations elsewhere in the country. The New Orleans agency certainly was an important one, but the volume of business there was much less than that which the branch had garnered. The Bank of Louisiana, the Louisiana State Bank, the Union Bank, and the Citizens Bank all dwarfed the Merchants Bank, and sundry other commercial and improvement banks in that city equaled or exceeded its capital and volume of business.[123]

The one location outside of Pennsylvania where the United States Bank actually expanded its operations was in Mississippi, and by 1841 virtually every bank in that state was hopelessly tied up in the ruin of the nation's largest bank. It is no exaggeration to say that the history of banking in antebellum Mississippi is the history of the Bank of the United States and its Pennsylvania successor. There can be little doubt either that the fate at which befell the United States Bank and its illustrious founder, as well as its Mississippi correspondents, fostered a highly negative view of banks among the state's inhabitants which persisted into the postbellum decades. The infamous bond repudiation, which effectively debarred the state from international capital markets down to the present day, stemmed from the underwriting activities of the United States Bank and its inability to support the market for the state's bonds in the London and Amsterdam markets.

Nicholas Biddle heartily embraced every improvement project that emanated from the state legislature, and the United States Bank subscribed heavily to the stock issues of the West Feliciana Rail Road and Banking Company at Woodville and sundry others. It is, however, a gross exaggeration to characterize conditions in Mississippi prior to the Panic and suspension in 1837 as endemic 'wildcat' banking. Indeed conditions there rather contradict contemporary perceptions that the crisis in 1837 had its origins in expansive credit facilities and over issuance of bank paper. True, the state chartered a total of nine improvement and seven commercial banks in the years from 1833 to 1838. But it is well to remember that only the West Feliciana Rail Road and Banking Company, the Commercial and Rail Road Bank of Vicksburg, and the Agricultural Bank, which was merely the successor of the Bank of the State, had become fully operational before the crisis in 1837. The Commercial Bank of Natchez, for example, only commenced purchasing domestic exchange in the last week of March 1836. It discounted little in the way of local paper until the fall of that year, and its first season of operations yielded little but protested paper.[124]

It is doubtful that the Mississippi legislature's plethora of banking charters had any real impact on the nation's monetary woes: most came too late in the decade to have contributed to the rise in monetary stocks and subsequent price rise in 1835 and 1836. It is much more likely that banking facilities in the state on the eve of the Panic were no larger than they had been in 1832. The withdrawal of the Natchez branch of the Bank of the United States in 1835 and 1836 reduced credit facilities by $3.5 million. The Planters Bank absorbed $1 million of local paper from the branch into its portfolio. The Agricultural Bank merely assumed the assets and liabilities of the old Bank of the State, leaving only the improvement banks chartered in 1835 to account for any rise in baking capacity prior to the Panic. Of the three improvement banks, only the West Feliciana Rail Road and Banking Company and the Commercial and Rail Road Bank of Vicksburg appear to have been operating. The bulk of their resources were consumed in building railroads, not expanding credit facilities for area planters.

Some of the newly-chartered banks only commenced operating in a very nominal way; either they never raised the requisite capital to begin discounting or they almost immediately passed into liquidation in the wake of the 1837 Panic and suspension. In December 1837, eleven Mississippi banks reported aggregate loans and discounts of $29 million a 20 percent increase over that which nine banks had reported in January of that year. But the increase is misleading: all of the banks were overwhelmed with portfolios of protested domestic exchange and protested bills and notes, and these categories of paper may account for substantially more of the aggregate portfolios than the seeming increase reported in 1837.[125] While loans and discounts do appear to have doubled in the years from 1832 to 1837, from $10 million to $19 million, a substantial part of the increase may have originated with the Bank of the United States' expansive exchange purchases in 1835.[126] Aggregate circulation was remarkably stable from 1832 to 1837, hovering around $5 million for the state banks. Circulation did rise 50 percent in 1837, but much of the increase may be accounted for by the inability of the banks to retrieve their paper from the market in the wake of suspension and the issuance of post notes.

In the immediate aftermath of the suspension, Mississippi bank notes were quoted at small discounts in the New Orleans market, the only national money market in which such paper was regularly quoted. By 1841 the rates of discount for the best Mississippi banks was 5 percent for the Commercial Bank of Natchez, 20 percent for the Agricultural Bank and the Planters Bank, and 70 percent for the Commercial and Rail Road Bank of Vicksburg. Thereafter, the notes of the Planters Bank and the Commercial and Rail Road Bank further eroded in value.[127]

One factor alone, however, seems to account for the sudden upsurge in aggregate circulation reported for Mississippi's banks in 1837; the state legislature's authorization to those banks to issue post notes with maturities of from six to thirteen months. The purpose was to enable the banks to prepare for resumption by allowing them to reduce demand obligations without accelerating the process of curtailments of their portfolios. The best banks largely replaced their demand notes with post notes; insolvent institutions issued post notes but were unable to curtail their portfolios enough to retrieve their demand notes from circulation. The components, then, of what passed for circulation in the state after the suspension changed dramatically, from demand obligation to obligations which could only be tendered for specie or its equivalent at some future date, presumably after resumption was fully effective among the state's banks and their correspondents elsewhere in the country.[128]

At issuance post notes were already at a 5 percent discount; they never enjoyed the currency of demand notes. The practical effect of post notes was to enable those holding Mississippi money at the time of the bank suspension to eventually realize those funds elsewhere in the country at some sacrifice. Post

notes made the process of debt liquidation more orderly, but did little to coun-
teract the contraction of credit facilities which had precipitated the crisis in
the first place. Bank money continued to lose currency and the risks of further
depreciation increasingly were borne by the communities in which those banks
did business. The localization of risks of holding bank money and the eventual
liquidation of all of the banks in the 1840s largely explains the hostility to them
in subsequent years.

The Last Days of the Natchez Branch

The credit contraction which would lead to the Panic and suspension in 1837
was already well underway in Mississippi in the summer of 1835 when the
Natchez branch of the Bank of the United States commenced its heavy purchases of domestic bills. This action brought temporary relief to the local
economy, postponing for another season the inevitable disappearance of the
credit facilities formerly afforded by the branch. The action, however, did nothing to stabilize the market for local paper, a species already purged from the
branch portfolio.[129] The exchange dealers, however, availed themselves and
their clients of what was afforded, retiring their local notes with bills on their
agents in New Orleans, Philadelphia, and New York, hoping that a loosening
of the stringency in those markets would permit their agents to find the means
to meet their bills when they came due. As previously mentioned, the state
banks then doing business, namely the Planters Bank, the Agricultural Bank,
the Commercial and Rail Road Bank of Vicksburg, and the much smaller West
Feliciana Rail Road and Banking Company, appear to have increased their discounts of local paper in response to the branch's expansive exchange purchases
which stood at $4 million in March 1836.[130]

The branch cashier, Thomas Henderson, actually anticipated a favorable
response to his institution's heavy purchases of domestic exchange. On 23
October 1835, he wrote to the cashier of the Nashville branch that he had 'no
doubt it w[ould] be for the interest of the local Banks to circulate the Notes of
the U. S. Bank that m[ight] come into their hands', because those notes then
commanded a premium in the local market of at least 1 percent. On 2 January
1836, he advised the cashier of the New Orleans branch that he was much in
need of the notes of his branch which had accumulated in that city, no doubt
to continue his heavy purchases of exchange. That he expected the local banks
to find it advantageous to give currency to the circulation of the Bank of the
United States indicates how dramatic the changes had been in the constitution
of the local money market. The paper of the Bank of the United States was simply more valuable than the paper of any local bank; hence, the Planters Bank,
for example, could capture the customary return on its own notes of 1 percent

by paying out the notes of the Bank of the United States as it was tendered for deposit.[131]

The premium being paid in the local money market for the circulation of the Bank of the United States was great enough to support the shipment of over $200,000 specie to Philadelphia from the branch's vault in the weeks before the closure. In normal times it would have been more economical to have sold the branch bank's specie in the local market and obtained a check for the proceeds payable in Philadelphia. That it was more economical to ship specie indicates that the premium for paper suitable for remittance was higher than the costs of shipping specie.[132]

The premium paid for good remittance paper was enough to draw specie out of the banks in the Lower Mississippi Valley, and it is interesting that some contemporaries traced the pressure to the preparations of the Bank of the United States for its withdrawal from the region. Thomas Barrett & Co. of New Orleans, for example, advised their Philadelphia correspondent, Jackson, Riddle & Co. on 16 March 1836, that the lackluster cotton markets could be blamed on the 'heavy drain made on our Banks for specie for exports-and to the want of the U. S. Bank'. In truth, however, the parent bank at Philadelphia was losing specie rapidly, its hoard having fallen from $16 million in the spring of 1835 to $8 million by January 1836. The large premium for bills payable in the East and the drain of specie away from the Bank of the United States indicates that the financial system was contracting even as prices approached their zenith.[133]

Serious problems surfaced in the branch's exchange account in December 1835 and January 1836, even before the purchases for that account had reached their maximum of $4 million. On 31 December 1835, Thomas Henderson requested the cashier at the New Orleans branch to return to Natchez seven acceptances of Bogart, Hoopes, totaling $30,000 provided they had not been protested for nonpayment already. Firm acceptances under protest were also to be returned so they could be paid at Natchez by Passmore Hoopes, the partner resident in that city. Henderson assured Peter Bacot, the cashier, that the 'House of B. & H. possessing the confidence of the community w[ould] be aided by the Banks [of Mississippi, and he hoped] … w[ould] go on with their business without further difficulty'. A few days later he wrote to another correspondent that the Natchez banks had granted Hoopes 'the indulgence required. The great confidence and friendly feeling manifested to Mr. Hoopes at this time [had to] … be gratifying to him'. Henderson too was likewise 'much pleased to see it'.[134]

Bogart, Hoopes was the New Orleans branch of a syndicate of interlocking partnerships that included houses in Natchez and Vicksburg. Joseph H. Moore & Co. represented the enterprise in Natchez, Passmore Hoopes being a general partner in that firm and in the New Orleans affiliate as well. In the fall of 1835 Bogart, Hoopes had come under acceptance for $500,000 of domestic bills drawn in Mississippi by its affiliates and sold to the Natchez branch which had then remitted them to New Orleans for collection. Bogart, Hoopes had accepted all of the bills as they were presented, but as the bills matured found itself unable to meet all of them. There can be little doubt either that the partnerships had come under heavy obligations to other purchasers of their paper, namely the Planters Bank, the Agricultural Bank, and most certainly some of the New Orleans banks.[135]

During the month of January as much as $120,000 of the New Orleans bills were arranged by allowing the Natchez affiliate, Joseph H. Moore & Co., to draw new bills at long dates on Bogart, Hoopes at New Orleans. The branch had resorted to this expedient in 1834 to forestall heavy defaults in the exchange account. Since then, firms operating in the Lower Mississippi Valley had increasingly resorted to the domestic exchanges to finance their activities, as permanent funding sources in the form of local accommodations had contracted. The rescue of Bogart, Hoopes and its affiliates, a temporary relief measure, was nothing more than an accommodation loan which took the form of domestic bills of exchange. By the spring Henderson thought it expedient to open similar facilities for other mammoth firms.[136]

In February 1836, it had become apparent that Bogart, Hoopes would require even more time to meet their acceptances, so the state banks in Mississippi resolved to extend one-half of the firm's paper for twelve months provided the Bank of the United States would do the same. Henderson strongly recommended to James Saul, the agent of the Bank of the United States at New Orleans, to accede to the arrangement. Bogart, Hoopes could meet their engagements 'much sooner if they [were] ... enabled to go on with their business, than [would be the case] ... if they stop[ped] payment'. He reminded Saul 'that in cases of failure, the delays in collections [were] ... usually great, probably three times as great as the extension asked for by the House'. Saul alone could authorize the compromise, which Henderson assured him would prevent 'a great deal of embarrassment to the House and to many worthy Planters whose names ... [were] on the Bills'. A conciliatory attitude permeated much of the thinking about how banks and other creditors should respond to defaulting clients, especially in the early years of the crisis. No doubt allowing debtors more time to meet their engagements yielded better results than forced sales of income producing property. But as time passed and the banks' own obligations depreciated in value, the incentives increased for debtors to avoid payment altogether.[137]

Bogart, Hoopes' creditors in New Orleans, especially the banks in that city, were unwilling or unable to extend them relief beyond the summer of 1836, and in consequence the arrangement which Thomas Henderson had proposed to James Saul, to extend one-half of the firm's paper until the winter of 1837, never was consummated. By 21 August 1836, the balance in the protested exchange account stood at $450,000, the bulk of the protests having stemmed from the suspension of Bogart, Hoopes and its affiliates in Mississippi. Most of the bills were settled in subsequent years by taking bills receivable from the parties to each bill under protest, but in June 1841 the protested exchange account still showed a balance of $212,000. Most of the debits in the account can be traced to bills on New Orleans, payments made on account of the bills receivable and subsequently protested for nonpayment. On 2 April 1840, a new account was opened for protested bills and notes that had originated at the old branch. On 30 June 1841, the balance stood at $321,048.30. On that same date, $131,811.59 of the local accommodations, as well as $35,919.03 of domestic bills of exchange, were still being carried on the books as good loans. Virtually all of this paper can be traced to the suspension of Bogart, Hoopes and its affiliates in January 1836. Seven hundred thousand dollars of claims then were carried on the books of the branch, as a debt owed by the late branch to its late parent, the Second Bank of the United States, until the failure of the United States Bank of Pennsylvania in 1841.[138]

In the years from 1836 to 1841 the conglomerate of firms which had been Bogart, Hoopes, slowly unwound its operations, its list of impressive 'names' leaving the firm behind and making the best arrangements they could for taking up the paper for which they were liable, either directly or contingently. Most had counterclaims against the firm for the proceeds of the last year's crop still in the hands of the managing partners when Bogart, Hoopes and its affiliates suspended. It was useless for them, however, to claim setoffs; the paper for which they were liable either as drawer or indorser had been sold to the branch whose representatives now had every right to demand payment from them individually irrespective of their claims against the partnerships.

Once a commercial firm suspended, collecting its bills receivable was a protracted struggle which often lasted for years as clients attempted to escape liabilities for which they were only contingently liable and open new credit facilities in order to carry on business. Partners in suspended firms often formed new partnerships, with names similar to the old ones, and attempted to conduct business as before, even as they carried on the liquidation of their defunct firms. Their new endeavors frequently met with failure. Joseph H. Moore, the managing partner of the Natchez firm which bore his name, informed Thomas Henderson more than a year after the firm's suspension that it was 'out of their power, at t[hat] time to meet the payt.-or to get any good Commission House to accept for them', and thereby assume a portion of the indebtedness they owed to the branch. '[M]any of their Customers finding since the failure of the House that they could obtain no further facilities ha[d] failed to pay their debts & they [were] … obliged to sue them which put it out of their power to make prompt payment themselves'.[139]

The Natchez branch's heavy purchases of domestic bills in the fall of 1835 consisted of a few ninety-day bills and a great many bills which would not mature for another six months. The resolve to buy only ninety-day bills had long since been abandoned; hence many protests occurred after the expiration of the charter. Thomas Henderson continued to serve as the agent of the late Bank of the United States and in 1836 assumed the new position of cashier of the Commercial Bank of Natchez. He transacted most of the business connected with his bank's agency for the United States Bank of Pennsylvania. On 30 December 1836, he wrote to Samuel Jaudon at Philadelphia that he 'was making little progress in collecting the outstanding debts'. In at least one instance he agreed to receive twelve-month bills on New Orleans to settle paper already under protest, a compromise that the old bank never would have acceded to. By way of compromise Joseph H. Moore even proposed transferring mortgage notes payable in from one to five years in satisfaction of his late firm's large debt. That the proposition was eventually accepted indicates how difficult collections would become in subsequent years as economic depression took hold.[140]

The United States Bank was beset by difficulties; much of the paper sold to the Planters Bank and similarly situated institutions in the west had fallen under protest in the summer and fall of 1836. Those banks were already in arrears on their installments even before the complete breakdown of the exchanges in Spring 1837. The late bank's notes flowed back to Philadelphia more rapidly than anticipated, and by the end of 1836 even small emissions of new paper by agents in the west strained the new bank's resources. Henderson apologized to Jaudon in February of 1837 for one unfortunate incident that showed all too well the pressure being brought to bear on the nation's largest bank:

> I regretted to learn that the President of the Planters Bank of Tennessee should have pursued a course with notes of the B. U. S. obtained directly from the Commercial Bank so very different from the understanding with him - We had good reason to believe from his assurances that the notes in question would not reach Phila. in less than 5 or 6 months from the time they were issued - I hope that we may not have been so grossly deceived in many cases.

Clearly conditions had deteriorated rapidly over the course of 1836, and not just in consequence of the issuance of the specie circular and the Bank of England's decision to stop discounting the paper of the principal firms in the Anglo-American trade. Certainly these events contributed mightily to the loss of confidence in the domestic exchanges and the further contraction of credit facilities which were mediated through those exchanges. But the problem of obtaining paper suitable for remittance was already manifest by the spring of 1836 as is evidenced by the huge drain of specie out of the Bank of the United

States. The outflow began in the summer of 1835 and continued unabated thereafter.[141]

Even as the United States Bank was obtaining its Pennsylvania charter, Nicholas Biddle was finalizing arrangements to raise funds for its operations by borrowing in Europe. The 'present plan [was] ... to borrow in Europe what ... [was] want[ed], in anticipation of what ... [was] due for the sales on long credits to the Bank of the debts due at the Branches'. As he explained to one correspondent 'the Bank [had] made long investments, so as to draw an interest during the two years allowed to wind up. The consequence [was] ..., that [their] ... funds [were] ... locked up & a good deal beyond [their] ... immediate control-and [they were then] ... endeavoring to get them back so as to provide the means of an active business'. To this end Samuel Jaudon had been dispatched to Europe 'where alone these funds c[ould] be cashed. Until the Bank g[ot] back its capital, which [was] ... a work of time' they would of necessity have to curtail all their usual lines of business.[142]

The Bank's initial borrowing in Europe on various securities was about $6,500,000, a modest sum considering its vast resources. In the United States the exchange premium on foreign funds was then rising; that alone assured the Bank a profit as it drew down its credits abroad. But the costs of realizing funds in Europe to service those loans were also rising, and during the summer of 1837, in the immediate aftermath of the national suspension, the sterling premium ranged from 22 to 25 percent in the New York market. During the remainder of the year, it ranged in the mid-teens then fell back to pre-suspension levels. During the remaining years of its life the United States Bank returned repeatedly to the European market for funds; its liabilities there exceeded $13 million in 1841. The Pennsylvania legislature chose to protect the American creditors and simply ignored the claims of merchant bankers in England and the Netherlands.[143]

Much has been written about the United States Bank's cotton speculations that commenced in earnest in the summer of 1837, but the explanations put forward by some historians have bordered on the bizarre. There can be no doubt that the losses were heavy in 1839, the second season in which the Bank's nominees operated heavily at various points in the South and in Europe. Total losses may well have reached $4 million during the course of that year. But a great many less apparent advantages flowed from the speculations which offset some of the losses and must be taken into account when assessing their relative importance in contributing to the Bank's ruin. Heavy advances on improvement stocks in 1835 and 1836, at the top of the market, greatly weakened the balance sheets; agreeing to take largely worthless stocks from Thomas Biddle & Co. in satisfaction of the firm's huge loans cost the Bank upwards of $5 million. Advancing $4 million to the Treasury on the bonds which the Bank had issued to liquidate the government's stock in the old bank and meeting the $2

million installment which matured in 1840 also pressed heavily upon available resources. The cost of servicing the European loans more than doubled in
1837: default was inevitable after the second suspension in 1839. There can be
little doubt that the primary impetus behind the Bank's cotton operations was
the need to raise foreign exchange to service the European loans.[144]

Any assessment of the factors leading to the collapse of the United States
Bank of Pennsylvania in 1841 must include its inability to realize its Mississippi
claims in short term commercial paper, rather than long term local paper.
The extent of the Mississippi claims in the summer of 1836 were relatively
manageable, consisting of the Planters Bank's principal and interest notes of
$1,200,291.30 and the protested exchange account at the late branch which
stood at $441,169.50 on 1 December of that year. But during the preceding
year the Bank had also acquired large stock positions in three Mississippi banks;
the Commercial Bank of Natchez, the West Feliciana Rail Road and Banking
Company and the Commercial and Rail Road Bank of Vicksburg. Those purchases stemmed from Nicholas Biddle's overly optimistic views concerning the
future course of economic development in the state and may have added an
additional $1 million to the bank's portfolio there. By 1841 additional invest-
ments, interest arrears, and damages had swelled that portfolio to almost $6
million, roughly equivalent to one-third of the state banks' combined loans and
discounts in 1836. In 1838 the bank obtained the underwriting contract for
the state of Mississippi's Union Bank bonds, a $5 million offering which came
to market in 1839, a less than propitious time for raising money in Europe on
issues guaranteed by a sovereign state. While the Mississippi claims were problematic in 1841 they still ranked among the bank's assets.[145]

The Commercial Bank's Agency and the Breakdown of the Exchanges

While voluminous financial records of the Commercial Bank of Natchez have
survived, the officers' letterbooks, except for scant entries by the cashiers of
the Brandon and Holmesville branches, are nonexistent. The financial records,
however, are so complete that the Commercial Bank's inauspicious beginning and premature end can be traced with relative ease. In many respects the
Commercial Bank was a continuation of the old branch, its principal officers having served the Bank of the United States in those same capacities. The
president and cashier of the Commercial Bank, Levin R. Marshall and Thomas
Henderson respectively, had held the same positions at the branch prior to its
closing in March 1836.

The Commercial Bank's limited operations in the months preceding the
Panic is indicative of the difficulty of assessing the relative impact of Mississippi's

banks on the domestic exchanges and their complete breakdown in the spring of 1837. The account for discounted local notes at the office of the parent bank showed only $698,052.30 of outstanding paper on 30 April 1837. Discounts of local paper at the branches may have increased this sum another $100,000. Purchases of domestic bills stood at $1,520,947.12 on 28 February 1837; thereafter the balance in account fell precipitously to a little over $100,000 on 30 June 1838. During the remainder of the Commercial Bank's lifetime, the account was more or less dormant.[146]

The Commercial Bank was the agent in Mississippi of the United States Bank. In November 1836 a total of 55 bills with an aggregate value of $386,651.06 were purchased for the exchange account of the principal. For purchasing and guaranteeing those bills the Commercial Bank received the decidedly un-princely sum of $963.13, or 0.25 percent of the amount of the purchases. But the relationship had other compensations, not the least of which were the various agencies performed for the Commercial Bank by the United States Bank and its affiliates in Philadelphia, New York, and New Orleans. On 19 November 1836, the United States Bank's exchange account with the Commercial Bank was credited for $521,000, which probably had been earned in consequence of the United States Bank having received tenders of the circulation and checks of the Commercial Bank as they accumulated at various points in the East. Those notes and checks were then returned to the issuer, the Commercial Bank, and the United States Bank's account was credited for the same. Having the United States Bank as a guarantor of the Commercial Bank's circulation in eastern cities was a powerful incentive for maintaining the relationship, even if the direct monetary compensations were scant.[147]

The United States Bank also remitted its own circulation to its Natchez agent in payment of the exchange purchased for its account. While there generally had been no profit for a bank giving currency to the demand obligations of another bank by paying them out at its counter, the disruption of the exchanges in 1835 and 1836 had rather changed things. Those wishing to remit funds from Natchez to points east were in dire need of paper suitable for remittance, and premiums for such paper rose steadily in 1836 in the money markets of the west. The Commercial Bank profited handsomely, and at no risk to itself, by selling the obligations of the late Bank of the United States and its successor, the United States Bank of Pennsylvania, to those in Mississippi in need of remittable funds. Even checks at long date commanded a premium in the Natchez market in the closing months of 1836. Henderson mentioned to Samuel Jaudon in a letter dated 2 December 1836, that he was aware that Levin R. Marshall, the president of the Commercial Bank, had already advised Jaudon that they had received 'the two parcels of notes per Ella Hand and Chester which [he] hope[d] ... w[ould] circulate as extensively as when the office [the late branch] was in business'.[148]

The difficulty of finding a medium suitable for remittance was particularly acute in the summer of 1836. Most of the banks in the Lower Mississippi Valley had ceased checking on correspondents at the North until shipping commenced of the new year's crop of cotton, thus assuring an almost simultaneous realization of funds with which to meet any checks the banks did sell. Sight exchange was virtually unobtainable, the incidence of sixty- and ninety-day sight bills for remittance purposes having largely become the norm. There can be no doubt that correspondents viewed such bills as a less desirable medium for remittance than sight bills.

The marked differences in perceptions respecting sight and long dated exchange poses serious problems for any attempt to extrapolate a pattern of interest rates in a particular locality at any given time by calculating from quotations the spread between sight and long dated bills. Even sight bills contained an interest component. If a sight bill on New York was quoted at par in the New Orleans money market, then it can be assumed that New York bills were at a slight premium in that market. Usance and travel time in the 1830s was approximately three weeks from when the bill was remitted from New Orleans until it was paid at New York. On the same date that a sight bill on New York was quoted at par in the New Orleans market, a sixty-day bill on the former city might be quoted at a discount of 1.5 to 2 percent.[149]

Did the time value of money alone account for this difference? The question must be answered in the negative. Long dated bills were simply not as desirable as sight bills in the money market. Predicting the cost of money and credit availability at New York two or three months hence was a risky business. The drawee might well default when the bill was presented for payment. Moreover, the best firms generally only dealt in sight bills; long dated bills usually were the province of second tier firms. A reputable firm's sight bill simply commanded more value in the local money market than other grades of paper. Sight bills were in greater demand than long dated bills, a factor that of course influenced prices for different grades of paper. The spread between quotations for sight and long dated bills is not, then, pure interest. The market graded and valued paper just as it did cotton. It is, then, virtually impossible to separate out with any degree of accuracy an interest component from the spread between sight and long date bills.[150]

As previously mentioned it is not certain that published quotations even reflect an interest component. When sixty-day bills are quoted at a discount it seems probable that some portion of the discount is an interest charge. In rare instances where long dated bills actually commanded a premium it can be argued that the interest component disappeared altogether. The key to understanding this issue is to realize that domestic exchanges were ruled by the same economic laws that ruled international exchange. The U.S. was on a specie standard; the dollar had precise definitions in terms of both gold and silver.

For all intents and purposes, only gold and silver were real money, i.e., were tenders in private transactions. But it was usually cheaper to remit using a credit instrument like a bank note, a check, or a bill of exchange. If the premium on exchange became too great, debtors would send specie instead, as a cheaper alternative. Conversely, if exchange slipped too far below par it would pay to 'import' specie from the other city. The net effect was very similar to an international fixed exchange rate regime - exchange rates could fluctuate but in normal times only within a band a few percentage points on either side of par.

The great British nineteenth century political economist John Stuart Mill held a similar view:

> Let us suppose that all countries had the same currency ... and ... let us suppose this currency to be the English. When England had the same number of pounds sterling to pay to France, which France had to pay to her, one set of merchants in England would want bills, and another set would have bills to dispose of, for the very same number of pounds sterling; and consequently a bill on France for £100 would sell for exactly £100, or, in the phraseology of merchants, the exchange would be at par. As France also, on this supposition, would have an equal number of pounds sterling to pay and to receive, bills on England would be at par in France, whenever bills on France were at par in England.
>
> If, however, England had a larger sum to pay to France than to receive from her, there would be persons requiring bills on France for a greater number of pounds sterling than there were bills drawn by persons to whom money was due. A bill on France for £100 would then sell for more than £100, and bills would be said to be at a premium. The premium, however, could not exceed the cost and risk of making the remittance in gold, together with a trifling profit; because if it did, the debtor would send the gold itself, in preference to buying the bill.
>
> If, on the contrary, England had more money to receive from France than to pay, there would be bills offered for a greater number of pounds than were wanted for remittance, and the price of bills would fall below par: a bill for £100 might be bought for somewhat less than £100, and bills would be said to be at a discount.
>
> When England has more to pay than to receive, France has more to receive than to pay, and vice versa. When, therefore, in England, bills on France bear a premium, then, in France, bills on England are at a discount: and when bills on France are at a discount in England, bills on England are at a premium in France. If they are at par in either country, they are so, as we have already seen, in both. Thus do matters stand between countries, or places, which have the same currency.[151]

A large part of any bank's exchange business was buying and selling bills on distant places. Rarely are buy and sell quotations for a single institution available, but even in instances where such information can be gleaned from the financial pages, it is not safe to assume that that difference was wholly interest.

A bank expected to sell the paper it bought at an advantage because it added value to the bills it bought and then sold by indorsing or guaranteeing them. The spread between buy and sell varied according to the reputation of the bank whose indorsement appeared on the paper.[152]

The disappearance of sight bills from the New Orleans and Natchez markets preceded the actions of the Bank of England to curb the speculation in American securities and commodities by raising the discount rate and more importantly declining to discount the paper of the principal Anglo-American houses in that country. It also preceded the issuance of Andrew Jackson's (in)famous specie circular. This is not to say that those developments did not contribute to the chaos in the domestic and foreign exchanges with ruinous consequences for everyone. But serious problems were evident in the money markets of the Lower Mississippi Valley well before the Bank of England and the Jackson administration acted out of self-protection.

On 24 May 1836, the New Orleans firm of Byrne, Hermann & Co. - whose failure in March 1837, along with its affiliates-Herman, Byrne & Co., Samuel Hermann & Co., Byrne, Reynolds & Co., and Thomas Barrett & Co., is often identified as the precursor of the coming Panic and suspension -- advised its Philadelphia correspondent, Jackson, Riddle & Co. that 'they had tried in vain for several days past to procure Bank checks at sight or something else that would' pass as a cash equivalent in Philadelphia and place Jackson, Riddle in funds to meet their acceptances coming due there. They seemed more hopeful a few days later that they would be able to remit sight checks, but their ability to remit such paper depended on whether they could discount some of their clients' long dated paper at the banks. If the banks proved unwilling to furnish the sight checks Byrne, Hermann urged Jackson, Riddle to immediately negotiate in the Philadelphia market any of their remittance paper, namely long dated sterling bills, in order to meet their acceptances then maturing. Jackson, Riddle was to make the negotiation regardless of the prevailing rates.

> We did not expect such a continued pressure in the money market with you, as your letters indicate, and are much at a loss to account for it; as things here are decidedly easier than they were a few weeks since, and we find that long paper passes freely from 11 @ 12%. We must again repeat our desire that you will not hesitate to make our remittances available at the rates going in your money Market (should they not prove available to you in Bank) it being no part of our desire to subject you to the slightest inconvenience to meet your liabilities on your account.

Byrne, Hermann and its affiliates at Natchez and New Orleans had followed a pattern of dealings typical of exchange dealers. The sterling premium fluctuated enough over a period of months to make it advantageous for the holders to postpone the sale of their bills in order to capture any rise in the premium.

Sterling tended to glut the New Orleans market during the shipping season, so it generally was more advantageous to sell in eastern markets where demand for sterling was greatest to answer the need of importers for paper suitable for remittance abroad. The decision of a holder to postpone cashing a sterling bill in a local market also was affected by the course of domestic exchanges. During the summer months the exchange tended to be in favor of New York, Philadelphia, and Boston and against the exporting cities of the South. An exchange dealer at New Orleans could draw on New York or Philadelphia at sixty days sight, sell that bill in the local market and apply the proceeds toward the purchase of a sight check on the North from a local bank to meet the draft when it matured. This maneuver allowed the New Orleans exchange dealer to borrow short term at near zero rates and thus postpone the sale of his long dated sterling bills. Another approach was for the firm to purchase less desirable paper in the New Orleans market at a heavy discount and then resell it in that market at a profit by adding value to it with the firm's endorsement. But the firm could also profit by selling its own bills on the North at the best rates of the market and then covering these bills with remittances of sight checks. The firm captured the New York exchange premium which more or less offset interest costs.[153]

The business of exchange dealers encompassed a great deal more than simply the arbitrage of bills payable in different markets, bills predicated on actual sales of staples and produce then in transit. Byrne, Hermann negotiated the paper of its planter clients at various New Orleans banks and drew on the resulting credit facilities at those institutions to support its exchange dealings. In one sense the firm was in direct competition with the banks in its exchange dealings, but those dealings also gave tone to the local market and supported the circulation of the banks throughout the region. As Nicholas Biddle observed, exchange and not the issues of sundry local banks was the primary circulating medium of the country.[154]

In the early years of the 1830s the opportunities were plentiful for parlaying local credit facilities into domestic and foreign exchange operations, and firms like Byrne, Hermann availed themselves of every opportunity to expand their two principal lines of business, i.e. obtaining local discounts for firm clients and speculating on changes in the course of exchanges and resulting the rate differentials. A portion of Byrne, Hermann's profits derived from the firm's ability to sell its own bills at the best rates and add value to paper it purchased for resale.

Among the seven firms which dominated the Anglo-American trade in the 1830s was Francisco de Lizardi & Co., a firm with offices in London, Paris, and New Orleans. After the Bank of England's resolve in August of 1836 not to discount any bills drawn on those firms by American correspondents or receive the same as collateral security, Lizardi's addressed a very full report to the Governor and Deputy Governor of the Bank of England on exchange dealings in New Orleans. The report noted that 'nearly the whole trading community [were] ... at one and the same time sellers of Exchange'. The rates of discount commanded by the banks of New Orleans were high, but they owned their prosperous condition mainly to 'their dealings in the home or foreign exchanges ... which enable[d] them to divide regularly 8 pc. per Ann[um]'. The two increases in the Bank of England's discount rate in the summer of 1836 were certainly an inconvenience, but that burden paled in importance to the closure of the Bank's discounting facilities to the seven firms and their American clients. Lizardi's was careful to call the Governor's attention to the fact that the prevailing sterling premium at New Orleans was then quite high relative to rates elsewhere in the Unites States. '[W]hile at New York the rate had been at 7 and 8 pc. for some time past, at New Orleans Exchange on London ha[d] not varied from 9 to 9 ½ pc. prem'. Lizardi's reason for making this observation was simple: it wished to reassure the Bank that exchange dealings at New Orleans mitigated in favor of a high sterling premium which retarded exports of specie from Great Britain to the United States. The Bank of England was not only losing specie from its vaults but wished in all events to avoid a repeat of the disastrous collapse of sterling in the American market in 1834.[155]

Prior to 1835 the sterling premium at New Orleans had ruled from 1.5 to 2.5 percent below the New York premium for sterling. The difference was in large measure accounted for by factors other than the two cities' distances from London. New York was a primary center for imports, hence there was a greater demand in that market for sterling for remittance purposes. The facilities for cashing sterling bills at New Orleans were also more limited than what the New York market could offer.[156]

Interest rates in the New Orleans market may well have been higher than comparable rates at New York, a factor which should have operated to suppress the premium at the former locale relative to the latter place. That the sterling premium at New Orleans now ruled above New York's, is a clear indication of the difficulties which beset the money markets of the Lower Mississippi Valley in the wake of the withdrawal of the Bank of the United States. Assuming the Bank of the United States had continued into the summer of 1836 its huge purchases of domestic bills, and provided adequate credit in the locations on which they were drawn, the surge in the sterling premium at New Orleans probably never would have taken place. The pressure for good remittance paper was so great in the summer of 1836 that Byrne, Hermann actually paid the New Orleans premium for sterling to cover firm acceptances coming due at Philadelphia. On 16 June 1836 they remitted to Jackson, Riddle bills totaling £10,000 drawn by Manuel DeLizardi & Co. of New Orleans on Francisco DeLizardi & Co. of London to cover firm acceptances then about to mature.

They authorized the Philadelphia firm to cash the bills in that market so as best to 'promote [their] … interest'. They had purchased sterling at a 9.5 percent premium, knowing full well that the prevailing rate at New York was only 7 percent. They had elected to follow this expensive route because they knew that the Philadelphia firm would not be able to convert bank checks or bills on the North at long dates into cash. Assuming Jackson, Riddle would not immediately require cash to meet Byrne, Hermann's acceptances, the former firm was 'to hold the Bills for awhile, rather than sell them at a loss'. The New York premium seemed poised to rise and might reach 12 percent if the United States Bank exported specie to England rather than 'directing bills to be drawn'. Even a small loss of specie from the banks to meet bills coming due abroad could drive up the price of sterling bills enough to permit Byrne, Hermann to recoup its investment. In another letter Byrne, Hermann noted that a bank had promised them sight checks but 'the cashier subsequently found he could not draw, and as all [their] … Banks [were] … [then] in the same situation', they had been forced to wait. Finally, they had arranged to purchase a check for $10,000 at 1.25 percent premium drawn by the Bank of Louisiana. Interest for time and usance meant that the actual premium was higher by at least 0.25 to 0.5 percent. Sixty-day bills on New York then ranged from par to a discount of 0.5 percent. Clearly sixty day bills did not command as high a premium as sight bills; so, it can be seen that interest charges alone will not account for the spread between sight and sixty day bills.[157]

Like Bogart, Hoopes, the firm of Byrne, Hermann belonged to a syndicate of partnerships operating at New Orleans, Natchez, Vicksburg and sundry other smaller communities in the Lower Mississippi valley. The partnerships in New Orleans included the firms of Hermann, Briggs & Co., Samuel Hermann & Co., Thomas Barrett & Co., Reynolds, Byrne & Co., and Briggs, Lacoste & Co.. The syndicate's principal correspondent in New York was Josephs & Co., which in turn was affiliated with firms in London and Paris. These interlocking partnerships created credit facilities for each other through the medium of cross acceptances for mutual accommodation. Thomas Barrett & Co., for example, accommodated Byrne, Hermann by drawing bills in its favor on their Philadelphia correspondent, Jackson, Riddle & Co., which Byrne, Hermann then negotiated or sold at New Orleans. Thomas Barrett & Co. then remitted sterling bills or sight checks on the North to Philadelphia to meet the acceptances there as they matured.[158]

The great syndicates also accommodated each other, as the following example will suffice to show. On 27 January 1834, A. B. Gill, a resident of Natchez, 'drew a Bill of Exchange, or Draft, for the sum of Four Thousand five hundred & forty-nine dollars & ninety-nine cents, on W. Bogart at New Orleans' without the latter's authority and without funds in hand to meet the bill. The bill was payable twelve months after date and it was endorsed by William H. Gill, 'an accommodation indorser without interest'. The Bill was drawn to the order of the great slave trader, Isaac Franklin, to pay a debt 'and was indorsed and delivered to said Franklin as his property'. Bogart had refused to accept the bill when it was presented to him, and afterwards refused payment as well. The bill was duly protested for non-acceptance and nonpayment. At the special instance of the partners of Byrne, Hermann & Co., Bogart Hoopes had agreed subsequently to accept another bill drawn by Gill, payable on 27 January 1836, or two years after the first bill had been drawn, to take up the protested bill. Bogart, Hoopes alleged that the partners of Byrne, Hermann & Co., had agreed to guarantee the bill's payment at maturity, and the former firm, relying on the latter firm's guaranty, had accepted other bills drawn by Gill. According to Bogart, Hoopes the firm of Byrne, Hermann had subsequently defaulted on its guaranty, and that as a consequence Passmore Hoopes had been sued by Isaac Franklin in 1837 and judgment taken against him personally for a debt arising from a transaction already three years old. It must be assumed that Byrne, Hermann had offered some inducement to Bogart, Hoopes to accommodate Gill with credit facilities.[159]

Sterling still ranged above 9 percent at New Orleans as the shipping season neared and only briefly dipped below that level in October 1836. Thomas Barrett & Co. still found it difficult to obtain sight checks on the North for remittance purposes noting that the banks were still 'checking but sparingly'. There are strong indications that the spread between sixty-day bills and sight bills on the North actually widened during the fall, in part because of the lamentable effects of the specie circular and the actions of the Bank of England. Over the course of the previous summer, sight bills on New Orleans had sold at their usual discount of 0.75 percent. The spread between sixty-day sight bills on New York at New Orleans and sight bills on New Orleans at New York was 6 percent in the months from September 1836 to April 1837. By the winter the sterling premium at New York was at or near the New Orleans rate. The exchanges within the United States were already so chaotic by the late fall of 1836 that the reliability and accuracy of quotations generally must be questioned.[160]

The high discount rates for exchange on New Orleans in the New York market clearly indicates that a contraction of existing credit facilities was taking place at that location. The usual purchasers of exchange on New Orleans simply lacked the means or the willingness to buy. The typical buyer was a commodities speculator who should have found the huge discount attractive enough to buy exchange on New Orleans in order to purchase cotton there for shipment elsewhere. The contraction at New York manifested itself in New Orleans by a rise in the premium for exchange on the North and Europe. In this sense the events leading up to the 1837 Panic were similar to those in 1834: the price of exchange on the western cities collapsed in the New York market and the premium for exchange on New York rose at those locations. But this time the sterling premium did not disappear; rather it started rising and continued to rise until it reached an unprecedented 25 percent at New Orleans and 22 percent at New York.[161]

On 7 October 1836, Thomas Barrett & Co. expressed their hope to Jackson, Riddle & Co. that 'the Merchants Bank 'arrangement' with the U. S. Bank', whereby the latter institution had purchased a controlling interest in the New Orleans bank, would mark the beginning of a period of ease in both their money markets. 'Doubts [had been] ... expressed as to the action of the [Louisiana] ... Legislature on the subject. [The firm, however], ... believe[d] no permanent opposition c[ould] be established against the Project'. If the past was any guide, the legislature would defer to the state supreme court on any questions respecting corporate charters, and the justices were 'decided Bank men'. But such optimism clearly was misplaced. The New Orleans firm soon advised its Philadelphia correspondent that they had been unable to negotiate the two notes for $27,471 remitted previously and were returning the same in hopes that the paper would find a better market at the North.[162]

By the spring, firms up and down the Mississippi River were suspending, finding it impracticable to go on. Thomas Henderson wrote to Samuel Jaudon from Natchez that he had just returned from a visit to New Orleans 'made in consequence of the failure of the House of Hermann, Briggs & Co. which' was much to be regretted because Levin R. Marshall, the president of the Commercial Bank, was 'deeply involved with them'. He continued:

> An arrangement has been proposed of which I presume you have been informed for Messrs. Reynolds, Marshall & Byrne to renew the firms of Reynolds, Byrne & Co. & Reynolds, Marshall & Co. for the purpose of liquidating the business of R. & B. & Co. & B. L. & Co. [Briggs, Lacoste & Co.] the Bank granting them 9, 12, 15, 18, 21 & 24 months to make the payments. The proposal I believe will be acceded to by the Banks in New Orleans & this place and I hope by you as it will probably enable Mr. Marshall & Mr. Reynolds to get out of the difficulty without severe losses and will I suppose prevent other heavy failures.

On March 17 Roswell L. Colt wrote to Nicholas Biddle from New York that '[g]reat regret ... [was] felt for the fate of the Josephs ... [The firm's] liabilities with the N. O. houses [was] ... 2 Millions for acceptances & 400,000 remitted'. A few days later he lamented that he saw 'no chance for the Josephs to go on and [that] it would be cruel in the Banks to extend new large aid to them, if this c[ould] only be done by curtailing the aid which ...' ought to go to the general merchants of that city. He spoke wistfully of what might be accomplished if Biddle had 'a million Sterling at [his] ... command'.[163]

Suspension

The events leading up to the national banking suspension in April and May of 1837 have been extensively chronicled. The Jackson administration's issuance of the specie circular in July 1836 effectively debarred tenders of bank notes to purchase government lands. Henceforth only specie, namely gold or silver, would be accepted at the government land offices. Contemporaries claimed the specie circular drew specie away from the nation's commercial centers in the East toward the West where most of the land transactions took place. The circular, then, precipitated a contraction of credit facilities in eastern money markets as specie flowed inland away from the coasts.[164]

Peter Temin, however, has observed that there is 'no evidence that the Specie Circular pulled specie to the West in either 1836 or 1837. The Specie Circular, therefore did not bring on the suspension of payments by denuding Eastern banks of specie'. Temin contends that there are strong indications that the circular almost immediately acted to suppress land sales in the West, but at least temporarily the fall in land sales may have sustained the inflationary price trends evident in 1835 and 1836 by drawing money heretofore destined for land purchases into other speculations such as commodities. Temin also discounts the effects of the distribution of the federal surplus which commenced on 1 January 1837, and clearly he is correct in this regard insofar as most of the depository banks in the West, including the Agricultural Bank and Planters Bank of Natchez, were unable to cash the Treasury warrants tendered to them.[165]

Temin focuses on the action of the Bank of England in the summer of 1836, the 25 percent rise in the discount rate and the closure of discounting facilities to the leading houses in the Anglo-American trade. Clearly the Bank of England was hemorrhaging specie from its vaults and necessarily acted to protect its solvency. But, according to Temin, the Bank of England's actions caused the price of cotton to fall, and in consequence consignees in England, who had advanced heavily on the new crop, were unable to recoup their advances from sales in a falling market and so were unable to keep their own credit facilities current. Important houses in England and the United States failed almost simultaneously in March and April 1837 by which time the Panic was in full swing. Temin notes that '[t]here is no evidence of a 'diversion of specie' to the west; the suspension was due to the crisis in international trade. The extent of the crisis in New Orleans and the high incidence of failures among merchants and brokers confirms this hypothesis'. He continues: '[h]ad the pressure originated with the Specie Circular or the distribution of the surplus, the pressure would have been concentrated first in the West or in New York, the city most drawn upon for interstate transfers, and not New Orleans, where bank deposits of the Federal government doubled in late 1836 and only small interstate transfers were demanded' for the distribution of the federal surplus. The sterling premium did rise in the last quarter of 1836 between 2 and 3 percent over gold par, but his was not enough to cause significant exports of specie.[166]

According to Temin, '[s]ince the problem originated in international trade, the financial pressure was strongest among merchants, brokers, and factors rather than banks. If the crisis had originated with the government's actions the pressure would have been felt first by the banks'. The incidence of mercantile embarrassments may, he says, indicate a problem in the trade sector or success- ful efforts by the banks to curtail credit facilities at the cost of the solvency of their customers.[167]

It should be noted, however, that the nation's banks were not equally situated *vis-à-vis* each other, either geographically or financially, and the vulnerability of their portfolios to the unfolding crisis seems to have varied considerably from region to region. Moreover, the exchange dealers themselves were at least the equals of the banks in rationalizing the nation's monetary system. The relation- ship between exchange dealers and banks was a symbiotic one: banks cashed the dealers' paper and dealers gave currency to the banks' notes. Once the deal- ers suspended and commenced liquidating, their bankers had little choice but to follow. The surviving commercial correspondence is scant for firms in the Lower Mississippi Valley, and it is difficult to say whether extant archives are at all representative of conditions generally. In any event, the availability of specie in the market rarely was mentioned.

A severe pressure was evident in the money markets of New Orleans and Natchez well before the proclamation of the specie circular and the actions of the Bank of England became widely known. Sterling at New Orleans ruled above the New York rates by at least 2 percentage points until late autumn 1836 when the two rates converged. Traffic in sight checks between the two cities showed some remarkable tendencies during that year. The spread appears to have widened to 2 percent, the course of exchange being decidedly in favor of New York. In September 1836, the spread widened to 4.5 percent, a clear indication that there were few takers of sight checks on New Orleans in the New York market. The high premium for sterling at New Orleans, relative to its price at New York, indicates also a scramble for paper that would suffice for remittance purposes. A credit contraction was underway even before the events of July and August came crashing down on the nation's money markets.

The specie circular may have had no identifiable effect on bullion flows in and out of banks in the United States, but it certainly presaged ill for the note issues of most banks, especially those in the West. One response of the money market was to bid up sterling, a medium of exchange payable in the proven money of another country unlikely to default by suspending specie convert- ibility. It must be assumed, too, that rates of exchange for checks on other western cities such as Nashville and Louisville were even more depressed than those for New Orleans in the New York market. Exchange on New Orleans at Natchez was at a premium of at least 1 percent and possibly more in 1836. Another response was to cease redeeming one's obligations in specie and thus default altogether. The pressure to suspend varied considerably from institution to institution, even in a single city.

The role of specie as a monetary regulator was nominal. Nicholas Biddle considered making national and international commercial settlements contingent upon coin as the primary medium of exchange, rather than commercial credits, as 'scarcely less barbarous [than] ... the savage mode of barter'. 'Credit then -credit in the simplest form of Bills of Exchange is the true element of all commercial dealings'. In a lengthy letter to Baring Brothers he observed that the whole commerce of the United States was grounded in trade acceptances. Purchasers of western produce bought on credit, either with bills on New Orleans or notes which when they matured were paid with bills on that city. The export trade at New Orleans generated huge amounts of sterling that could be liquidated there, or remitted elsewhere when the sterling premium was too low. When the price of bills on England was depressed 'the shippers, instead of selling to the New Orleans banks their bills on London, [would] sell them their bills on the North drawn on commercial houses, to which [sterling bills] ... or orders to draw on England [were then] ... forwarded in hopes of selling them at a better rate to meet their acceptances [coming due at the North]'.[168]

Two months before the New York banks suspended, Roswell L. Colt wrote to Biddle and pleaded for the United States Bank to offset the effects of the contraction by issuing post notes, i.e., notes redeemable in specie on a specified date in the future, rather than on demand when tendered. '[W]e shall have a great number of suspensions - I find the discredit which as been thrown on out of town Bank Notes, begins to have its effects on the City Banks - R. Nevins - the great purchaser of foreign Bank Notes, tells me all those who sell to him foreign Bank Notes-in exchange for city Bank Notes - immediately draw the Specie to their great annoyance'.[169]

Another letter from Colt on 25 March 1837 rather clearly indicates how distorted rates of exchange among America's cities had become by that date. He urged Biddle to issue post notes payable at six months 'against first rate business paper, payable at the South, & West at 5 months, and charge 5 ½ percent exchange less ¼ percent for difference of time'. He thought the six-month post notes might also be used to purchase five-month business paper payable at Boston, 'with 3 percent exchange, certainly 2 1/2' which would result in a handsome profit to the Bank. The post notes could also be cashed in the New York money market at the legal rate of interest. In all the commercial centers interest rates then ruled well above the legal rate. In the New York market exchange on western and southern cities could only be cashed at disastrous rates of discount. If the Bank could issue its post notes, which were non-interest bearing, at par and charge a substantial discount of 5.25 percent on the paper it purchased with those notes, then clearly rates of discount on six-month bills in the New York market which were payable at the West and South must have been upwards of 10 percent. Colt also believed that a fall in commodity prices, which he thought was as inevitable, would bring the 'rate on Interest down to the legal rate, if not lower', a good indication that usury laws were largely ineffectual. Colt even suggested that the Bank issue bonds payable in London in 8, 10 or 12 months, with a 5 percent coupon, which would be readily sold in New York to those in need of safe remittance paper.[170]

In subsequent days Colt sent more advice to Biddle. The Bank might, he said, issue post notes payable in sterling at Baring Brothers on specified future dates which would be immediately absorbed by remitters and thus 'stop the drain of Specie', as the post notes could be cashed immediately in Europe. The rate of exchange on the post notes could be fixed at 10 percent less 'the differences of Interest between the excess of time over 90 days' that the post notes had to run and the maturities of the bills of exchange purchased with the post notes. He had no doubt that the Bank could sell six-month sterling post notes at a 12 percent premium and still 'charge Interest on the time the Notes [bills of exchange] taken in payment had to run over 90 days'. Issuing post notes payable at Baring Brothers would obviate the necessity of any formal acceptance of those notes when tendered at the firm's counter.[171]

'The whole [New York] community … [was] alive on the subject of [Sterling] Post Notes', according to Colt, and the Brown brothers had already committed to making all of their remittances to London in this species of paper. Moreover, the Browns had 'advise[d] all … [their] Friends to make such remittances, instead of buying Bills-and all the Bill Buyers [had said] … they w[ould] take them at once' which would bring down the sterling exchange rate to 9.5 or 10 percent 'where no more Specie w[ould] be sent'. Colt also noted that federal depository banks in New York were then preparing for the distribution of the second installment of the government's surplus, which placed great demands on their resources.[172]

By the end of March the specie hoard at the United States Bank had fallen to $1,400,000 and more drafts on that reserve were yet expected. Still the Bank had been able to sell its 12-month post notes for cash in the New York market at a 12 percent discount. The Morris Canal and Banking Company, whose president was E. R. Biddle, Nicholas's cousin, had issued six-month post notes that could only be cashed at a discount of 22.5 percent.[173]

The United States Bank did sell some sterling bonds in the New York market in early April, at from par to 4 percent premium, which was equivalent to a discount rate of from 12 to 16 percent a year. Colt strongly recommended against further sales at those rates and to hold for at least a 6 percent premium and sell only for cash. New York money, which was then at a premium relative to the local transaction media of other American cities, could then be used to buy undoubted bills 'drawn against the cotton shipments which w[ould] be made under the present low price of that article'. Here then is a very early revelation about the exigencies which would drive the United States Bank and sundry other institutions into the commodities market. A splendid opportunity was unfolding for arbitraging among a chaotic array of domestic exchange rates. There was also a pressing need to make cotton, in the form of sterling bills, answer for specie as banks strained to keep their interbank accounts current. Profit and necessity were at the centre of what would come to be known as the United States Bank's cotton speculation, not altruistic motives to support the price of America's commodities, and prop up the whole commercial community, as some historians have claimed.[174]

On 18 April Colt again wrote to say that the United States Bank's credit was so much better than that of any other institution in the market that it could cash its post notes at or near par and buy 'Bills drawn against cotton shipments at present low prices on any favorable terms'. The New York banks would be only too glad to cash the post notes to 'meet their payment in July for the 9 Millions [which] the Deposit banks [were] … to pay out'. In this very troubled financial environment even relatively small inconveniences took a high toll; a loss of a few hundred thousands of dollars of specie from the banks over a few days left the money market in a deep state of gloom. He then added:

> The importation of 31 Millions of specie & retaining it with us has lowered the value of the cotton crop to at least that amount - of the 1,600,000 [bales of cotton] we hold certainly 1,200 M & the fall has been near 30 Dollars per bale - The Benton gold experiment has cost the cotton growers more than the whole value of this excess of Specie.

Specie imports in the early part of the decade, and their retention in the United States, lay at the root of the ongoing credit contraction, according to Colt. There can be no doubt that specie did become a significantly more important component of the nation's money supply as one decade came to a close and a new one commenced, but the relationship between a surging supply of specie and expansive credit facilities predicated on that supply its tenuous. Specie's rise in importance seems to have had more to do with the wholesale discredit of much of the circulation and an overall contraction of credit facilities. This development did not necessarily follow from a steady accumulation of specie in the country in the years from 1831 to 1834 and its subsequent deployment in a massive expansion of credit facilities that could not be sustained.[175]

Peter Temin rather minimized the practical effects of a suspension of specie payments by the banks. 'In the 19th Century [a suspension meant that] the banks refused to fulfill only one of their obligations, and they continued to fulfill others. In fact, since they were no longer obligated to maintain the price of their notes and deposits in terms of gold and silver, they were able to issue them more easily than before'. A decision of Louisiana's supreme court offered a somewhat less sanguine assessment of the consequence of suspension for the banks and their collections. When bank notes ceased being convertible into gold or silver, 'they lost the character of bank notes, and became mere evidences of debt, which fluctuated in value as the reputation of the bank for solvency increased or diminished'.[176]

From the moment banks suspended, their notes steadily lost currency and value, and most banks in the Lower Mississippi valley adopted a rigorous program of systematic curtailments of their discount lines. Only by retrieving their liabilities from the marketplace could the banks ever hope to return the value of their notes to par and thus insure the value of their stockholders' capital. Note depreciation was costly indeed; customers who could find the means could purchase such paper in the market at steep discounts and tender it at face value in settlement of their debts. The forces of curtailment and depreciation were more than sufficient incentive for most banks to reduce their outstanding liabilities.

Far from passing their notes off more freely, as Temin suggests, banks even in Mississippi managed to reduce their demand liabilities; so much so, that by 1839 Stephen Duncan could advise his Philadelphia correspondent that the parent of the Planters Bank had but $53,000 of notes outstanding. The parent and its seven branches then had a combined circulation of only $400,000. The Agricultural Bank with a capital of $2 million and one branch had an outstanding circulation of only $200,000. The Commercial Bank's curtailments had been so successful that its demand notes were then quoted at par in the New Orleans market.[177]

A bank suspension did not, then, result in monetary pressure giving way to a monetary ease as Temin contends. Nominal rates may well have fallen in the aftermath, but that consequence only obscures the reality that credit facilities were now foreclosed to virtually everyone. Banks in suspense were banks in liquidation. Default was tantamount to bankruptcy.[178]

The most pernicious consequence of a suspension was the loss of currency of bank notes. Solvent customers availed themselves of the opportunity thus afforded and tendered depreciated paper in settlement of their claims. They also took their business elsewhere, to exchange dealers and brokers who could pay specie or its equivalent in bank paper for advances on cotton consignments or purchases of the same. In the case of the Mississippi banks the loss of exchange business was immediately apparent. What remained were portfolios of bills receivable which could not be cashed except at discounts of up to 50 percent in the local market. The only 'new' loans contracted by the banks were renewals of such paper. Whatever was realized from collections flowed out to creditors; namely depositors, note holders, and banks and agents elsewhere whose remittances were not under protest. As Temin notes, specie did become a significantly more important component of the money supply.[179]

The banks of New Orleans are reported to have suspended on 13 May, three days after the banks of New York stopped redeeming in specie. In truth the last set of quotes for sterling and franc denominated exchange, as well as sixty-day sight bills on New York and Philadelphia, was 22 April. Thereafter all quotations were reported in the *Price Current* as 'Nominal'. This condition persisted until 14 October when quotations for sterling and franc bills again became available on a regular basis. Quotations for sight and time checks on New York began being reported again on 24 February 1838, ten months after the commencement of suspension.[180]

With the banks of New York moving inexorably toward resumption in late 1837 and early 1838, the premium for sight checks and sixty-day sight bills on that city at New Orleans reached 7 percent for the former and 5 percent for the latter. As the banks of Louisiana prepared to resume on 1 January 1839, the domestic exchanges gradually returned to pre-suspension levels. Sight checks on New Orleans in the New York market also recovered. In August 1837, they had reached a nadir of 11.5 percent discount. By February 1839 they were again quoted at par, but declined rapidly thereafter as the probability of a second suspension steadily increased.

Cotton, Bonds, and Resumption

Nicholas Biddle could describe the banks of Ohio as 'nominally specie paying' as early as March 1836. The same could be said of other banks in the West, the exception being those of New Orleans, which were among the best situated in the country until the events of July and August 1836. It is perhaps ironic that the course chartered by Biddle for the United States Bank of avoiding local discounts and cashing only first-class domestic and foreign bills of exchange never could be implemented. The bank's inability to repatriate its capital from the western branches and heavy advances on improvement stocks in the closing years of the old bank's existence caused the new bank's operations to assume a character very different from what Biddle seemed to contemplate when he wrote to the cashier of the Pittsburgh branch of the United States Bank.

> [M]y own wish was to avoid if possible, scattering the funds of the office to places from which they could readily be recalled. The strength of the Bank will hereafter be in the concentration of its means. The Bank too, being no longer charged with the regulation of the currency & the exchanges, has no special interest, as it once had to bring the exchanges down to the lowest limit of price. That duty is devolved on others-and the bank now, instead of making the rates-takes them as it finds them-I would not therefore take bills on remote places without a full

remuneration (of course, a moderate one) for the loss of time and the difficulty of getting back our funds.

The bank's means were indeed circumscribed, and on 30 August 1836, Biddle advised one correspondent that '[o]wing to the derangement of the exchanges, a great demand exist[ed] at present in the cities, which absorb[ed] all the disposable means of the bank'.[181]

By January 1837 Biddle was imploring John Minturn, the president of the Merchants Bank of New Orleans, a bank wholly owned by the United States Bank, to send to Philadelphia immediately any funds collected there for the account of the late branch in that city. Minturn was to remit only bills on the North, England, or France and refrain from purchasing any bills on Natchez. Funds were wanted at Philadelphia to 'meet our circulation as it comes rapidly in, and here we can use to great profit any surplus'. The state banks whose accounts remained unsettled with the late branch were to tender immediately 'specie, or drafts on the North, or Exchange on the North, or foreign exchange at low rates. Unless they c[ould] do th[at], they ... [were] insolvent'. There was more profit to be gained from buying exchange than discounting local paper at 6 percent, the legal rate allowed by Louisiana law. Here, then, is evidence of one of the chief mechanisms for circumventing state usury laws. Requiring a debtor to settle his bills with the money of another city or country permitted the creditor to capture the prevailing premium in the local market whether he cashed his debtor's bill in the local market or sent it on for collection.[182]

By the beginning of 1837 the only mode available for remitting money from the West to the East was merchants' bills which according to Biddle were not 'perfectly safe'. Mercantile failures in late 1837 foreclosed any drawing of checks by the banks in the West on their correspondents in the East; so the only way open to those in need of remittance paper was to forward bills drawn by merchants and exchange dealers. The failure of one New York firm, Hamilton & Cole, threatened the solvency of the Union Bank of Florida. John Gamble, its president, wrote to Biddle on 22 April from Columbus, Georgia, urgently soliciting the aid of the United States Bank. The firm had advanced substantial sums to Florida planters on their forthcoming crops by means of bills of exchange drawn on New York. The Union bank had cashed the bills for the holders and then sent them on to the United States bank for collection. The Union Bank had then anticipated the proceeds from the maturing bills by selling checks on its correspondent. The firm's suspension meant that the maturing acceptances would not be paid and the bank's checks on Philadelphia would be dishonored unless the United States Bank extended credit to the Florida bank and protected its checks. The aid appears to have been forthcoming. Among the assets assigned to the John Bacon et. al. trustees in 1841 was a claim against the Union Bank of Florida for $240,151.96, and it is safe to assume that that claim had originated four years before.[183]

John Sommerville, formerly the cashier of the Nashville branch of the Bank of the United States and now the president of the Planters Bank at that location, required similar aid. The suspension of Yerger, Chaffin & Co. had left the bank without the means to redeem its notes accumulated at New Orleans. His bank required a credit of from $200,000 to $500,000 at the Merchants Bank to take up its obligations at New Orleans. He thought the resulting balance against his bank could be settled in two years. Sommerville even proposed making use of the notes of the old Bank of the United States then on hand at the Nashville office if opening a drawing facility at New Orleans was inconvenient. If the United States Bank afforded his bank a credit facility, the entire portfolio of $5.5 million would be available from which to select collateral securities.[184]

The anecdotal evidence suggests that many banks in the West and South already were *de facto* in suspense by the beginning of 1837. Both the Planters Bank and the Agricultural Bank of Natchez were federal depository banks, with upwards of $1 million of government deposits. The Agricultural Bank had prepared for the distribution of the federal surplus in January 1837, and subsequent distributions, by purchasing bills of exchange on points where the Treasury's warrants were to be paid. The bank's purchases of domestic bills had aggregated to $2,200,000 during late 1836 and early 1837. Of this amount $1,840,000 returned to Natchez and New Orleans under protest even before the general bank suspension. In 1838 the Agricultural Bank tried again to honor the government's warrants drawn on its deposit, this time by purchasing bank checks on points in-state and out-of-state where the payments were to be made. But the checks too came back protested for nonpayment. The bank next tried to sell its own bonds and raise sufficient funds to pay the government's claims with interest. But the bonds found no market in the wake of the second suspension in 1839.[185]

The Agricultural Bank's experience shows how even a well-run bank with a large, paid-in capital could be paralyzed by events beyond its control. In truth it had only received the government's deposit in 1836 and then the tender had been made with its own paper and the paper of other banks, not gold and silver. By receiving and crediting the deposit the Agricultural Bank effectively assumed responsibility for the condition of the paper it received, and presumably used the paper to set off its liabilities with the issuing banks. The deposit probably did not cause the Agricultural Bank to increase its local discounts, but it certainly required the bank to increase its purchases of domestic exchange in order to accumulate funds at various places on which to check when the Treasury's warrants were presented. The bank thus sustained serious damage even without a hemorrhage of specie from its vaults. If a large number of bills fell under protest, the bank's own means were effectively immobilized regardless of the vigilance of its managers. Paying out the deposits in a suitable medium of exchange was a complex business even in the best of times. Both the depository banks at Natchez would have fared much better if they had never engaged to perform the government's business. But it is also clear why these banks wanted the deposits. Some portion of the tenders were made with their own notes which of course supported their note issues and kept them current. Also, deposited items often included the obligations of New York and Philadelphia banks, paper which was more than suitable for remittances to cover a bank's own checks on points east. Good remittance paper had become increasingly difficult to obtain after 1834.[186]

Weeks after the suspension, Nicholas Biddle wrote to a Boston correspondent that the United States Bank's claims in the Lower Mississippi Valley were all perfectly secure. 'In regard to Natchez, all of the bills bought there [had been] … *guaranteed* by the Commercial Bank. When they became suspended, the Commercial Bank [had] proposed at once to take the whole on itself' provided the United States Bank gave the Natchez bank a year's time at 9 percent interest to liquidate the claim. He did not, moreover, anticipate any losses from the bills under protest at New Orleans, only delay in collecting them. His assessment clearly was very wrong.[187]

Temin suggests that in a post suspension environment, because most people in a locality were both debtor and creditor, bank paper continued to circulate, the disadvantages of tendering coin seemingly outweighing concerns about the relative worth of each bank's obligations. Even in a single locality banks tended to pull apart. At New York, advised Roswell Colt, 'the banks when they receive[d] a deposit enter[ed] in the Bank Book received in Bank Notes - this they th[ought] w[ould] exonerate them from the obligation of paying out Specie - under their new business - and as in a short time their old Balances w[ould] in this way be liquidated … they w[ould] only have to prepare for their circulation'.[188]

The Natchez banks behaved much the same way as the New York banks. On 25 June 1838, Thomas Henderson recounted to the first assistant cashier of the United States Bank his experience with depreciating currencies. Having forwarded certificates of deposit issued by the Bank of Vicksburg to that city for his credit, he found that he could only realize his funds in the money of the Brandon Bank and 'other uncurrent Notes - there [was] … a difference [in the Natchez market] … of 10 to 15 per Cent between those & what … [were] considered current bank Notes'. In September he advised a representative of the Philadelphia bank that his account had credit by a certificate of deposit issued by his own institution, the Commercial Bank, and a draft on the Agricultural Bank.

[T]hese credits are in what are termed here 'current Bank Notes of the State' by which is meant the notes of Banks in good standing in other parts of the State than this City - You will see the distinction in the Certificates of Deposit made by the Bank here, particularly those of the Commercial Bank, which are expressed payable in 'current bank notes of this State' or of 'the city -' the latter are preferred as they can be deposited here to bear interest which cannot be done without much inconvenience if at all with the Country Banks.

The Agricultural Bank paid its dividends in the notes of banks outside of Natchez. Such notes were termed current bank notes of the state but were not as desirable as current bank notes of the city. Prior to suspension a bank generally tried to refrain from circulating any paper but its own. But now efforts to bring in notes perforce necessitated paying out the balances of other banks that lacked the means to keep their accounts current.[189]

During the summer of 1837 Nicholas Biddle made serious exertions to quietly purchase specie in the market to strengthen the United States Bank's reserves. But his chief concern, aside from gathering the needful to meet the first installment to the government, was finding the means to service the United States Bank's debt in Europe. Sometime during the summer he resolved to ship cotton on the bank's own account or the account of its agents in order to meet the obligations coming due there. He wrote to C. A. Davis at New York on 20 September that the bank had 'contract[ed] a heavy debt ... [in Europe] which it ... [had] to provide for. It chose to employ its own officers to attend to that business. What right ha[d] any body to complain? ... [T]o pay this debt it [had] ... to buy bills of exchange'. What then compelled the Bank to buy those bills from the merchants of New Orleans, who had failed, drawn on merchants in London and Liverpool, who had also failed? When the bank took a bill of exchange 'it w[ould] have the security of the bills of lading as the best endorser'.[190]

The extent to which bills of exchange, accompanied by collateral securities, had been trafficked in prior to 1838 is not known. This species of exchange, however, became commonplace in the years after the suspension of 1837 and quotations for bills of exchange with attached bills of lading were reported regularly thereafter in the New Orleans *Price Current* until after the Civil War. It is interesting that such bills, presumably the most secure of all bills, never commanded as high a premium as bills drawn by first rate houses on their foreign agents.[191]

Only weeks after the onset of suspension, Roswell L. Colt summed up in a single sentence the exigencies which were driving Nicholas Biddle and his Bank toward what would come to be known as the cotton speculation. 'If the newspaper reports of the value of ... [United States Bank notes] on the Mississippi [were] ... true, [Biddle] ... c[ould] make an immense business by letting [his] ... New Orleans Bank purchase cotton ... and ship to Barings & [the United

States Bank then] … draw against' those shipments at a 20 percent premium in the New York market, sell the bills, and obtain funds to redeem its notes.[192]

Making cotton answer for specie was an idea also much in vogue among the banks of Mississippi. W. H. Shelton, the president of the Mississippi and Alabama Rail Road Company at Brandon (better known as the Brandon Bank), wrote to Biddle on 10 July that his bank had excellent prospects of gaining control over from 60,000 to 80,000 bales by direct purchase and advancing on consignments. Cotton exchange would enable his bank to redeem its circulation at the North and meet its foreign liabilities and 'to prepare … at home with exchange to answer in place of specie all demands' made on the bank. Biddle responded by writing to his agent in Mississippi, George D. Blaikie, with instructions to approach Shelton and purchase or advance on the cotton at the rate of two-thirds of its value. He was careful to authorize a variety of modes for settlement of the transactions. One approach would be to deposit proceeds of the purchases and advances to the credit of the Brandon Bank at the United States Bank in Philadelphia. The Brandon Bank could then sell drafts on that fund to people in Mississippi and realize a huge premium for exchange. Therefore, the price paid or advanced for the cotton would be something less than the prevailing prices in the local market. Another approach would be to deliver post notes of the United States Bank, payable at six months, directly to the Brandon Bank. In that case also, because the post notes were relatively more valuable than the paper of any Mississippi bank, the amount paid or advanced would be less than prevailing local market prices.[193]

By buying and advancing directly the United States Bank and the banks of Mississippi were engaging in activities somewhat beyond their customary purview. Cotton's traditional market makers, the factors, were indignant over the course of conduct exhibited by the banks. John B. Byrne, a partner in several of the failed partnerships which had comprised the syndicate of Hermann, Briggs & Co., wrote to Washington Jackson that it was difficult to obtain consignments from the cotton planters because of the competition from the banks which was driving up prices in the local market. 'The corner so far produced by the Miss. banks … [was] operating very injuriously on the interest of cotton Factors, Grocers & others … & w[ould] delay their collections at least a year'. He predicted that the banks would 'certainly pay dear for the preference they … [were] seeking'. Moreover, because the banks' notes were technically under protest in consequence of the suspension, any holder could attach the bales once they reached New Orleans. As Joseph H. Moore had complained, because his house could no longer afford to extend credit to their customers, they had abandoned the firm without paying their debts.[194]

The United States Bank's cotton speculations were conducted under the name, and to a limited extent the control of, the old and respectable Philadelphia firm of Bevan, Humphreys & Co. Matthew Bevan had for many years been a director of the parent of the late Bank of the United States. At the bank's behest a new firm composed of May Humphreys and Edward C. Biddle, Nicholas' son, was established at Liverpool, to handle operations in England. There can be little doubt, however that the officers of the United States Bank were largely involved in the collection of cotton at various southern ports and that all of those who consigned cotton to the firms, such as the Brandon Bank, understood that their undisclosed agent was in fact the United Sates Bank, not Bevan, Humphreys or Humphreys, Biddle. The firms appear to have had over 150,000 bales under their control during the 1837-1838 shipping season. Such a huge business would have been impossible without the vast resources of the United States Bank, which were at the command of the partners, and all of those who dealt with the firms knew that they were dealing with the Bank.[195]

All of the Mississippi banks shipped cotton for the reasons given by Shelton of the Brandon Bank: to redeem their notes, pay foreign debts, and accumulate exchange that would answer for specie. Their operations were spectacular indeed. In the early days of January 1838, the old-line Natchez firm of Bennett, Ferriday & Co. thanked Washington Jackson for favoring them with an offer of a credit facility with his Liverpool correspondent, but the firm had already obtained an 'undoubted letter of credit' from one of the most respectable houses in Liverpool, authorizing advances at the rate of £8 pounds sterling per bale 'which with exchange amount[ed] to nearly $40. p. Bale', a rate well above what Jackson was prepared to offer them. 'The heavy operations of the Mississippi Banks & the high prices which they [were] … paying or advancing to the planters, ha[d] taken out of [their] … control a large quantity of cotton'.[196]

James Hagarty, one of Biddle's agents in the South, wrote to him from New Orleans that the price of cotton in the transaction media of that market had advanced well beyond the point where it would be profitable to ship to England. There were many reasons, he wrote, for not only sustaining present prices but to advance them as well, not the least of which was the large operations of the Mississippi banks. By 31 March 1838, the Commercial Bank at Natchez had advanced $1,512,387.28 for shipments of cotton on its own account. By September 1839, it was clear that the huge shipments, which had aggregated to at least 30,000 bales, had resulted in a loss to the bank of nearly $400,000. Twenty-five thousand bales had gone to the Browns at Liverpool, and Baring Brothers and George Green & Sons also had received small consignments. But no shipments were made to Humphreys, Biddle which is surprising because the United States Bank bought most of the Commercial Bank's sterling bills. All of those who shipped for the account of the Commercial Bank were credited with the Natchez premium for sterling, which ranged as high as 16 percent over the course of the shipping season. None of the Natchez banks shipped to Humphreys, Biddle, the Planters Bank preferring to operate largely through Dennisons and the Agricultural Bank bestowing its business on the Browns.[197]

The recovery of cotton prices in southern markets in consequence of the huge demand for the commodity to substitute for specie resulted in a corresponding decline in the sterling premium at New York and New Orleans. Another factor depressing sterling was the Draconian efforts of the New York banks to resume specie payments, curtailing credit facilities to importers who absorbed so much of the sterling exchange. Concern was evident, particularly at New Orleans, that the low price of sterling would cause specie to flow to the United States from England. But by the summer of 1838 the price of sterling in New Orleans money was rising, and in July it ranged from 12 to 13 percent, about double the rate at New York.

The resumption of the New York banks, however, took a savage toll on the domestic exchanges, and this consequence may be of greater significance in the unfolding of subsequent events than sterling's relative depression at New York. Sight checks on New York again became unobtainable in the New Orleans market and the premium on sixty-day sight bills rose to 4.5 percent. Sight checks on Philadelphia were at a 3.5 percent discount in April and May 1838. Exchange dealers like Washington Jackson found it profitable to buy sterling bills at New Orleans, send them on to New York for sale even at the prevailing low price in that market, and then purchase sight checks on Philadelphia with the proceeds. The fund thus created at Philadelphia could then be drawn on by selling sixty-day sight bills at New Orleans at a premium. The result was a profit of at 3.5 percent on the arbitrage in New Orleans money. That such large profits should accrue from an arbitrage suggests a crisis in the domestic exchanges of monumental proportions.[198]

The demand for cotton by financial institutions may have lent enough support to the market to offset the effects of resumption at New York at least temporarily. Under normal conditions resumption at New York would have greatly depressed the prices of all commodities. The chaos in domestic exchanges was a speculator's paradise, and no doubt their heightened level of activity stimulated the cotton markets of the South, and Liverpool as well. But over the course of the spring and summer cotton prices fell enough in England to insure large losses to the banks of Mississippi that had shipped on their own accounts. Only those who had shipped to Humphreys, Biddle found their positions protected by the firm which thanks to the seemingly limitless aid of the United States Bank's agency in London held on until the autumn, at which time prices recovered enough to guarantee a profit. There were many more losers than winners in 1838, a fact that is overlooked by many in previous examinations of the Bank's cotton speculation. The relative success of that operation, however, was a bad example for others.[199]

The Natchez banks appear to have largely discontinued their operations by 1839 having sustained heavy losses. The Planters Bank may have lost as much as $1 million; the Commercial Bank about $400,000. Thereafter the Agricultural Bank, and the others as well, continued to ship small quantities but their cotton speculations were largely over.

The great planters were the next to catch the fever. Accounts of the fabulous profits which had accrued to the bank's syndicate fed the frenzy. Ironically, shipments to Humphreys, Biddle dropped dramatically to less than one-third of the previous year's volume. This appears to have been due principally to Nicholas Biddle's retirement from the Bank in April 1839 and his successor giving the bank's business to other firms. Biddle's personal success in the speculation undoubtedly attracted a great deal of attention and unfortunately envy.[200]

But the cotton speculation was also the bank's lifeblood in England, and as the London agency, under the able management of Samuel Jaudon, supported Humphreys, Biddle over the summer and autmn of 1838, so the firm directed all of the proceeds from cotton sales in the late autumn to Jaudon. The bank was thus able to meet all of its engagements in England in the autumn of 1838.[201]

The cotton speculation accomplished what Biddle had hoped it would do - furnish the bank with the needful to meet its huge engagements in England. But preserving the bank's credit in England came at a high price. The three Natchez banks shipped no cotton to Bevan, Humphreys or Humphreys, Biddle, but the United States Bank nevertheless furnished them with extensive credit facilities in the Philadelphia and New York markets. The bank of course wanted the sterling bills drawn by the banks on their agents in England - the Browns, Barings, Green, and Dennisons. Those facilities permitted the banks and their customers to discharge many of their obligations at the North, which paradoxically strengthened the position of the New York banks and their resolve to maintain specie convertibility. But the proceeds of cotton sales in England failed to cover the bills drawn against the consignments. This left the United States Bank with huge unsettled balances against the Natchez banks that consisted of various species of paper. Demand notes and post notes collected at Philadelphia aggregated to well over $1 million by the summer of 1838. Total claims against Mississippi's banks now approached $5 million; the Commercial Bank, upwards of $1 million; the Planters Bank, nearly $2 million; the Agricultural Bank, $700,000; and the Commercial and Rail Road Bank of Vicksburg, $1,200,000.[202]

There can be little doubt that Biddle's strenuous exertions to win the underwriting contract for the $5 million of bonds authorized by the Mississippi legislature in 1838 to capitalize the Union Bank stemmed from his mistaken belief that the new bank, rather than opening discount lines, would absorb enough of the circulation of the other banks to make resumption in Mississippi a reality rather than an illusion. Only with resumption could the claims be liquidated and the funds repatriated to Philadelphia where they were much needed.[203]

During the summer of 1838 Biddle met with the three commissioners charged with negotiating the bonds. In early August the terms on which the bonds would be sold were settled. On 31 August 1838, he wrote to Samuel Jaudon at the bank's London agency that the United Stated Bank was making great exertions to aid the banks in the South and West in their efforts to resume. 'Among the things which ... [had been done was] one which w[ould] come under ... [Jaudon's] care, ... [namely] the purchase of five million of Mississippi State Bonds, 5 p. ct., payable in London, endorsed & guaranteed by the Union Bank of Mississippi'.[204]

On 2 October 1838, Biddle sent the bonds to London convinced that the guaranty behind them was unassailable. 'As to the character of the state & its councils', he wrote, 'the ascendancy of such men as Mr. J. C. Wilkins, the commissioner to sell the bonds-Dr. [Stephen] Duncan & others whom ... [Jaudon] kn[ew] personally, ... [was] the best guarantee for the fidelity with which the state w[ould] fulfill its engagements'. Indeed, the bonds had been negotiated 'for the purpose of bringing back the state to a sound condition of currency, ... and the whole state w[ould] resume specie payments on or before the first of January next'. He fixed the sell limit at par, even though the Bank had paid par value for the bonds. But the Bank, he continued, had 'received some advantages in the payments'. The bonds were to be paid for without interest in installments of up to twelve months; moreover, they were mostly to be paid for at Natchez and New Orleans.[205]

Biddle revoked his previous sell limit for the bonds in a subsequent letter to Jaudon, a letter which suggested that the Bank was receiving substantially more advantages from the arrangement than his former communication had indicated.

Your Mississippi bonds have such a margin that you can afford to sell them low if necessary. We have taken them at par, which gives us four & six pence (4s. 6d) for every dollar. We pay one million on the 1st of November, by which time we receive arrears of interest on one sett of coupons, to the amount of $111,000 - Then we pay in New Orleans, 1 million on the 1st of November - 1 in Jany. - 1 in March - 1 in April - all these in N. Orleans. And in July next, 1 million in Natchez, which Mr. Marshall will pay out of our old Commercial Bank debt, running on 'till then at 9 per cent. All this time we pay no interest on these installments - So that on the whole, I deem it a tolerable bargain - the more as by buying Mississippi paper & putting it into New Orleans paper, a saving has been made: Having said this much, I forebear to fix any limits - leaving it to your good judgment - only I would convert it.

The arrangement thus contemplated was this: the bonds were to be paid for over the space of a year without interest, the whole while interest was accruing on them for the benefit of the holder. New Orleans and Natchez money was to be tendered, dollar for dollar, as each installment became due. The sterling exchange premium at those places ranged from 7 to 14 percent during the period in which the installments were paid. In order to meet interest and principal payments, which were payable in London, the state would have to purchase sterling at market rates that were substantially in advance of four shillings, six pence to the dollar. Even a small decline in the local money over the lifetime of the bonds would substantially raise the borrowing costs to the state.[206]

The United States Bank clearly needed to sell the bonds immediately; even the advantages surrounding their negotiation could not compensate for the fact that the purchase would increase the bank's demand liabilities at an inconvenient time. The stock of specie at Philadelphia 'ha[d] been considerably diminished by the resumption'. Much depended on a successful resumption by Mississippi's banks, the date for which was 1 January 1839. Biddle expected to be able to tender the mass of notes and checks of various banks in Mississippi, which had accumulated at the United States Bank during the suspension, and thus realize their full value. He advised W. W. Frazier, his agent at New Orleans, to purchase additional lots of Mississippi paper in the local money market.[207]

Biddle prepared to meet the first installment coming due at New Orleans by sending Frazier interest coupons, which had already accrued, from the bonds to the amount of $111,605, new notes of the United States totaling $740,000, New Orleans bank notes for $110,000, nearly $600,000 of Mississippi bank paper, and drafts on various locations where the United States bank had funds for $248,099.58. 'With respect to the Mississippi notes', he wrote, he thought that 'as the Mississippi Banks approach[ed] the period of resumption and as their crops c[ame] down to New Orleans, their paper w[ould] rapidly appreciate'. He hoped Frazier would be able to convert it with little inconvenience in order to meet the installment.[208]

Only one week after sending the paper to meet the first installment at New Orleans, Biddle wrote to James C. Wilkins, one of the bond commissioners and president of the Planters Bank, evidently indignant over the course about to be pursued by the Mississippi Union Bank. He perceived clearly that all of his plans for a meaningful resumption in Mississippi were unraveling. He reminded Wilkins that in making the negotiation he had been 'influenced entirely by a desire to assist the Banks of Mississippi in their effort to resume, and the plan by which it … [had been] proposed to accomplish this was, that the Union Bank, having a credit established at New Orleans, could draw on it for the notes of the other Mississippi Banks; thus being a creditor of the other Mississippi Banks, settle with them gently and kindly'. Biddle had been chagrined to discover that the Mississippi Union Bank had called in all of its demand notes and substituted post notes not payable until August of 1839, 'so as to reach beyond the last installment'. He had also learned that the bank would refuse all tenders of Mississippi bank paper to meet the installments, insisting on specie. He admonished Wilkins that '[i]f such a proceeding were adopted it would be neither more nor less than a sheer fraud'. The payment of specie 'was never contemplated by any one … for a single moment'. The loan had been made at a low rate of interest, and it was ludicrous to assume that the bank 'would go to the expense of sending specie to New Orleans, when its own notes were worth 15 or 20 per cent more than those of Mississippi'. If specie were demanded, specie would not be paid. If the Union Bank issued post notes, Biddle assured Wilkins, its credit and that of Mississippi would be ruined.[209]

Far from absorbing the uncurrent circulation of Mississippi's banks, the actions contemplated by the Union Bank almost certainly guaranteed a rapid depreciation of all outstanding paper. But tremendous pressures were being brought to bear on the Union Bank, both inside and outside the state, by those desperate for a medium of exchange suitable for remittances to points East. Biddle had to abandon any thought of tendering his accumulation of Mississippi Bank paper to meet the installments, and that paper eventually made up a portion of the claims against the Mississippi banks which were assigned to the John Bacon et. al. Trustees in 1841. Two-thirds of the bonds could not be sold, but were transferred in pledge to bankers in the Netherlands and in England as collateral securities for loans made to the bank's London agency.[210]

Resumption

Most of the banks in Mississippi resumed redeeming their obligations in specie on 1 January 1839, the same date set for resumption by the banks of New Orleans. On 28 December 1838, Biddle wrote to John Minturn, the president of the Merchants Bank of New Orleans, that it would be 'imprudent as well as useless' for the United States Bank to further aid the banks' efforts to resume. He expressed his disappointment over the course pursued by the Union Bank, but still he hoped that that bank and the Natchez banks would do their part in supporting 'their less prepared neighbors' as the date for resumption neared.[211]

Biddle was somewhat curt in his reply when the Whig congressman from Mississippi, Seargent S. Prentiss, applied to him for a loan from the bank. The bank 'having made its arrangements for Louisiana & Mississippi, [was] … no longer desirous of purchasing bills on those States'. He had labored without success to negotiate Prentiss' bill on Mississippi with private capitalists: all had insisted upon an indorser resident at Philadelphia 'as an indispensable security, & [had] declined discounting the bill'. Biddle assured Prentiss that the Bank was ever ready to serve him, and to that end had made an exception and discounted his bill. He enclosed the proceeds in the form of a draft for $6,345 on the Bank's agent at Washington.[212]

Biddle received regular intelligence about the conditions in Mississippi after resumption from James Hagarty, one of the agents he sent to the South to purchase cotton and contract consignments for Humphreys & Biddle. On New Year's Day, Hagarty advised him that no part of the first installment for the Union Bank bonds had been met with the Mississippi bank paper that had been sent to New Orleans for that purpose. One of the cashiers of the Union Bank had been in New Orleans the day before 'on the subject of the first installment and [had] suggested to the President and Cashier of the Merchants Bank that they might possibly be able to set off some part of this Miss. money against it but they [had] both said it could not be done'. In consequence, cashier W. W. Frazier had delivered the notes to Hagarty who was to take them to Mississippi 'and there convert them into Northern or New Orleans funds'. Hagarty was apprehensive that it would be a 'difficult matter to find northern funds there to such an amount $1,068,935'.[213]

The Mississippi and Alabama Rail Road and Banking Company, the Brandon Bank, was one of the banks which did not resume along with the banks of Natchez and Vicksburg. Some of its cotton at New Orleans had been attached by note holders in the course of reducing their claims to judgment, but according to Hagarty the bank had been successful in persuading all but one of the creditors to lift the attachments in return for confessions of judgment which bore 5 percent interest until paid. Still, its credit was 'as much prostrated as ever'.[214]

Resumption at New Orleans did not reopen the banks' discount lines. In fact, according to Hagarty, '[m]oney matters continu[ed] very uneasy … and all parties having bills to draw on the North complain[ed] bitterly of the Banks', because they declined purchasing their exchange. Hagarty thought the banks were pursuing a particularly ill-advised course in that northern exchange could 'always be converted into cash' and their dormancy undermined public confidence.[215]

Mississippi bank paper still traded at heavy discounts in the New Orleans money market. The post notes of the Union Bank were at a discount of from 4 to 5 percent and could only be redeemed when tendered at Jackson with checks on New Orleans which commanded a 1 percent premium. The discount on the post notes was large enough, however, to cause Hagarty to inquire of Biddle whether it would not be useful to buy the post notes in the New Orleans market, tender them to the bank at Jackson, pay the premium for the checks on

New Orleans, and thus reduce the amount of the installments yet to be paid for the bonds by as much as 4 percent on the funds converted in that way.[216]

Hagarty's primary duty was to exchange the Mississippi bank paper for northern funds after the banks resumed there. He left New Orleans for Natchez and other points in the state in late January 1839. His first stop was the Planters Bank where he attempted to exchange $180,000 of the bank's paper for checks on New Orleans and the North. The bank's officers informed him that they were not prepared at that time to meet the tender with remittable funds. Thomas Henderson of the Commercial Bank proposed to satisfy the balance against his bank with a check of the Union Bank on New Orleans at par on March 1. The Agricultural Bank, represented by Stephen Duncan, after much deliberation, likewise agreed to cover its account with checks on New Orleans. Hagarty was chagrined to discover that all of the Natchez banks claimed the right, accorded by local custom, to pay their certificates of deposit, 'when made payable in current money in what they call[ed] current notes of the State', which meant satisfaction with tenders of notes of banks located all over the state. Accepting such a tender would occasion much inconvenience and risk. The banks also proposed to settle tenders of their post notes with sight checks on the North, but demanded a 3 percent premium for the checks. Demand notes would likewise be met with sight checks but at a charge of 1.5 percent. Hagarty accepted Duncan's offer, even though it meant foregoing all interest on the account until March 1, the date set for payment at New Orleans. But the payments there could be used to offset the installment due the Union Bank on that date and 'the Exchange at par instead 1 ½ & 3 pct. [premium] w[ould] cover the interest' that the United States Bank would forego.[217]

Resumption in Mississippi was an illusion and developments over the course of the winter and spring left no doubt that many of the banks would suspend once again. The Agricultural Bank found it impossible to arrange for sight checks on New Orleans and in 1840 settled the claim with a transfer of bills receivable from its portfolio. The Commercial Bank likewise failed to fulfill the agreement consummated with Thomas Henderson and instead on 19 June 1839 negotiated 1,000 bonds of £225 each to the United States Bank, one half payable at the London agency on 1 March 1841, and the other half on 1 March 1842. The issue was valued at $1 million exclusive of exchange and effectively absorbed most of the United States Bank's claims against the Commercial Bank. The Planters Bank also issued bonds, but the United States Bank found no takers.[218]

It appears that the United States Bank never found a market for the Commercial Bank's bonds, but instead transferred them to one of its London bankers, Morrison, Cryder & Co., as collateral security for that firm's huge loans to the bank. A similar bond issue of the Merchants Bank of New Orleans likewise passed into the hands of Morrison, Cryder & Co., but the assets of that bank were deemed to be of sufficient quality to justify the firm's purchase of the bank from the failed United States Bank in 1841. The subsequent liquidation of the Merchants Bank proved to be a highly profitable operation for Morrison's, and the firm was the subject of much talk about the skill and financial acumen of its partners. Even the Commercial Bank's bonds were eventually redeemed, as were all of its other outstanding liabilities, and the shareholders actually saw a portion of their capital returned to them in the 1850s, a highly unique, laudable occurrence.[219]

On 25 January Hagarty advised Biddle from Vicksburg that as he had become 'better acquainted with the position of the Banks in Mississippi, ... [his] confidence in their ability to meet their circulation on demand ha[d] exactly been in that proportion diminished'. The banks had in fact no circulation at all, 'their notes instead of returning gradually upon them, ha[d] been bought up and return[ed] in large masses and they ... [were] afraid to discount and issue new notes lest they should be immediately returned and specie demanded; in consequence ... there [was] no material in which they c[ould] make their collections'. The president of the Commercial and Rail Road Bank had already informed Hagarty that any demand on his bank for an immediate settlement of the $350,000 of demand and post notes held by the United States Bank would force an immediate suspension. Ironically, according to Hagarty, the only banks with a circulation were those which had not resumed '[A]s their notes d[id] not return upon them, they furnish[ed] the chief circulation of the place'.[220]

Hagarty's subsequent letters contained more baleful news. That the banks of Mississippi had not suspended once again was due primarily to the sufferance of the United States Bank, whose interests in the state were simply too large to allow any resort to coercion. All of the banks which were still nominally specie paying looked largely to the Union Bank for salvation, and it appears that the credit facilities afforded that institution by the negotiation of the $5 million of Mississippi bonds were largely consumed in a vain effort to support the credit of the Planters Bank and the Commercial and Rail Road Bank of Vicksburg. It is likely that the state's bonds accomplished little beyond a more orderly liquidation of debts already several years old. The Commercial and Rail Road Bank, for example, proposed settling $259,167.76 of its debts with post notes bearing 7 percent interest and payable in 12, 13 and 15 months in Philadelphia. In addition the bank was then in negotiations with the Union Bank 'for the notes of that Bank which it effected' would be tendered to the United States Bank in place of the post notes.[221]

By 1839 the outstanding circulation of the principal banks in the state aggregated to no more than 20 percent of their liabilities, the bulk of their debts consisting of unsettled balances owed to banks elsewhere in the country, as well as merchants in the United States and in Europe, interest-bearing certificates of deposit, and of course the shareholders' remaining capital. The negotiation of the bonds actually contributed to the United States Bank's becoming the principal creditor of Mississippi's banks. The bank's operations at New Orleans had involved heavy purchases of the paper of the principal banks in the state, the purpose being to draw down the credits created by the negotiation of the bonds with calls for demand and post notes of those banks. Absorbing the surplus circulation was an indispensable prerequisite to resumption. But simply supporting the credit of the existing banks did little to offset the massive contraction of credit. Even with much reduced demand liabilities hanging over them, the banks could do little in the way of expanding their discount lines.

The level of activity in the Commercial Bank's cash account shows dramatically the paralysis that affected all the banks after resumption. Upwards of $6 million of paper cleared the account each month in October, November, December, January, and February. In March 1837 activity in the account fell to $4 million, and in June only $1 million of debits and credits passed through. Activity surged in the late fall and early winter to near pre-suspension levels, largely in consequence of the bank's huge advances on cotton and heavy selling of sterling bills, but the account was in deficit upwards of $800,000 throughout the period, about double pre-suspension levels. Over the course of 1838 activity remained well below pre-suspension levels, occasionally rising above $2 million. During the first six months of resumption, activity in the account averaged $2.5 million each month, still well below pre-suspension levels. Over the summer the average was just $400,000 a month. In the last three months of 1839 average monthly activity was $876,179.86. Thereafter levels of activity ranged from 10 to 20 percent of those maintained in 1836 and 1837. Combined net debits and credits were so small after March 1842 as to indicate a virtual state of dormancy.[222]

The overall condition of the Commercial Bank accurately reflects the health of the best banks in Mississippi. Its principal corresponding banks in Mississippi were the Planters Bank and the Agricultural Bank. There is every reason to suppose then that the deterioration of the Commercial Bank's cash account indicates a growing paralysis at the other Natchez banks. The Commercial Bank's cash account also shows how tentative resumption was in Mississippi. A reopening of discount lines and large exchange purchases should have accompanied the return to specie, but credit facilities were still contracting across the country. As the needful was gathered, often at great sacrifice, to liquidate one balance, no new facility opened to offset the one that had been closed. As mentioned before, it is ironic that all of the good efforts of the United States Bank in Mississippi probably accomplished little beyond supporting the resumption of the New York banks. Those with claims in Mississippi were able to close out their positions at some sacrifice. They did not reciprocate by opening new facilities. On 25 January 1839, Thomas Henderson wrote to John Andrews, the First Assistant Cashier of the United States Bank, that '[c]ollections ... c[ould] only be made in what ... [were] termed current 'Bank Notes' ... [that is] the notes of Banks in the State in good standing not payable in the city [of Natchez]'. The notes of the Natchez banks had been 'almost entirely withdrawn from circulation & every one that c[ould] be found ... [was] immediately presented at the Counter for payt. in Northern checks, notes of the Bank U. States or specie-not by the Citizens ... [of the area] but the Northern holders of them-Money of every kind ... [was] scarce'. On 28 March he advised Andrews that the Commercial and Rail Road Bank of Vicksburg had once again suspended.[223]

Hagarty wrote to Biddle that he did not consider 'any of the institutions in Mississippi ... entirely safe-they all except the Union [Bank] ha[d] enormous suspended debts and there ... [was] literally no sound circulation in the state out of which collections c[ould] be made'. The suspended debt was indeed staggering. On 30 June 1840, notes and bills under protest at the Commercial Bank aggregated to $1,392,518.51. Notes and bills in suit stood at $620,540.55. The Protested Exchange Account still showed a balance of $105,179.59 outstanding. Only $66,094.62 remained in the Exchange Account itself. Excluding a favorable balance in the Profit and Loss Account, the bank's principal income producing assets were $604,256.11 in discounted local paper. After 1837 it would be difficult to represent the operations of even the best banks in Mississippi as indicating any thing more than a condition of *de facto* liquidation.[224]

The anecdotal evidence certainly indicates that anyone with a claim in the state was attempting to settle it and cease operations. Hagarty confirmed Henderson's intelligence. The Union Bank, moreover, was about to issue more post notes payable in New York and Philadelphia which the merchants of those places, who had claims in Mississippi, had already authorized 'the marshall to receive ... in payment of executions' on judgments previously taken. He expected a further depreciation in the value of the notes and recommended purchasing them to tender when the last installment for the bonds came due. On 2 April he reported that the situation was deteriorating rapidly. The post notes of the Natchez banks, which bore 5 percent interest, were then at a discount of from 15 to 20 percent in the New Orleans market. Those of the Brandon Bank were at a 50 percent discount, and he expected the new post notes of the Union Bank soon to be selling at a 20 percent discount.[225]

In February Hagarty had strongly advised against extending any further aid to the Brandon Bank and recommended rejecting that the bank's proposal to secure its debt with a pledge of the business paper of planters endorsed by the directors. '[I]f the Debtors of the Bank, whose paper [was] ... offered as security had any means at all, they would [he wrote] make every effort to bring them into action at th[at] ... moment when they c[ould] buy Brandon money at 40 to 50 p. ct. discount and pay their debts with it to the Bank at par'. Hagarty thus stated succinctly the forces that were gaining the ascendancy in Mississippi. Soon enough those who stood to gain from a rapid depreciation of bank money would overwhelm those whose interest it was to preserve the solvency of the banks. Nor would conditions in Mississippi differ markedly from those in Pennsylvania, or in any location where the banks joined in a second general suspension in October 1839.[226]

Conclusion

Over the summer and autumn of 1839, Stephen Duncan, the last president of the Bank of the State, dispatched a steady stream of advice from his home in Saratoga Springs, New York, to William D. Minor, the president of the Agricultural Bank, the successor of the Bank of the State. His great object was to settle as quickly as possible the government's claim for the deposit, which had been made three years before, and the claim of the United States Bank. He meant for the claims to be settled in that order. Fearful that the Treasury would coerce the payment by suit, which would result in a fire sale of the bank's best assets, Duncan had been instrumental in persuading the bank's directors to transfer upwards of $600,000 of bills receivable to the United States Attorney for Mississippi as security for the deposit. '[N]ot to provide for the Govet. debt out of the first collections would', he wrote, 'subject the assets of the bank, to the seizure of the Marshall & a forced sale at a ruinous sacrifice-and ... the effect of this would be, to force all our debtors to take advantage of the ... [bank's] loss of credit'. His hope was that the United States Attorney would proceed to suit on the transferred bills receivable to the federal district court and recover the debts in specie as a third party transferee of the Agricultural Bank.[227]

Duncan strongly recommended that the Agricultural Bank buy cotton when it could be done without increasing note issues. What he proposed to do was use the paper of other Mississippi banks that remained to be retrieved from the Agricultural Bank where it had been tendered prior to and after suspension. The 'probable' loss he estimated at $6 a bale, but this was better 'than holding on to the post note currency, which c[ould] be made available in no other way, in meeting [the bank's] ... engagements'. A loss of even $10 a bale would be, he argued, bearable if it allowed the bank to meet its cash engagements and dispose of uncurrent bank paper.[228]

Paying out the circulation of other banks and refraining from issuing one's own paper had become routine practice after 1837. The Agricultural Bank paid its dividends in the notes of the banks of the state in good standing, not its own demand and post notes. None of the banks that resumed in 1839, according to

Hagarty, ever obtained a circulation. The ease with which the best banks gave currency to the obligations of inferior rivals suggests how dramatic were the changes wrought by the first suspension. The whole world of accepted banking usage and practice had been turned upside down.[229]

By early August, Duncan was advising that the banks of New York must suspend once more, and it could only inure to the credit of the Natchez banks if they outlasted the eastern banks. He could do nothing with the bonds that the bank had proposed to sell at New York and use the proceeds to take up its debt to the United States Bank. The best offer he had received was for '76' which was equivalent to an annual interest rate of 32 percent. The United States Bank was 'in a bad way. Her agents [were] … sitting on post notes at 1 ¼ & 1 ½ percent disct. per month in any city of the Union'. Duncan even reported on the famous issuance of $1 million of nine- and twelve-month post notes by which the United States Bank was 'enabled to make a pretty good demonstration of strength which only call[ed] for increased efforts in the banks elsewhere to maintain their credit ….[T]he chord c[ould] not be drawn much tighter'. When the banks of Philadelphia again suspended in October he urged Minor to '[b]uy Cotton, or advance on cotton to the full extent of your collections in the currency of other Banks'.[230]

The effects of the second suspension were disastrous. Sight checks on Philadelphia in the New York market fell to a discount of 5 percent in November, 7 percent in December and remained at that level throughout the winter and early spring. Sight checks on New Orleans initially fell to a 10 percent discount, but then recovered somewhat in December. They remained at a 5 percent discount during most of 1840 and generally traded above Philadelphia, perhaps because the extent of the exposure of the most important banks of New Orleans to the vicissitudes of the United States Bank were limited. Contemporaries certainly saw the United States Bank's second suspension as bringing ruin to all the banks of Philadelphia. The important New Orleans banks did permanently resume in May 1842, about the same time as those of Philadelphia.[231]

During the early days of resumption in Mississippi, Duncan had seen clearly enough that the contraction of credit was by no means over. He admonished Jackson, Todd & Company of Philadelphia that the conduct of the eastern money markets towards his state, which was predicated on the assumption that a second suspension there was imminent, would become a self-fulfilling prophecy. 'Your northern Banks & Branches have been acting toward our banks, ever since their resumption, as though a second suspension was inevitable, and if any thing could have caused a second suspension, it would have been the course thus pursued. But they will see, that their calculations are erroneous; & that although they have crippled us, they cannot break us'.[232]

The Agricultural Bank, the Planters Bank, and the Commercial Bank did remain nominally specie paying banks until after the suspension at Philadelphia. The aid they received from the United States Bank, in the form of forbearance from pressing its huge claims upon them, did allow for the liquidation of other claims. The banks of New York did not suspend a second time, and the United States Bank's support of resumption in Mississippi contributed in some measure to their ability to withstand the pressure for a second suspension.

The banks of Mississippi certainly importuned the New York banks for aid in supporting resumption. On 29 September 1838, Biddle addressed a letter of introduction to Charles A. Davis, an influential figure in the New York banking community, on behalf of Charles Davis of Mississippi, a representative of the Planters Bank.

> My friend and your namesake, Mr. Davis, of Mississippi is negotiating with some of your New York Banks to take some bonds of the Planter's Bank, bonds that are very safe and bear a very good interest. We have taken some of them ourselves-but I really think that your city ought to take some, and not throw upon Philada. the whole burden of the resumption in Mississippi. You have all the trade with that state-You are more benefitted than we are by the resumption - and it is a shame for you all not to take a share in helping them out.

Biddle requested that his recommendation not be made public 'suppos[ing] it would prejudice Mr. Davis' object'. Davis wrote from New York on 1 October that he expected little from the New York banks in the way of aid, and in a subsequent letter he remarked that there was not a bank in his city which did not 'shake in its shoes' when it crossed the Hudson River to do business out of the state. Thus the banks could find few incentives to support the credit of their brethren in Mississippi. Biddle responded that under prevailing conditions New Yorkers could only collect their claims at a loss of from 15 to 20 percent. 'If Mississippi ow[ed] New York 4 or 5 or 6 millions, and New York by lending ½ million c[ould] give an additional value of several million to the debt, should she not do so?'[233]

That the inhabitants of Mississippi were net debtors of New York financial interests is a highly relative assessment and must be evaluated in a context of failed commercial firms in New York, Philadelphia, and London. When huge firms like Joseph's, Timothy Wiggin & Company, Wilson's, and Wildes' failed, their consignors generally had no better claims on their assets than that of a general creditor. The firms' claims against their consignors for advances, evidenced by trade acceptances, were of course assets of the firms which during the crisis were either discounted or transferred as collateral security to their bankers. The consignors, i.e., the planters themselves or their immediate consignees, were still immediately liable for the full amount of their acceptances even if they recovered only a fraction of their own claims against the failed firms at some distant time. As a practical matter, the failed firms had been unable to cover their acceptances because of the dramatic contraction of credit facilities in the locations where they operated. New York was the center of the import trade. When goods were shipped from that point to the South, New York merchants drew bills on their agents there and discounted them at local banks. Much of this paper returned to New York under protest, and the banks indeed became net creditors of those in Mississippi who had failed to meet their bills. At the same time, a plethora of New York firms which had failed were net debtors of British exporting interests and their bankers. Trade patterns, rather than a simple debtor/creditor dichotomy, explains much about how the crisis developed in the late 1830s. In this respect Temin's assessment seems entirely correct.[234]

Speaking of Temin, trying to fix the blame for the crisis on the policies of the Bank of England was an idea that enjoyed some currency even among contemporaries. Nicholas Biddle articulated it all succinctly to Samuel Jaudon in October of 1842:

> The view I wish to present is this - That in the midst of the issues of the State Bonds, & the expansion of the currency here stimulated in fact by the abundant currency of England in 1838, & the early part of 1839, the Bank of England was forced into a very rapid curtailment to protect itself. The advance of the West Indies indemnity - the return of the East India company's money, the demand for coin to export for grain all obliged the Bank of England to take a very restrictive course & to discredit as much as possible investments of American securities - How far all this can be proved, you were on the spot, can tell-but I am anxious to have the best information & especially to have any printed documents which may illustrate the matter.

At that moment Biddle was anxious to direct public anger away from himself, and it is not surprising that the Bank of England provided him with a convenient scapegoat. It was after all an English institution. Biddle may never have transformed the Second Bank into a central bank, but he certainly showed that he could affect the arrogance the job demands. He never doubted his ability to create money to meet the exigencies of the moment.[235]

Jaudon wrote from New York two days later and referred Biddle to *The Report From The Select Committee on Banks of Issue of The House of Commons of 1840*. The *Banker's Circular* he reckoned also contained 'a good deal in relation to the destructive effect of the restrictive course of the Bank of England upon American securities'.[236]

Biddle obtained a copy of the House of Commons *Select Committee Report* from Henry Cary. Cary referred to Jaudon's remarks about the testimony of George W. Norman of the Bank of England and agreed that he was 'certainly a crack witness'. But he thought Biddle should read the question and answer at number 2476 wherein he would discover to his surprise that a depositor who left gold with the Bank of England and then drew checks on that deposit did not 'enjoy the same facility for purchasing which … [was] enjoyed by his neighbor who walk[ed] the street with his pockets filled with notes of the Bank of England, or Sovereigns!' Norman, he opined, enjoyed considerable reputation, but did not evidence more in his testimony than a facility for money matters comparable to that of the bank presidents and cashiers of Philadelphia.[237]

There can be little doubt that events in England exacerbated the financial crisis in the United States in the 1830s. But it is also true that the course of events in the United States made themselves felt in England. The collapse of the sterling premium in 1834 in the United States was largely the work of the Bank of the United States. There is also good cause to believe that specie retention in the United States, which Temin says was the basis for the upsurge in credit in 1835 and 1836, can be traced to the actions of the Bank of the United States. Certainly the bank's movement in the direction of liquidation in 1835 contracted credit facilities throughout the country, especially in the West. The transformation of local discounts at the western branches into domestic bills payable at points East, at least initially, tended to encourage an upsurge in credit, with inflationary consequences.

ASSIGNMENTS, PREFERENCES, AND TRUSTS: THE FAILED BANK OF THE UNITED STATES IN THE COURTS OF MISSISSIPPI AND THE NATION

Few episodes in American political history have generated as much scholarship as the 'Bank War' between Andrew Jackson and the Second Bank of the United States. Economic historians have debated whether the bank was a central bank, its role as a monetary regulator, and the national economic consequences of its removal. Some argue that the bank exercised a significant influence over the nation's credit markets in the early antebellum decades, contributing to a consolidation of those markets; a trend which legal historians say was helped also by a federal judiciary sensitive to the needs of interstate business. Tony Freyer, for example, has explored the work of federal courts in the antebellum decades and concluded that those courts were instrumental in the formation of a body of commercial law that satisfied the needs of an expanding market economy.[238]

As important as federal courts were in shaping a national commercial law, it is difficult to imagine a national institution that weighed so heavily on local markets as the Second Bank of the United States. Indeed, the bank as regulator of domestic exchanges, it can be argued, was the most significant national institution in the years before 1836, immersed in every important market and linking those markets together in a great national system.

In the ongoing debate over the commercialization of the common law to satisfy the expansive needs of a market economy, much of the scholarship has come to focus on negotiability and the transferability of contracts. Morton Horwitz writes: '[n]o development had a more shattering effect on American conceptions of the nature of contract than the necessity of forging a body of commercial law during the last decade of the eighteenth century. At the heart of all commercial problems lay the question of negotiable instruments and of whether the American legal system could assimilate the principles of negotiability into a conception of contract that had been forged in a precommercial society'. Recent studies by Freyer and James Stephen Rogers persuade us that Horwitz's characterization is entirely too sweeping. Rogers argues that negotiability as a legal doctrine was insignificant in the development of a body of legal rules regulating bills of exchange, at least until the nineteenth century. The instances where holder in due course status would have been of critical importance were simply missing from the kinds of commercial transactions where bills were in general use in the decades before the Civil War.[239]

The findings presented here do not fit well with any of these characterizations. The transferability of contracts to good faith holders, more or less freed from equities between the original parties, was recognized in the wilds of Mississippi probably from the organization of the territory. The state's economy was deeply immersed in national and international markets, its principal industry being staple production. Credit institutions not only functioned in Mississippi prior to statehood, they were pervasive in the organization of its economy. Only after the 1839 depression savaged local credit markets did the state legislature and judiciary attempt to narrow, and then reprobate, existing authority to assign credit contracts in certain instances. To characterize such changes as rank debtor relief measures, however, is rather crude and misses the exquisite permutations and ironies that often color credit relations in general.[240]

Little is known about the operations of the Bank of the United States in the localities where it had branches. Work on the successor institution chartered in the state of Pennsylvania has tended to focus on cotton speculations and the inevitable failure that must result from presumably 'unsound' banking practices. Scholars generally date that failure to February 1841 and pay little or no attention to the winding up of the bank's affairs.[241]

The story here begins in May 1841 when a special stockholders' meeting voted to make assignments of the bank's most valuable assets for the security of several classes of creditors. The transfers were preferences, but seemingly allowable ones. The largest and most important of those assignments was to secure the bank's notes and deposit liabilities. The trustees named in that assignment were John Bacon, Alexander Symington, and Thomas Robins, known collectively as the 'John Bacon et. al. Trustees'. The work of that trust in redeeming the bank's demand and post notes from circulation and paying the depositors by collecting the claims assigned to it, particularly collections in Mississippi, is the subject of this examination. The operations of the Bacon Trustees in Mississippi not only represents a unique and complex mediation process between debtor and creditor but raises questions about previous characterizations of antebellum credit relations and the law.[242]

The Bacon Trust assignment compassed $12.5 million of assets, making it one of the largest enterprises in the United States. Forty-one percent of the assets were in Mississippi. The Mississippi claims, aggregated with those in Mobile and New Orleans, accounted for 71 percent of all the trust's assets. The Lower Mississippi Valley was home to an even larger percentage of the assets deemed good. (Among the assets assigned to the trust was $1 million of stock in the Morris Canal and Banking Company of New Jersey which turned out to be worthless.)[243]

As vast as the trust's connections with Mississippi was, an accounting of those assets does not fully represent the extent of the United States Bank of Pennsylvania's connection with that state. In 1838 the bank had underwritten a $5 million bond issue of the state of Mississippi, the proceeds of which capitalized the Union Bank of Mississippi. The United States Banks' London agency sold $2 million of these bonds to European investors and transferred the remaining $3 million to London and Amsterdam bankers as collateral security before the bank failed. The London agency had also negotiated $1 million of bonds issued by the Commercial Bank of Natchez to Morrison, Cryder & Co. The United States Bank had taken these bonds from the Commercial Bank, its agency bank in Natchez, in 1839, in satisfaction of defaulted domestic exchange claims that had been purchased at Natchez for the account of the United States Bank and balances then owed to the Philadelphia bank by its Natchez affiliate. The United States Bank's dealings in Mississippi had been its most extensive area of operations outside of Pennsylvania, the state of its incorporation. Every bank in Mississippi enjoyed a connection with the United States Bank. The Bank's extensive involvement in Mississippi certainly had contributed to its problems, but it is also certain that its failure had insured the bankruptcy of every chartered bank in the state. The United States Bank certainly was a factor in the Mississippi legislature's conviction not to charter another bank, a conviction that it kept for the remainder of the antebellum period. [244]

The United States Bank's deep involvement in Mississippi owed something to Nicholas Biddle's long experience as the government's banker, manipulating the country's exchanges so the Treasury would have the means to service the foreign debt. Biddle evidenced a deep interest in the state; it was rich and many of its prominent citizens had close ties to Philadelphia. He bought Mississippi bank stocks for his own account was well as for that of the United States Bank. No state, he wrote, 'in proportion to its population ... [gave] the greatest amount of produce saleable for cash'. To Biddle 'cash' meant sterling exchange, acceptances that created credits for Americans to spend in England. Mississippi was 'probably the richest agricultural country existing ... [producing] an exportable cash ... [crop] of bale of cotton for every soul in the state, and if [one] ... divid[ed] the produce by the white population (supposing the produce to be 15 or 16 million of dollars) ... [there were] more rich proprietors than ... any where else assembled'.[245]

Of the $5 million of Mississippi claims transferred to the Bacon Trust, $700,000 had originated at the Natchez branch of the old Second Bank of the United States. These claims were already 5 years old when the Bacon Trust received them. All had stemmed from domestic bills on New Orleans, drawn at 60, 90, and 120 days date, and discounted at the branch by exchange dealers in Natchez. In its heyday, the Natchez branch had discounted on an ongoing basis for local dealers upwards of $2 million of domestic bills. The traffic in domestic bills had rather loosely paralleled long term advances to cotton planters by their commercial agents in New Orleans, New York, and Europe, a mechanism that guaranteed consignments to those same agents from the producers of southern staples. Such bills had taken the form of trade acceptances, but in reality they had been accommodation loans complete with endorsers or securities. After the general suspension in April 1837, most of those claims had been converted into promissory notes secured by the same accommodation endorsers. In 1841 many such notes were under protest for nonpayment.[246]

The branch had likewise discounted upwards of $2 million of local accommodation loans on personal security. By 1835 the Natchez branch, acting on instructions from Philadelphia, had reduced the portfolio of local accommodations to $1 million. The Planters Bank of Natchez had purchased those loans at par on a credit of 4 years with interest. Six years later $500,000 of this claim still remained unpaid.[247]

The United States Bank of Pennsylvania had also afforded substantial relief to the Planters Bank in 1838 to assist it and the other Natchez banks with resumption in January 1839. Two million dollars of the assigned claims were against the Planters Bank and represented the balance owed on the purchase of the branch portfolio and bonds at 12 and 24 months which the Planters Bank had transferred to the Bank of the United States in lieu of a cash settlement of the balances against it. The agent of the Bacon Trustees would later claim that the inability of the Planters Bank to settle that account in 1840 with sight bills on the North had been 'the cause in great measure of the failure of the late bank of the United States'.[248]

The mode of settlement finally arrived at between the Planters Bank and the Bacon Trust provoked extensive litigation in the courts of Mississippi and led ultimately to the United States Supreme Court. The events leading up to the decision of *Planters Bank vs. Sharp* and its companion, *Payne, Green & Wood vs. Baldwin, Vail & Hufty*, and the implications of those decisions for the development of the negotiability doctrine in American law will occupy the remainder of this examination.

The Taking of Bills Receivable

In the winter of 1840, Joseph Cowperthwaite, the cashier of the United States Bank, traveled to Mississippi to assess the condition of the claims there. He found little to be optimistic about, concluding that the only way the Planters Bank, and similarly situated institutions, could settle would be with transfers from their portfolios of bills receivable, much of which were already under protest. Specie resumption in Mississippi had been merely nominal, a fact Nicholas Biddle had been apprized of by his special agent there in the spring of 1839. By 1840 all the Mississippi banks were again in suspense and clearly operating in a liquidation mode. Dealings in domestic exchange after the first suspension in April of 1837 had likewise been merely nominal. Some bills had been sued on immediately, but most had been converted into new obligations drawn in the form of promissory notes payable in 12 months. Interest on such claims, not discounts from domestic exchange and bills and notes, now accounted for most bank earnings. In this state of things, it was inevitable that bank notes and other liabilities would depreciate in value and steadily lose currency.[249]

Parties to an acceptance under protest for nonpayment had simply contracted a new obligation that was known as a bills receivable. The new instrument contemplated a liquidation of the debt over a period of years. From a bank's perspective this mode of settlement had two advantages: the statute of limitations commenced running anew, and the necessity of filing suit was obviated. Short term credits thus became long ones, and it was just such claims that the Bacon Trust was now obliged to take if something substantial was going to be salvaged from the ruin. But taking such claims meant that many of Mississippi's most prominent citizens would now become debtors of the Pennsylvania trust. Not only would the trust have the management of hundreds of individual accounts, but its representatives might expect open hostility from hard pressed debtors.

Taking bills receivable in lieu of cash settlements was not an innovation. The Bank of England had sought to discount such bills in the London market in 1839 to support its own impaired credit. The Agricultural Bank of Natchez had transferred $1.2 million of bills to the United States Attorney as collateral security for a judgment against the bank, predicated on government deposits that had remained unsettled after the first suspension in April 1837. The Agricultural Bank had postponed execution on the government's judgment by further securing it with personal guarantees from some of the wealthiest men in southwest Mississippi. Stephen Duncan, the great Natchez planter and financier, acted as agent for the bondsmen and advisor to William J. Minor, the bank's president. Duncan had hoped the United States Attorney would sue on the bills in the federal district court and obtain judgments in specie and thus preclude the possibility of the debtors making a legal tender of depreciated bank liabilities. He estimated that the bank would lose 40 cents on every dollar it raised by cashing its bills receivable in the market. The bank would have to receive cotton from its debtors, credit their debts at premium prices, sell the cotton at a loss, receive its own demand and post notes in payment, and then convert those notes into specie at a loss. He feared that the United States Attorney would cause writs of execution to issue and levy on all the bank's assets. A forced sale of the bills would yield pennies on the dollar, something the bank's debtors knew and hoped would occur. Unlike other bank creditors, the government had few incentives to make the most from the bills. Indeed, there were those in the Van Buren administration who would have welcomed a fire sale of the bank's assets.[250]

Bank suspensions created perverse incentives for debtors and creditors of such institutions. A debtor had good cause to postpone payment for as long as possible, assuming he could tender depreciated bank liabilities in satisfaction of a claim. A creditor had every reason to preserve the value of any collateral placed in his hands as security for bank liabilities such as demand and post notes. Assuming it was collectable, a bill receivable would retain its value. The Bacon Trustees felt 'compelled in self defence rather than remain with the prospect of losing all, to make selections from … [the Planters Bank's] bills receivable'.[251]

Prior to 1840 the best legal authorities in Mississippi probably would have subscribed to the view that a good faith holder of a bill receivable was relieved of any equities existing between the original parties to the instrument. He could in other words recover the amount stated in the instrument in good funds. However, it is difficult to imagine a more important defense, or one more likely to be raised in any contest in the nineteenth century, than the right of a debtor to tender a creditor's own obligations in satisfaction of a debt. The instances where a debtor was likely to assert a defense against a holder in due course were cases where the debtor could claim a setoff against the holder's transferor, usually a bank, rather than some other defense such as a failure of consideration.

In 1840 the Mississippi legislature passed a law ostensibly intended to guarantee that the banks would resume specie payments within a year's time. Compliance with the new law and resumption within the time specified was a practical impossibility for most banks. The law was a coercive measure, intended to force the banks into liquidation, voluntarily or involuntarily, guaranteeing that bank debtors could tender depreciated notes in payment and precluding transfers to bank creditors who might attempt to recover specie or its equivalent in paper.[252]

The act barred the banks from dealing in cotton, restricted stock speculations to $100,000 per institution, outlawed the issuance of post notes, limited circulation to 3 times the amount of specie 'actually in the vaults', and mandated specie redemption of all notes within a year's time beginning with those of $5 or less which were to be redeemable 45 days hence. Direct liabilities of an individual or firm were not to exceed $20,000 and contingent liabilities were not to exceed $50,000. The act strictly prohibited loans to officers and directors. Assuming that the banks of the state would find it more expedient to voluntarily liquidate, the act provided for the continuance of such corporate powers as were necessary for the completion of the liquidation within 8 years. Bank debtors were to have up to 6 years to pay off their loans.

Having suspended, all the Mississippi banks were technically in violation of their charters. The act effectively barred the banks from undertaking operations, such as shipping cotton on their own accounts, which might have aided in resumption. The act seems to have assumed a tacit forfeiture of every bank's charter, and this may have figured in the rationale for including a provision making it 'unlawful for any bank … to transfer by endorsement or otherwise, any note, bill receivable, or other evidence of debt' and in the event of a transfer, authority to defend on that basis in a collection proceeding. If the banks were operating in violation of their charters, perhaps the legislature had the power to reform their acts of incorporation unilaterally and retroactively. A supplemental act required that the banks should at all times 'receive their respective notes, at par, in the liquidation of their bills receivable and other claims due to them'.[253]

The Act of 1840 evidenced a high level of sophistication about the conduct of banks: its primary objective was to make bank creditors and stockholders absorb all the loss from currency depreciation. Stephen Duncan studied the legislation and gave his opinion to William J. Minor.

> I think from a cursory reading of the Bank Law your Bk. would be more favored, under a repeal of the charter by the Executive Quo Warranto - than by a surrender - In the former case you are not obliged to grant the 6 years extension [to the debtors] & you are only obliged to have one examination by a commissioner - In the latter case, you are obliged to be examined annually & pay the expense of the examination - The only objection to the former-is, that you are prohibited from dissolving until all your liabilities are paid - This will be considered by a succeeding Legislature – Besides - there would be a better prospect of being reinstated on fair terms - if repealed by Quo Warranto than if you surrendered. That you will be compelled to adopt one of these cases I have now-no doubt - If you determine to accept the Law - would it not be well to confirm to the very letter of it-by paying only your 5' now-your 10's in July - & c & c - as you don't mean to use your p. n. [post notes] any more – this - it appears to me would be your best course - It requires reflection previous before action on so important a step.[254]

Prior to the act, a debtor clearly could tender a bank's own liabilities in satisfaction of his debt, and he could likewise tender those same liabilities to a third party transferee of the bank provided his own evidence of indebtedness had been transferred after maturity. The Mississippi legislation, however, was intended to accomplish more than codifying recognized defenses. Its abatement provision could be interpreted as a penalty clause subjecting the offending bank to an absolute forfeiture of any claim that was transferred in violation of the act. The provision certainly was ambiguous, but it would be crucial in the United States Supreme Court's decision to grant writs in the cases of *Planters Bank vs. Sharp* and *Payne, Green & Wood vs. Baldwin, Vail & Hufty*.

Laws supportive of debtor rights were not unique to Mississippi. To make its assignments the United States Bank needed the Pennsylvania legislature to exempt it from a bond requirement for those charged with liquidating corporate property. The legislature predicated that relief on the trustees receiving in payment of debts due to the bank or 'to them at par, the notes or other evidence of debt issued or created by said bank'.[255]

Nicholas Biddle, now openly hostile to the institution over which he had once presided, wrote to one legislator during the debate of the relief bill that:

> There is a thing about the Bank bill which I think the Western people ought to know. The purpose of it is to enable the Bank to transfer to Trustees the debts of the Pittsburgh, New Brighton & Erie branches. This puts them entirely under control of these Trustees who may collect the debts as they please - instead of having them paid to the Directors at the branches - the friends & neighbors of the debtors - They are in fact sold out to strangers - I think the Directors of the Branches should remonstrate against such a transfer & the western men will be very wrong if they assent to any such bill. There is besides another very serious disadvantage to the debtors. They contracted the debt to the B. U. S. of course they have a right to pay in the notes of that Bank & while the notes are at a depreciation they can pay their debts easily. But if he is transferred to other banks or other Trustees in Philada., he must of course lose his chance of paying in notes of the Bank - and he will have to pay in any currency these banks may require, however difficult it was to get such currency in the west-If I were a western debtor I would oppose the transfer.

Biddle counseled the legal representative of one debtor that 'things ... [were] going as badly as possible at the Bank & [that in consequence] debtors w[ould] have favorable opportunities of settlement with depreciated paper'. Under those circumstances he advised raising cash and buying the bank's notes 'when they reach[ed] the lowest point', a strategy which he had already adopted in settling his loans.[256]

Biddle even applied to the Merchants Bank of Baltimore for a loan with which to purchase some of that institution's claims against the Bank of the United States.

> The notes [of the Bank of the United States] are at a discount of about thirty one percent, but in order to purchase I must make a sacrifice on the sale of stocks

which will I hope sell better hereafter, my idea would be to purchase your draft on the B. U. S. at say 25 pr. cent discount with my note payable in one year with interest & of course adequate collateral security-that which happens to be most convenient is the Philada. & Baltimore Rail Road.

The cashier of the Merchants Bank declined his offer, explaining that his bank had already attached adequate property of the Bank of the United States to fully secure its claim.[257]

Creditors sued out writs of attachment in New York, Baltimore, New Orleans and other places where the bank had property. The United States Government sued in the state courts of Louisiana to set aside the assignments and had writs of garnishment served on hundreds of the bank's debtors in New Orleans. The prospect of protracted litigation caused the bank's liabilities to depreciate rapidly in the money markets of New York, Philadelphia, and New Orleans. By the winter of 1842 the demand notes and post notes of the United States Bank had depreciated more than the issues of the best Mississippi banks including the Planters Bank. Paradoxically, that state of things substantially simplified the enormous task of reaching a settlement with the Planters Bank.[258]

Joseph L. Roberts' Mississippi Agency

The Bacon Trustees soon determined that their business in Mississippi would require a full time agent who was resident there. In July 1841 they chose Joseph L. Roberts, a native Philadelphian and career employee of the Bank of the United States. Roberts had risen to become cashier of the Norfolk branch of the old bank. Biddle had subsequently given him the management of the Insurance Bank of Columbus, Georgia, one of several banks acquired by the new bank after its 1836 incorporation in Pennsylvania.[259]

Roberts finally arrived in Natchez in November 1841 and opened negotiations immediately with the officers and directors of the Planters Bank. Levin R. Marshall and Thomas Henderson, the president and cashier respectively, of the Commercial Bank, the agency bank of the Bank of the United States at Natchez, assisted him in his lengthy negotiations. They cautioned him to expect the Planters Bank to 'dispute every thing they c[ould] & ... not admit any charge for exchange either between Philada. & New York or between New York & [Natchez]'. The exchange claim was nearly $50,000; it represented the costs of purchasing exchange on New York at Natchez to meet the Planters Bank's principal and interest payments on its bonds due there on a particular day. The United States Bank had made the payments in New York for the Planters Bank. On that date at Natchez, New York exchange had been at a substantial premium, a difference the Bacon Trust claimed it was entitled to recover. H. D. Mandeville, the Planters Bank's cashier, argued that it was a 'fictitious' charge because on that day 'the Bk. U. States [had] held those very Bonds in her vaults in Philada'. Roberts answered that such an 'assertion [was] beyond his [Mandeville's] knowledge … that when the Bonds were made payable by the Planters Bank & were not met by them, but by others, the parties … holding them had a right to demand payment according to the value of the money where & when due'. The Planters Bank continued to insist that there could be no claim for exchange, and as new problems arose and the prospects for making collections worsened, Roberts simply dropped it.[260]

Roberts and the representatives of the Planters Bank could claim with some justification that the settlement was predicated on an understanding reached two years before when Joseph Cowperthwaite was in Mississippi. But the Act of 1840, which postdated that understanding by one month, nevertheless figured in the negotiations and the actual transfer of the bills receivable in the spring of 1842. Roberts had occasion in 1845 to reflect on the significance of that legislation for the mode of transfer that had been adopted in 1842. The bills receivable were notes made payable to the 'President, Directors & Co. of the … Bank, not 'or order'-the Notes being joint obligations, or rather the securities signing under the Principal on the face, the holder of any Individual Note or notes here, without the note being endorsed to them, c[ould] always … [bring] suit in the name of the Bank 'for the use of' the holder or anybody else-for the reason it was thought best not to have the notes … endorsed over to [himself or the trust], particularly as all the debtors knew of the law passed to prevent a transfer of Bills Receivable (thou' the law was generally believed to be unconstitutional)'. If any of the debtors refused to pay, their notes could be returned to the bank 'in the same situation as … received, … without endorsement'. Subsequent litigation in state courts would, however, result in a decision which seemed to say otherwise, that the mere fact of transfer prevented even the original payee from collecting on re-transferred bills.[261]

Roberts complained about the 'mortifying' conduct of the Planters Bank, 'their faithlessness', and obfuscation, during the negotiations, but it is remarkable that the bank ever consummated the transfer. The bank faced a hostile community, the Act of 1840, and the State of Mississippi, its largest shareholder. The transfer stripped the bank of its best assets, leaving its notes and other liabilities virtually unsecured. Roberts wrote to the trustees:

> Tis reported that after we get our 2 million, that there will not be a million (indeed not more than one half of it) left in the Planters Bank that will be good for anything - & I fear it is but too true, their expense (lawyers principally) are $80,000 a year & they ought to be but $20,000.

Depositors and holders of demand and post notes certainly ranked concurrently with bond holders and general creditors. The Planters Bank was making a preferential transfer to the trust, albeit an allowable one.[262]

The Act of 1840 was supposed to discourage dispersal of bank assets to pre-ferred creditors during the course of liquidation. 'Amalgamation' was a term that enjoyed wide currency in the 1840s, not just in Mississippi, but in the North as well, as bankrupt corporations of every description attempted to reorganize. It assumed that all creditors were equal and entitled to the same dividend from the assets of a failed corporation. Shareholders, too, could assert an equality with creditors in such cases. In more fortunate circumstances, creditors and shareholders combined in a new enterprise and began business anew.[263]

Clearly Mississippi benefited if it eventually came in for a share of the dividends from the Planters Bank liquidation: if shareholders got nothing, the loss to the state would be disastrous. The state had sold $2 million of its bonds to finance its capital contribution and had relied on dividends from the bank to service those bonds during the 1830s. If shareholders received nothing from the liquidation, Mississippi taxpayers would have to shoulder alone the burden of redeeming the bonds. The state, then, had a vital interest in preventing transfers of bills receivable to preferred creditors, especially from the Planters Bank portfolio.[264]

In April 1842 Roberts could finally report to the trustees that he would be allowed to select 'from the best of their paper at the Parent Bank & Branches - & so having selected certain debts - the Planters Bank [would] … collect & the same for [his] … account'. In cases where the debtors were disposed to make 'an entire new arrangement', he would tender a corresponding amount of bank liabilities to the Planters Bank and 'give more time, on the debts being well secured', and the debtors agreeing to pay part with the current funds, part with the United States Bank's own demand and post notes, and part with Planters Bank demand notes. Many of the debtors acquiesced, according to Roberts, because Planters Bank obligations were then 'of higher value in the Market, than the Notes of the Bank U. States by from 5 to 20 percent according to the fluctuation of Miss. Bank paper, as well as of that of the Bk. U. States …. As Planters Bank obligations were higher … by holding the paper as recd. from the Bk., [he] … could compel the debtors to pay in Planters Bk. obligations-hence, the … inducement, for them to give … new notes payable in the <u>Notes of the Bk. U. States'.265</u>

Contracting anew with the debtors should have obviated most of the problems respecting an unlawful transfer of bills receivable, and settled any question about what constituted an acceptable tender. Unfortunately the trust was still locked up with the Planters Bank, insofar as debtors of every description could tender Planters Bank notes. Some debtors refused to make new arrangements which obliged Roberts to accept full tenders from them of Planters Bank money. His accumulation of Planters Bank notes grew steadily: their conversion into bills on the north or obligations of the Bank of the United States depended on conditions in the New Orleans money market. Most of the time, the demand for Mississippi money was merely nominal, and sales of large blocks depressed prices significantly.[266]

The Planters Bank faced increasing pressure to make a general assignment in conformity with the Act of 1840. New legislation in 1843 gave local authorities an additional weapon with which to coerce the banks, the so-called 'Quo Warranto' law. Under its provisions the district attorney in a county could file a bill in the circuit court to enjoin any further actions by a bank, including collection proceedings against debtors, where the officers and directors were alleged to be operating in violation of the charter. On 8 June 1843 the stockholders of the Planters Bank voted to make an assignment to three of the officers, all of whom Roberts held in low regard. Rather than retrieve the bank's liabilities from circulation, Roberts ascertained that the assignment had 'commit[ted] such a suicidal act, as to provide, or give permission [to the assignees] for getting out & selling her insolvent & depreciated obligations, & thereby increase the[ir] liabilities, or the depreciation of them, in a three fold degree'. This measure, no doubt, was intended to defray the costs of the liquidation, but Roberts clearly saw it differently.[267]

Within six months of the Planters Bank's general assignment, a court decision sustained an exception to the legality of the transfer to the Bacon Trustees. Two claims upon which the Planters Bank had brought suit previous to the transfer were 'decided against the Bank; one on the ground that the transfer... to the Bank of the U. States was illegal; & the other on the score of usury'. A bill of exceptions had been filed in the proceeding and was being readied for submission to the High Court of Errors and Appeals, Mississippi's highest court. Roberts advised Samuel H. Lambdin, the president of the Planters Bank, that he had retained eminent Natchez lawyers John A. Quitman and John T. McMurran to represent the trust, and he recommended that the bank engage them to gain a reversal in the High Court. The bank was bound to defend the trust in suits involving the legality of the transfer. In years to come, the trust alone would bear the heavy costs of litigating the case of *Planters Bank vs. Sharp* to a final decision in the nation's highest court. The Planters Bank would soon cease to be; any warranties from it would prove to be worthless.[268]

Planters Bank vs. Sharp

A year passed before the High Court of Errors and Appeals heard arguments in the cases of *Payne, Green & Wood vs. Baldwin, Vail & Hufty* and *Planters Bank vs. Sharp*. Roberts advised Quitman and McMurran that while the case was of 'vast importance' the delay it had occasioned was costly. Pending a decision he had stopped suing on other claims, and without the threat of coercion by suit, debtors would force him to renegotiate their agreements. The new Quo

Warranto law of 1843, moreover, seemed to afford the debtors an opportunity for escaping payment altogether, assuming a forfeiture of a bank's charter destroyed the obligation to pay. Planters Bank money in consequence had declined steadily in value. The '[d]ebtors w[ould] move Heaven & Earth before they w[ould] pay anything else & not a dollar w[ould] be collected except at the end of the Law & of that' he would have his hands full.[269]

Roberts began to lose confidence in Quitman and McMurran and obtained the trustees' permission to hire the Vicksburg lawyer, George M. Yerger, to assist them in the High Court. Two more cases had been decided in the same court against the Planters Bank, and Roberts decided that 'if the paper sent up to the High Court ... [was] more regular than either one of the former cases sent up on the ground of the transfer' Yerger should handle the appeal.[270]

The transfer agreement had obliged the Planters Bank to defend the suits, but Roberts soon discovered that the state's recent quo warranto proceeding against the bank's assignees had altered the thinking of the bank's general counsel. Debtors at Woodville, 'wrong headed loco foco repudiators', had combined to hire the best lawyers in the state to fight the appeal and subsequently had retained the Planters Bank's lawyers, Montgomery & Boyd. Hearing rumors to that effect, Roberts had had an interview with Montgomery, and the latter had confirmed that he and his partner had agreed 'to protect' the Woodville debtors. He told Roberts that neither he or his partner had ever believed that the transfer was lawful, that Roberts had taken the bills 'knowing such a law to be in existence, & against the wishes of many of the debtors at the time'. Roberts reminded him that at the time of the transfer they had had no doubts that the law was unconstitutional; 'that whenever the question came up in law the Planters Bank were to join in the suit to establish their right to transfer, they being as much interested' as the trust. Montgomery replied that the bank had never sought their advice on matters then pending and that their original opinion on the validity of the transfer had been given long ago. They considered the Planters Bank 'as pretty much down now'. There would 'not be much pickings for them', and they had to look after themselves.[271]

The interview confirmed Roberts in his original estimation of Montgomery and Boyd, that the former was 'an unprincipled man', and the latter a 'matured, artful rascal'. If one could assume 'unhesitating rascality in Men, who consider[ed] themselves highly honorable & respectable, it ... [was] to be found deep rooted and abundantly in Mississippi'.[272]

Having retained Yerger, Roberts asked permission to also hire the Whig politician, Seargent S. Prentiss 'more on account of the character which he ha[d] obtained as a great Lawyer than any thing else'. The fee would be large, and Roberts detested his principles. He also knew that Quitman & McMurran would insist on comparable compensation and refuse to honor their original fee arrangement. Indeed, McMurran had said as much indicating to Roberts a 'want of principles in these Men [as well as], the most respectable and wealthy men of the Miss, community'. Prentiss, however, was retained by the other side, thus sparing the trust additional expense.[273]

The High Court of Errors and Appeals rendered decisions in *Payne, Green & Wood vs. Baldwin, Vail & Hufty* and *Planters Bank vs. Sharp* at its November 1844 term. The former opinion was far more important than the latter insofar as it explained the court's reasons for sustaining the legislature's power to prohibit the transfers. The circuit court had sustained a transfer of bills receivable from the Mississippi Rail Road Company to Baldwin, Vail & Hufty, a Philadelphia firm. The bank had transferred the notes by endorsement more than one year after the enactment of the prohibition. The endorsee, Baldwin, Vail & Hufty, had sued the makers, Payne, Green & Wood, and the circuit court had rendered judgment in their favor. Payne, Green & Wood had then applied for a writ from the High Court of Errors and Appeals.[274]

Chief Justice Sharkey reversed the trial court in a well-reasoned, carefully drawn opinion which in essence stated that the bank had derived all of its authority to negotiate its bills receivable from the general law of negotiable instruments, not expressly from provisions in its charter or any power incidental to its charter. Negotiability was an exception to the general prohibition against the assignability of claims, a statutorily created exception. 'As these laws ... [were] alterable at the pleasure of the legislature', Sharkey argued, 'the corporation c[ould] not claim exemption for the effect of these alterations, unless by express stipulation the legislature ha[d] consented to grant such exception'. The legislature, he continued, had done nothing 'but take from promissory notes an incident they had previously given them'. The Mississippi Rail Road Company's charter did 'not guarantee to the corporation that such notes should remain negotiable'.[275]

Sharkey's reasoning had much to recommend it. He implied that the Mississippi Rail Road Company could still recover on the notes; so it followed that Baldwin, Vail & Hufty could retransfer the notes. But the decision was highly anachronistic, intimating a distinction between evidences of indebtedness drawn in the form of promissory notes and other commercial instruments such as bills of exchange. In fact the two notes transferred to Baldwin, Vail & Hufty had been drawn in Mississippi, but made payable at New Orleans, at sixty and ninety days date respectively. Probably the drawers had intended them to effectuate the same purpose which trade acceptances would have accomplished, i.e., to create credit facilities at New Orleans. Probably because no city merchant had been willing to accept the paper, thus guaranteeing payment, the instruments had taken the form of promissory notes. Both notes had been duly protested for nonpayment at New Orleans in 1839 and returned to the Mississippi Rail Road Company.

There can be little doubt that the Mississippi Rail Road Company would never have discounted the notes in this form had it not been desperately attempting to raise funds in New Orleans. Sharkey simply avoided the obvious - in 1837 domestic exchanges within the United States had collapsed. The ensuing debt liquidation had left all the Mississippi banks in a state of insolvency; few of the receivables transferred to creditors of those institutions had been anything more than ordinary commercial exchange when the parties defaulted.

There could be no doubt however that drastic action by the state was needed to rehabilitate the banks that could be saved and provide for an orderly liquidation of the rest. A balance had to be struck between bank creditors and stockholders on the one hand and bank debtors on the other.

Sharkey dissented, however, in *Planters Bank vs. Sharp*. The majority adopted the former opinion by reference. The legislature's purpose in adopting the prohibition had been 'to enable the debtors of the banks under all circumstances to pay their debts in the notes of the banks'. But the majority turned next to the abatement provision and rather ominously added that it was a 'penalty annexed to the transgression of th[e] statute. The consequence of such abatement they were not prepared to say. Perhaps the notes could be transferred to the bank and it could maintain a cause of action, but they would not 'volunteer an opinion in this respect'.[276]

Sharkey favored a reversal of the trial court: The Planters Bank had filed the suit precluding the transferee from recovering 'constitutional money'. The debtor might still tender the bank's liabilities in satisfaction of the debt; hence, the purpose of the prohibition had not been defeated. He reminded the majority that their former decision had expressly held that the Act of 1840 had in no manner prevented the bank from suing on the claims, presupposing a retransfer by the holder. 'Any Act impairing that right would be … unconstitutional'. Sharkey clearly was concerned about the majority's equivocal language respecting the bank's right to sue in the event of a retransfer. He was right to be, insofar as either decision was ever likely to be sustained by the Supreme Court of the United States.[277]

Assuming *Planters Bank vs. Sharp* did not obviate the possibility of a retransfer of the bills, thus permitting the Planters Bank to sue and collect, the Bacon Trustees still had good reasons for wanting to avoid a transfer. First, a retransfer might cost the trust its preference: probably it would only come in for a prorate share of any distribution to general creditors. Second, the tender of Planters Bank liabilities could not be refused, even from debtors who formerly had agreed to pay part in good funds and part in notes of the United States Bank. Many debtors were already in default on these agreements, having refused to pay anything in consequence of the decisions. Defaulters might eventually be held to be fully accountable for their debts in specie, not depreciated bank notes.

George Yerger must be credited with having advised Roberts to apply for writs of error to the decisions of the High Court of Errors and Appeals, thus affording the Supreme Court of the United States an opportunity to review the cases. Quitman and McMurran allegedly had advised him that he had no further recourse. Yerger, however, seems to have thought the decision of *Payne, Green & Wood vs. Baldwin, Vail & Hufty* better situated than *Planters Bank vs. Sharp* for obtaining a writ and gaining a reversal. The trust had not been a party in the former case, but Roberts advised Yerger that his principals would willingly share the costs of an appeal. The trust probably bore all the expense: John Seargent and G. M. Wharton argued both cases before the nation's highest court for the plaintiffs in error. These eminent lawyers had formerly advised the Bank of the United States and the successor bank, and were then acting as counsel for the Bacon trustees.[278]

Roberts wrote to the Bacon trustees stating that the debtors were then 'consulting lawyers (some of the most eminent) & they [were] encouraging the debtors not to pay [on the grounds that] ... the late decisions of the High Court of Errors and Appeals ... not only dis[s]olv[ed] all indebtedness on such claims but all debts which ha[d] been transferred by the Bank U. States or its Agency ... under any transfer or arrangement '. It was very important that their lawyers in Philadelphia 'should decide on the two cases sent up to the Supreme Court of the U. S. which ... [was] best to go upon, & one or both to be acted upon'. Gaining a reversal seemed a remote possibility in 1845, and Yerger urged him, pending a decision on the writ application, to compromise in large cases for one-half of what was owned, rather than allow such claims to be barred by the statute of limitations.[279]

The Supreme Court issued writs in the cases and rendered decisions at the January 1848 term sustaining the transfer of the bills receivable, declaring that the Act of 1840 as interpreted by Mississippi's highest court violated the contracts clause of the federal constitution, and permitting the transferees to recover in specie. Roberts immediately wrote to one debtor saying that his notes, when taken from the Planters Bank, became debts due to the trustees and 'due in the Notes of the Bank U. States or Specie'. He concluded: 'I told you long ago you had better settle the debt, but you told me you were advised otherwise'. The notes of the United States Bank were now at or near par in the New York and Philadelphia money markets.[280]

But the Court's decisions were rather messy, and their final disposition was heavy with irony. Levi Woodbury, no friend of the United States Bank, wrote for the majority, while Justice John McLean, one of the Court's most able commercial law specialists, authored a separate opinion, which dissented from the majority's conclusion in one important particular. Not surprisingly, Chief

Justice Taney and Associate Justice Daniel dissented. The bank's old friend and heavy borrower, Daniel Webster, argued the case for the defendants in error.[281]

The majority chose *Planters Bank vs. Sharp*, rather than *Payne, Green & Wood vs. Baldwin, Vail, & Hufty* for a lengthy exposition of the issues presented in both cases. Woodbury wrote that the bank's authority to negotiate its promissory notes derived not from the general law, but from its charter. 'In truth, promissory notes usually constitute[d] a large portion of the property of such institutions'. The bank 'as the legal holder of such notes, possessed a double right 'to dispose' of them; first, from the express grant in the charter itself, …; secondly, by an implied authority incident to its charter and business'. The power to transfer notes might 'well be regarded as an incident to [the bank's] … business as a bank to discount notes'. The bank needed to be able to assign or sell such notes 'to procure more specie in an emergency, or return an unusual amount of deposits withdrawn, or pay large debts'. If the bank could not settle claims against it with specie certainly it was 'much wiser and safer [to transfer notes] than to issue more of its own paper'. So far as the general law had any bearing on the subject, it was 'highly probable, that, by the principles of the law of contracts and commercial paper … [the bills] might be legally assigned or transferred everywhere, when not expressly prohibited by statute'. Mississippi 'by passing the law prohibiting the transfer of notes by banks, recogniz[ed] the previous right, as well as custom; to transfer them; otherwise' there would have been no need for such a prohibition in the first place.

Woodbury noted that the state court opinions indicated that the purpose behind the prohibition had been to require the banks 'to receive their own notes in payment of their debtors, though below par'. But '[t]hat design too, … still recogniz[ed] the prior authority to sell or transfer'. The legislation, however, was 'very invidious' because it singled out one class of property holders, the banks, and one kind of property, their bills receivable. The Act of 1840 had 'vitally changed the obligation of the contract'. Moreover, 'the State court in Mississippi appear[ed] finally to have thought [the abatement provision meant] that no suit at all c[ould] be sustained on such a note by anybody after a transfer'. If subsequently the state courts should adopt Judge Sharkey's dissenting opinion, or go back 'to what they appear[ed] to have before held in [*Payne, Green & Wood vs. Baldwin, Vail & Hufty*] - namely, that the right to sue by the bank, after a transfer, was not taken away, ' the extent to which the Act of 1840 impaired the obligation of contract 'might not be so extensive and clear'. It would still impair the contract in some respects; yet whether it did so 'as to render the obligation itself changed' could only be decided when such a case was presented for decision.

Woodbury proceeded to acknowledge that the Mississippi legislature had a vital interest in insuring that 'bill holders of the bank, when debtors [should have] the privilege of paying in the bills of the bank ... [and though] assigned by the banks, should still be open to set-offs by their debtors'. Such would be equitable 'and no more, probably, than they would be entitled to on common law principles, if an assignee purchased, [as indeed had happened in the case under review] after the promissory notes fell due, and perhaps with a knowledge of the existence of such a set-off'. But the legislature had 'adopted a shorter and more sweeping mode of attaining the end of preventing assignments which might embarrass or defeat setoffs'. The legislature virtually authorized the debtors to tender depreciated notes that had been 'bought up for that purpose' and thus gain 'an undue advantage over set-offs by other debtors in other matters'.[282]

Debtors speculating on bank note depreciation may have been morally reprehensible, but certainly it was not illegal, and it is impossible to divine the point Woodbury wished to make in this regard. Speculators created a market for the liabilities of suspended banks; unless some portion of the public was willing to hold such paper, no bank could ever gain a circulation let alone return to paying specie. Indeed, no suspended bank could resume unless its debtors created a demand for its liabilities.

The Act of 1840 had two important and worthwhile objectives: first, to discourage preferential transfers to certain creditors and, second, to provide a mode for liquidating the banks that were operating in violation of their charters. It seems clear that Woodbury would have had more difficulty finding that the Act of 1840 fatally impaired the obligation of contract without the obtuse language in *Planters Bank vs. Sharp* which only implied that a transfer in violation of the Act of 1840 might bar forever recovery by either the transferor or transferee. There was little support for such an inference in light of the act's overall objectives. A decision of the High Court of Errors and Appeals in 1846, two years before the decision of these cases in the Supreme Court, interpreting the 1843 Quo Warranto Law, had clearly affirmed the debtor's obligation to pay even after a bank had forfeited its charter.[283]

One circumstance that mitigated in favor of the Act of 1840's constitutionality was never raised at any stage in the litigation. In 1837 the Mississippi legislature had passed an act which authorized the banks to issue post notes 'not having a less period than six months, nor a greater period than thirteen months to run to maturity, nor of a less denomination than twenty dollars'. The measure clearly had been intended for the relief of the banks, then in a state of suspension, to enable them to expand their circulation in a way which avoided the obvious consequence of issuing demand notes, i.e., their immediate presentation for redemption in specie. The banks which issued post notes were relieved of any penalty for circulating liabilities other than those due on demand, and the legislation specifically stated that a bank which issued such notes would be deemed to have 'as validly accepted the provisions of th[e] act as if the same had been formerly accepted by resolution of its board of directors, and [would] ... be bound by all the provisions of th[e] act'.

The legislation contained a remarkable provision which barred a maker of a promissory note and his securities, who received post notes for a promissory note discounted at a bank, from defending at a subsequent time on the basis of a want or failure of consideration. Any bank which issued post notes was 'compelled to receive the same for any debt due to' it. Interest on the post notes was fixed at 5 percent per annum, and the issuing banks might loan them out at a rate not exceeding 9 percent per annum, which gave the banks a 4 percent spread. The legislature reserved the right to repeal the act in its entirety or any of its provisions at any time.

All the Mississippi banks had availed themselves of the provisions of this legislation and issued post notes. After the suspension of 1837 they had discounted little else but promissory notes. True, the 1837 legislation had not specifically barred the transfer of the promissory notes, i.e., bills receivable, by the banks, but by accepting the act's conditions, the banks had already voluntarily entered into a wholesale amendment of their charters. More important, the relief had been predicated on a bank's accepting tenders of its liabilities.

In light of the 1837 legislation, there can be little doubt that many of the provisions in the Act of 1840 were intended to be remedial or conservation measures. By availing themselves of the relief afforded in the 1837 law the banks had guaranteed unconditionally to accept tenders of their liabilities, a condition they might have easily evaded by transferring bills from their portfolios. In this context the Act of 1840's prohibition against transfers of bills receivable seems a logical next step, a mechanism for guaranteeing that the banks would perform that which they had already obligated themselves to do.[284]

Justice McLean dissented from the majority's conclusion as to whether 'the repeal of the law making notes negotiable by banks c[ould] effect the notes executed before the repeal'. He wrote: 'an individual holds a note, which, under the statute, is negotiable; but the statute is repealed. Does this take away the negotiability of the note? I think it does'. How was the obligation thus violated or impaired? 'A promise to pay A. B. or his assignee [was] ... no contract with the assignee until, the new contract of assignment ... [was] made. The promise [was] ... to pay the indorsee, if the payee of the note s[hould] indorse it'. There was then no obligation, so how could it be impaired? McLean agreed that had the charter of the bank included a special provision authorizing the negotiation of promissory notes, then no subsequent act might repeal or modify that authority without the consent of the bank. Clearly he had difficulty with Woodbury's finding such a power in the bank's charter, and incidental to it as well.[285]

Justice Daniel's strong dissent contained some excellent points. He called the majority's finding that the bank's authority to transfer its bills receivable derived from its charter, and not the general law, an 'extravagant' construction. The charter had specifically authorized the bank to discount bills and notes: absent that provision, he thought it impossible to infer such a power from the charter itself. Banks, he wrote, were 'created for the purpose of making loans, and this in a medium, in theory at least, equal to money; not for the purpose of borrowing, or raising means to eke out their daily existence by selling off their securities or their own paper'. Brokering 'the paper of their customers to put themselves in funds, [was] not …, therefore, one of their regular functions, and c[ould] flow only from an abuse of their functions'. Whatever power of assignment the banks had was 'conferred upon them in common with all other persons … by a general public law, subject at all times to modification or repeal by the authority which enacted it'.

Daniel found it particularly troubling that the transfer had taken place after the enactment of the prohibition. '[T]he notes [had been] … assigned after the enactment [had been] … an independent and posterior contract' forbidden by law. The plaintiffs in error had 'with full knowledge of the law, placed themselves directly in the attitudes of resistance thereto; for they ha[d] entered into an agreement explicitly inhibited upon the grounds of public policy, and this long after such inhibition was proclaimed to every person in the state'. There could be 'no merit in a combination, the effects and manifest purpose of which to deny to the holders of the notes of those banking corporations the power of making payment to them in their own currency'. By sanctioning such a result the majority had enabled those who controlled the banks 'to appropriate to themselves or their favorites the substance of those very note-holders to whom such a right of payment' could now be denied. '[N]o one c[ould] claim to have a perfect and vested right, through all future time, in the mere capacity to do an act, [in] … the absence of a law forbidding the act'. Such a pretension 'would forestall and prevent legislation upon every subject'.[286]

Justice Woodbury's opinion seems far more sensible where the suspended banks were in receivership, or were in a condition to resume operations within a reasonable time. In truth, none of the Mississippi banks had resumed after 1839; their portfolios were *de facto* in liquidation. Portfolios full of bills receivable, not commercial paper, indicates their true condition. The applicability of negotiability seems questionable. The absence of legal and governmental institutions for winding up failed banks, collecting their assets, and paying off creditors and stockholders is plainly evident. The decisions of both the High Court of Errors and Appeals and the United States Supreme Court indicates little awareness of the implications of suspension for bank charters and the conduct of those institutions in the aftermath of a suspension.

State and federal courts, however, continued to acknowledge a dichotomy, albeit a blurred one, between promissory notes and other kinds of commercial paper which was anachronistic in light of the realities of banking and money markets in general. The form of an evidence of indebtedness hardly mattered when all such instruments were intended to create credit facilities of some kind. Few were drawn against funds actually in the hands of a drawee. More often the acceptor of a bill of exchange, after paying the holder, transferred it as collateral security to the party who had placed him in funds to meet it. At some subsequent time the drawer might remit an 'accepted' bill so the drawee could discount that acceptance and reimburse his accommodating party, provided that party was still holding the original bill. Banks with weighty portfolios of bills receivable were out of the money market. They were simultaneously reducing their accommodations through rigorous curtailments and retrieving their notes from the money market. The right to transfer such a bill without the consent of the maker and endorsers was not free of ambiguities or equities.

Conclusion

Even after favorable decisions in the nation's highest court, Joseph Roberts still found it more desirable to compromise with debtors for something less than what they owed in specie rather than opting for litigation. Most of the bills receivable were for very large sums of money, from $100s to $10,000s. Debtors generally could hire lawyers and delay collection proceedings; moreover, Roberts had no desire to purchase any more acreage at sheriff's sales on account of the Bacon trustee.[287]

The trust was at various times in the decade of the 1840s the proprietor of as many as four plantations, and it probably ranked among the largest slaveholders in Mississippi. Roberts trafficked extensively in slaves; he preferred slave collateral when new agreements with debtors demanded additional security. The trustees in Philadelphia were not indifferent to the public opprobrium they would be subjected to if it became widely known in the North that the trust dealt extensively in slave property. The principals and their agent had good and ample reasons for making discreet out-of-court settlements with recalcitrant debtors.[288]

All of the Mississippi claims had their origins in commercial credit facilities. Individual bills and notes were mere evidences of indebtedness, debits and credits on open accounts. The accounts, not particular pieces of paper, accurately represented those ongoing credit relationships. The transferability of bills and notes was essential for making settlements, and it was recognized and acquiesced in by every participant. So long as bank liabilities, i.e. demand notes and drafts on correspondents in distant places, enjoyed wide currency and were acceptable tenders in lieu of specie, the suppositions underpinning the system never were questioned. But massive defaults in the commercial paper market, the breakdown of domestic exchanges within the country, and in consequence the suspension of the banks, resulted in a debt liquidation of unprecedented proportions.

The banks were convenient scapegoats for Whig, Democrat, and Loco Foco politicians everywhere in the United States. The enmity the banks attracted was not altogether undeserved. But misbegotten regulation schemes must be evaluated in their proper context. Andrew Jackson's war on the national bank had legitimated innate prejudices against banks and intensified a deep distrust of foreign capital and its local agents. State legislatures freely adopted coercive measures in the wake of the 1839 suspension, ostensibly to force the banks to redeem their liabilities with specie. In reality the true purpose was to force bank creditors and stockholders to absorb all the losses from currency depreciation. Such measures were largely ineffectual, but in the case of Mississippi they were successful in putting an end to chartered banking for the remainder of the antebellum period. Probably the Commercial Bank and Agricultural Bank at Natchez, and sundry smaller banks around the state, could have been saved had the state been less determined to forcibly liquidate every bank and instead adopted a reformation plan similar to the one implemented in Louisiana.[289]

Developments in Mississippi are especially interesting insofar as they involve negotiability and a state's power under the federal constitution to prohibit its application to certain classes of business paper. Clearly the states were not precluded from legislating in areas affecting commercial law, and it is improbable that in a federal diversity action a judge could have freely ignored relevant statutes and divined an applicable law from 'federal' common law. *Planters Bank vs. Sharp*, as finally decided in the Supreme Court, is ambiguous. It may be an indication that the role of courts in reshaping the common law to meet the needs of a commercial society was peripheral and not central to that process. Indeed, it would seem that financial markets were substantially in advance of judicial formulations that were anachronistic in their application to ongoing credit relationships. *Planters Bank vs. Sharp* was not a case where the nation's highest court transformed a class of contracts, heretofore nonnegotiable, into negotiable ones at the expense of a powerless debtor class. In truth, it was nearly the reverse. Many of the Mississippi debtors possessed ample means and honored their obligations in a timely fashion, whether to the Planters Bank or the Bacon Trust. Others opted not to pay and gambled that further depreciation in the value of bank liabilities would eventually inure to their benefit. Such men were highly sophisticated in their financial dealings and certainly aware of the possibility that someday they might be forced to honor their debts in good money and be barred from tendering the worthless liabilities of defunct banks. In the course of a decade, the financial markets, not the Mississippi legislature and not the state and federal courts, distributed the losses from currency depreciation to bank creditors and stockholders and bank debtors. The stockholders of the United Sates Bank and the Planters Bank never recovered a cent.[290]

THE BUSINESS OF MAKING COLLECTIONS

All business transactions here are made in New Orleans Bank Notes-they are the only currency - debts due to the Banks here when paid are made in their own depreciated paper - We shall have to receive the same for all Bills received from the Agricultural & Planters Bank - the other Bills Receivable we have here will be paid in U. S. Bank, Planters Bank & Agricultural Bank Notes -- Joseph L. Roberts to John Bacon et. al., Trustees - 15 November 1841.[291]

Joseph L. Roberts spent the remainder of his lifetime in Mississippi in the service of the Bacon Trustees, dying at Natchez on 28 March 1853. During those twelve years he acquired a plantation with over one hundred slaves, and so ably managed the trust's business that recoveries averaged better than 50 percent along with accrued interest and collection costs. Among the valuable properties that passed to the trust was the ownership of the Vicksburg to Jackson Railroad, the principal asset of the Commercial and Railroad Bank of Vicksburg.[292]

While Roberts' recovery efforts were indeed remarkable it is well to remember that others besides his principal were attempting to collect claims in Mississippi: Baring Brothers, the Brown brothers, even the Bank of England, all were large claimants with extensive ongoing collection agencies in the state. The Browns, for example, paid off the federal government's claim against the Agricultural Bank for the unsettled deposit and succeeded to its position as that bank's principal creditor. In consequence of their heavy involvement with Peter Lapice, a speculator with properties in Louisiana and Mississippi, they gained control of his four plantations. For more than a decade they managed his enterprises and invested over $100,000 in improvements.[293]

The business of making collections was tedious and time consuming, but it was a very worthwhile pursuit. That Roberts and other agents of out-of-state creditors realized millions for their principals speaks volumes about the capacity of the credit system to reconstitute itself after the disasters of 1837. Much of the debt passed into the hands of indigenous investors who for a variety of reasons saw value and opportunity in the claims of those who wished to repatriate their funds. If the 1830s had been a decade of heavy foreign involvement in places like Mississippi, through the medium of exchange, the 1840s were a time of liquidating a mass of defaulted bills and reordering credit relationships. By the 1850s the commerce of the region was largely in the hands of local capitalists.[294]

Each year Roberts sent hundreds of thousands of dollars back to the North, and he was able to negotiate this feat without the aid of banks. Most payments were in the form of bills on New Orleans factors. Those he sent to the city for collection which in most cases simply meant that his agent exchanged the New Orleans bill for a bill on Philadelphia through the agency of a bill broker. At no point in the transfer from Natchez to Philadelphia was any of the paper negotiated or discounted 'in bank'. It was all done 'out-of-doors'. A chartered bank's primary function of giving currency to paper obligations, then, could just as easily be performed by exchange dealers. Roberts clearly was aware of the fluctuations in nominal exchange rates as the following communication to his agents in New Orleans shows.

> The present serves to enclose the dft. of Js. H. Wilson on Messrs. Hill, McLean & Co. of your city [New Orleans] at 90 days date for $12,000 - with 6% interest from date - which please present for acceptance - (payable in New Orleans at par) - I waived the right I had to a Bill on them at sight payable at sight in Philada. funds (as you will see by the enclosed letter of advice) to accommodate Mr. Wilson & Hill, McLean & Co. taking the Bill at 90 d/d payable in N. O. at maturity in par funds - I do not want you to present the letter of advice, as they might then avail of accepting to pay in Philada. funds & so debar me of the benefit of the Exchange on the North at maturity - therefore if not simply accepted as payable in N. O. funds please have it regularly protested - it was understood by Mr. Wilson & myself when this dft. was given on time instead of sight that it should be paid in N. O. at par.

The course of exchange was then in favor of New Orleans and against Philadelphia, so to accept a tender in Philadelphia funds would have deprived the trust of the profit from a favorable exchange when New Orleans money was traded for that of Philadelphia.[295]

Many economic historians have reckoned that bank suspensions cushioned the impact of a financial panic, but the contrary seems to be true. Suspensions further contracted existing credit facilities; so, from the moment of suspension the banks worked furiously to restore their credit by resuming. The longer a suspension lasted the more business the banks lost to private capitalists; hence, it was essential to resume in order to keep the exchange business 'in bank'. After 1840 it would be difficult to describe the condition of Mississippi's banks as partaking of anything more than a state of permanent suspension. As noted several times above, they were *de facto* in liquidation. Current funds in the form of bills on cities outside the state, which passed into their possession, immediately passed out again into the hands of creditors anxious for remittable funds.[296]

Shortly after his arrival in Mississippi, Roberts presented the trustees with a grim report on the condition of their Mississippi claims. Lengthy discussions with individual debtors, whose claims stemmed either from the bills receivable taken from the Agricultural Bank or from the residue of protested bills held over at the late branch, had led him to conclude that some were 'pressed down as low as they c[ould] be having already more judgments against them than they c[ould] hope to pay & w[ould] therefore relieve themselves by benefit of the insolvent law'. Others, he continued, expected to pay in a few months time, but many had requested additional time of from 2 to 5 years and without furnishing additional security. The bonds of the Planters Bank and the Commercial and Railroad Bank, which constituted the bulk of the Mississippi claims, were yet to be settled.[297]

In some cases debt levels were truly staggering. Alexander McNeill, a member of the syndicate of Bogart, Hoopes and its affiliates and president of the Commercial and Railroad Bank of Vicksburg, had mortgaged his plantation and slaves in Louisiana to secure debt with an aggregate value of $143,950. The trust was the holder of one note for $16,500 secured by mortgage and the Planters Bank had two other notes totaling $29,000. One note owned by the trust had been transferred to the United States Bank's Natchez agency in 1838 as part of a settlement of Joseph H. Moore & Co'.s bills on Bogart, Hoopes, then under protest at the agency, amounting to $142,144.77. Five notes drawn by McNeill, amounting in all to $78,633.33 and secured by mortgage, were negotiated by Moore to the agency. Moore then transferred four more notes, secured by mortgage on 1,467 acres in Madison Parish, Louisiana and sixty slaves, for the balance of his debt. The McNeill notes had derived from a credit sale of a plantation belonging to Moore which then had been mortgaged to him to secure the credit portion of the sale. Often the general partners' principal capital contribution when forming a commercial partnership consisted of just such notes, i.e. mortgage notes which evidenced the credit portion of a sale of an entire plantation and slaves. A single credit sale might encompass the transfer of hundreds of thousands of dollars of property, the security interest which emanated from such a sale, evidenced by promissory notes for principal and interest, were much more suitable for collateralizing credit facilities than a pledge of the specific tangible assets of a plantation.[298]

Moore subsequently sold his plantation in Madison Parish to William Briscoe, and the Bacon Trust released him on $83,000 of his notes in return for a new guaranty from Briscoe. Thus commenced one of the most interesting chapters in Roberts' collection work in Mississippi, revealing a course of conduct on Briscoe's part that amounted to simple racketeering. William Briscoe, in modern parlance, was an 'operator'. He and his relative, Parmenas Briscoe, had been clients of the late branch from the moment it opened its doors at Natchez and had obtained extensive discounts from other banks in Mississippi and Louisiana as well. Parmenas Briscoe lent his name to one of the most infamous bills ever to come before Mississippi's legislature for regulating the banks. According to Roberts had the 'Briscoe Bill' of 1843 ever become law it would have 'nullif[ied] all the Banks as to their corporate privilege & power & the indebtedness of all persons due to them'. Roberts was rather too sweeping in stigmatizing the 'Briscoe Bill', or Quo Warranto Law, as it would later come to be called, but the Briscoes certainly seem to have been rascally characters.[299]

Many others besides William Briscoe saw in the general bank suspension a fine opportunity for speculation. The great New Orleans factor, Jacob Upshur Payne, for example, proposed purchasing $50,000 of the trust's claim certificates against the Commercial and Railroad Bank, no doubt at a heavy discount, in order to tender the same to the bank in full satisfaction of his brother's debt at that institution. Roberts believed that Payne's brother had 'a considerable amount of property pledged to the Bank' which he no doubt hoped to get released. But Roberts also surmised that Payne might be acting for undisclosed principals, possibly the same men then serving as trustees of the bulk of the bank's assets which had been assigned in 1840 for the benefit of creditors. If Payne were an agent of an undisclosed principal, then, his motive for wanting the claim certificates was clear. He could then purchase the notes of some debtor or debtors 'who ha[d] a large property pledged to the Bank … & proceed against th[eir] property'. Mississippians, he continued, 'are very smart, & they pride themselves on it, & are estimated higher by their fellow citizens generally whenever they can practice it adroitly & successfully, Viz. by deception, overreaching, outwitting & what we would call at the North a pretty strong sprinkling of swindling or fraud'.[300]

Steven Duncan provided yet another perspective on the subject of over-reaching by those who sought to take advantage of a neighbor's distress. He strongly recommended to William J. Minor that the Agricultural Bank accept the terms to be proposed for settling the protested bills of Bullitt, Shipp & Co., other wise the debt would be entirely lost. He was not at liberty to reveal the source of his intelligence, but thought it 'very desirable that the collaterals which Ferriday ha[d] place in the Bk., be transferred to the U. S. Bk. if possible' in satisfaction of the outstanding balance. 'I have great fear the whole debt will be lost. In these times the best men-will do-what under other circumstances - they would have been ashamed even to think of - All this is confidential'. If the firm's collateral securities turned out to be worthless, Duncan clearly thought it was better to slough them off on the United States Bank.[301]

In any event, from 1841 to 1846 William Briscoe had possession of the plantation on Roundaway Bayou in Madison Parish, Louisiana, exploiting its resources to the fullest and paying over little or nothing to Roberts. Roberts commenced proceedings to rescind the sale for nonpayment of the purchase price in 1844. 'Old Briscoe' threw up every obstacle to thwart Roberts in his collection work. He pled usury and want of consideration as defenses to Roberts' suit, all the while continuing in possession of the land and slaves and getting 'four crops off it & ha[ving] only paid one semi annual period of Interest'. Briscoe hoped to avoid paying his debt altogether, relying on the High Court's ambiguous decision of *Planters Bank vs. Sharp* as one defense to any collection proceeding, and also another debt predicated on a bill receivable which had been transferred to the trust by the Agricultural Bank. Another tactic Briscoe used was subjecting himself to the jurisdiction of Louisiana's courts and the proceedings which had been commenced there by the United States to set aside the United States Bank's assignment in Pennsylvania to the Bacon Trustees. In connection with that proceeding the United States Attorney for the Eastern District of Louisiana had taken the usual step of garnisheeing all of the trust's claims in the state. Any Mississippian indebted to the trust could subject himself to the Louisiana proceeding, confess his indebtedness to the trust, and wait to have the claim sold at sheriff's sale by the United States Attorney in New Orleans. The average bid for such claims was 25 cents on the dollar. Many Mississippians were able to arrange with financial interests in Louisiana to buy their debts when the sheriff auctioned them off. Roberts' protégé, Fielding Davis, resorted to this tactic, arranging to have Isaac Franklin purchase his debt to the trust.[302] Briscoe relented, however, and offered to re-convey the plantation on Roundaway Bayou back to the trust. He had given three notes evidencing the purchase price of $100,000. In exchange for their return he promised to re-convey the land and slaves, fixing their value at $85,000, the difference to be made up in a cash payment. Briscoe, however, had had possession of the plantation for six years and no doubt had collected a considerable income. He had exploited the property to the point of ruining it, and this fact in part accounted for his newfound willingness to re-convey it. On the debt transferred from the Agricultural Bank to the Trust he demanded an additional 5 years to liquidate it. Roberts estimated that the return of the plantation would cost the trust no less than $30,000 because of presumed defects in the titles to the land.[303]

The agreement with Briscoe was consummated on 18 September 1845, Roberts that day writing to the trustees that he had 'concluded it was our best policy to accept, though we may be cheated again'. In a subsequent letter concerning another property owned by the Trust, the Sarah Plantation, which Roberts then offered to buy, he wrote '[y]ou can have no idea the trouble and difficulties which arise' from credit sales of whole plantations, especially if the mortgage must subsequently be foreclosed, and 'much property will have to be bought in & sold again if we are to get any thing'.[304]

Briscoe it seems had assured Roberts that the property and slaves were entirely intact, and that nothing had been removed from the plantation except the surplus corn. Roberts, however, had intelligence that as many as one-quarter of the slaves had died during Briscoe's tenure, but having been barred from inspecting the property at a time previous to Briscoe's re-conveyance, he was in no position to know whether Briscoe had lied to further frustrate his efforts. On 20 January 1846, he appointed the Louisiana lawyer, Alonzo Snyder, to take legal possession of the property, hoping that this device would enable him to avoid a levy on the plantation by the United States Attorney. The United States Attorney it appears was receiving invaluable help from James Erwin, Nicholas Biddle's old confidant, in identifying trust property in Louisiana.[305]

Roberts next sent an agent to Louisiana to take charge of the plantation, fearing to go himself, lest Erwin effect service of process on him and so subject him to the proceedings in Louisiana, thus burdening the trust with the expense of a fight over the assignment of the Mississippi assets. What that agent found on Roundaway Bayou was truly appalling:

The time having arrived on the last day of Jany. & 1st of February for the delivery of the Briscoe plantation on Roundaway Bayou & apprehending some process to be made upon me [in Louisiana] at the instance of [James Erwin] to give trouble when I should be there at an appointed time - I determined to send Mr. William C. Bradley a person well versed in planting & all plantation matters, to receive Plantation stock & c & all appertaining to the same, accompanied by a good overseer whom I had engaged to take charge of the place - Mr. Bradley had just returned & reported a wretched state of things - Only 53 Negroes large & small; they received 60 Negroes with the place & their natural increase, inclusive of deaths, ought now to have made on the place at least 75 in number - several of the Negroes now there are sickly & inefficient from overwork & exposure - some frost bitten, some ruptured, some branded on their hips as runaways - all without shoes & most of them without winter clothing or blankets.- the stock in the same miserable condition & only 16 mules, (poor) instead of 36, no Horses - not Medicines & a few, very few, tools, farming utensils, & c &. The people had had nothing to eat for two days before Mr. Bradley got there - they (the Briscoe's) bagged up & moved off all the best cotton seed, leaving the most miserable refuse stuff.

Despite the deleterious effects of William Briscoe's tenure, the plantation soon was restored to good working order, and a year later Roberts could report that he expected the property to yield upwards of 500 bales during the shipping season. Roberts wasted no time in attempting to find someone to buy the property.[306]

It should be noted that Roberts was not a completely disinterested party and that reality may have influenced or colored his grim assessment to the trustees about the plantation's overall condition. He was already the proprietor of one plantation purchased from the trust and wanted to acquire additional property. Self-interest may have caused him to exaggerate the extent of the depredations.

Roberts' purchase from the Bacon Trust of the Springfield Plantation stemmed from a debt of Fredrick Stanton, evidenced by five bills receivable taken from the Planters Bank in 1842. The Stanton debt was $175,000, or almost 10 percent of the total value of all the bills receivable transferred from the bank. It consisted of a note of Fredrick Stanton of $90,066.24 and four notes of Stanton, Buckner & Co. indorsed by him and several clients of the firm with an aggregate value of $79,479.80. The notes were secured by a deed of trust that encumbered a plantation of 1,559 acres in Adams County and 130 slaves. At the time this debt was selected from the Planters Bank's portfolio 'it was considered one of the best-there had been 39,000 drs. more on it which was paid in the first year'. Stanton's business had consisted of commission houses in New Orleans, Natchez, and Yazoo City.[307]

But only one month after the transfer of the debt, Stanton applied for bankruptcy under the newly enacted federal statute. Roberts determined to oppose Stanton's getting a discharge from his debts because of the release of the indorsers on four of the notes and the fraudulent sale of the equity of redemption in the property encumbered by the deed of trust. Roberts waited for Stanton to file the schedules, which enumerated nearly $1 million of liabilities for which he was directly and indirectly responsible, and make application for his discharge. Stanton 'was taken by surprise' when Roberts appeared at his discharge hearing and threatened to object unless provision was made for the trust's debt. He claimed to be innocent of any collusive activity that might have prejudiced the rights of the trust and so furnish a ground for objecting to his discharge.[308]

Stanton claimed 'as to his endorsers being released he could not help that, nor was he aware of it until his Lawyer informed him of it afterwards, and that he would erase the report on his schedule made by himself that "they were released"'. He also agreed to arrange for the equity of redemption to pass to Roberts, thus clearing the way for the trustee to sell the plantation and slaves with the Bacon Trust having a priority claim on the proceeds. A year passed before a sale under the deed of trust could be made at public auction.[309]

The land and the slaves, which were subject to the deed of trust, were sold separately, and all told brought $68,000, about one-third of Stanton's debt. (Years later Roberts and other creditors brought an action to set aside Stanton's discharge on grounds of fraud and were successful in their efforts, although by the time a judgment was rendered Roberts was already dead.) The 'choice hands' were sold first, some 30 in number, and brought $13,125.32 'in specie'. After the choice hands were sold, Roberts' 'bids for the remaining lots altho low were not advanced on - there [was] … a large proportion of *female* infants & middle aged people … & some few very old people. In having bought nearly all the people it became necessary to buy the plantation, stock & c to keep the people together for & carry on the ensuing crop at least until the end of the year'.[310]

Roberts believed there was a surplus of slaves on the plantation and recommended that the land and 60 or 70 slaves with their children be sold together on a 3-year credit. The remaining slaves would 'have to be sold at auction for cash for the most they w[ould] bring'. He had purchased the land in his own name for the account of the trust, along with the stock and farming implements, for $15,000, which had been credited on Stanton's debt; the balance of $53,815.99 realized from the auction was solely attributable to the sale of 100 or so slaves. This was all, he advised, the trust was ever likely to see from Stanton's debt, except for some small dividends from his bankruptcy estate. Roberts had immediately hired out some of the slaves for $1,800 which he had applied to the expenses connected with the sale and running of the plantation.[311]

Roberts next proposed to buy the Springfield Plantation and its people from the trust for $70,000 'in United States Bank Notes [then at 60 percent of par in the New Orleans market] or such funds at the Trustees … w[ould] take'.

> Now having stated all the particulars to you, the place being bought in my name, the stock & c & the people (except the 15 sold) & that it may not appear on the books as belonging to the Trust & selling the same again, & believing that it may be a good investment for myself (I design the purchase of a stock farm at the North this summer) trembling for my investment in Bank Stocks which I have heretofore lost considerably, I now propose to take the whole purchase including to me any amount saved on the expenditure by the hire of the Negroes, also the sale of the 15 people to [L. R.] Marshall & the two Gillespie's & the $650 charged I have made against the property for care & attendance & pay the whole amount of the Nett proceeds of the sale in U. S. Bank Notes.

His tone was obsequious. 'If you think there is no impropriety in my becoming the purchaser, while I am acting as your agent, or any remarks would be made to the disadvantage of the Trust, or to me, let not a second thought be given to the subject & let this communication be considered Null & void except so far as it makes you acquainted with all the facts connected with the purchasing in of this property'. But he then cautioned that he would be hard pressed to find a better offer, both as to price and the length of time required to liquidate the credit portion of the sale. To underscore the risks inherent in planting he closed with a postscript warning that the recent decline in cotton prices would depress the value of land and slaves by 25 percent.[312]

Roberts clearly thought that a slave plantation was a better long-term investment than bank stocks. His whole professional career had been spent as a banker, and although he was already in his sixth decade, he was now prepared to embark on a new career as the proprietor of a large slave plantation. It is clear too, that to raise the funds necessary for the purchase of the plantation he needed to liquidate his portfolio of bank stocks.[313]

The trust had many incentives for selling the plantation to Roberts, not the least of which was his clearheaded assessment of the property's value and the fairness of the price he was prepared to offer for it. The primary asset of the Springfield Plantation were its slaves, and it seems clear that the trustees had qualms about conducting planting operations for extended periods of time using slave labor. Roberts wrote to Thomas Robbins and Alexander Symington and intimated that the extent of the trust's involvement with slave property had been intentionally concealed from the third trustee, John Bacon, lest he entertain some scruples which might result in a sacrifice of trust assets for the sake of moral niceties. '[I] f you think proper' he wrote 'to keep the whole subject, I mean the buying & selling slaves either for myself or the trust from Mr. Bacon you will please do so'. He next attempted to justify his own conduct with respect to the slaves on the Springfield Plantation. 'I have this business to do, buying & selling slave property, & if I become the owner of them for the time being that I may be in the South, say 2, 3, or 4 years more, I do it not only for some advantage to myself, but to better their condition-they have been treated badly, & tho' fed well, as to enough to eat, they had hardly clothing to cover their nakedness, some of them without a pallet to lay on-please answer my proposition in a day or two after receipt of this'.[314]

It was of course inevitable that the trust should become heavily involved with slave property. By allowing time to those who owed money, whether predicated on claims stemming from the late branch or the transfers of bills receivable, the trust became the largest financing agency in Mississippi. Nearly every claim against a domiciliary of the state, whether a direct recipient of a loan or an indorser, was a planting debt, the notable exceptions being the large claims against the Mississippi Railroad Company, the West Feliciana and Woodville Railroad and Banking Company, and the Commercial and Railroad bank of Vicksburg, all of which were predicated on loans to build railroads.

From the moment of his arrival in Mississippi, Roberts recognized the importance of slave property to the trust, not only in providing the means for liquidating huge debts, but as security for extensions of time to debtors in lieu of protracted litigation. But even mortgage debt could be, he wrote, 'quite uncertain, the slaves which ma[de] mortgaged debts most safe, [were] ... frequently removed & disposed of' beyond the reach of legal process. When Fielding Davis proposed in 1845 to transfer land to the trust in settlement of his debt, Roberts replied that it was not in his power to satisfy his wish. 'Negroes [on the other hand] c[ould] be sold & [thus] attain th[e] object [of the Trust] but land [could] not'.[315]

In the case of Henry Vick of Vicksburg, Roberts agreed to a transfer of land in partial settlement of his debt, provided Vick placed 15 good mules, farming implements, and livestock on the property. 'Negroes [however were] to be taken for the balance of the debt'. Roberts regarded the transfer of slaves as being nearly the equivalent of a cash tender; land was never so liquid. In one case Roberts agreed to raise his lien on a tract of land so that the owner could sell it on condition that the buyer furnished additional security in the form of slaves. The pledge of the slaves would, he argued, make the transaction perfectly safe. In fact, the slaves formed part of the consideration for the sale of the land. Roberts advised his agent that 'in case he [the seller could not] ... turn them [the slaves] into cash <u>immediately</u> which Negroes he was receiv[ing] from the [buyer] ... as cash in part payment [of the land], & as [the seller] ... m[ight] have opportunities of selling them' in which case the agent was to furnish a clear bill of sale when the proceeds were paid over to him. The seller 'also wish[ed] to have the Negroes (his own) sold from time to time to pay the balance of the debt due by him to us & other debts which he [was then] ... owing'.[316]

Over the years Roberts became very astute in valuing slave property. When David Stanton proposed transferring to the trust a male field hand, aged 34, at a price of $700 in the notes of the Agricultural Bank, Roberts answered that that sum was nearly double the value he had placed on the slave. Agricultural Bank money was very scarce and then commanded 75 to 80 cents in the dollar. The only solution was to 'sell your Negro & buy Agricultural paper to the amount of the principal & interest due on your debt will be the best way to test the value of each & close the matter- .... I call upon you to sell your Negro for the most you can get for him & settle the debt - good Negroes I am told will sell readily altho they will not bring high prices'.[317]

Only a few weeks before Roberts had pleaded for indulgence from the trustees in meeting the next installment on his debt for the Springfield Plantation. 'I endeavored' he wrote 'to sell 25 Negroes to enable me to remit <u>$10,000</u> on account of my own debt, but I could not do so unless I would let them go for <u>less than half</u> what they stand me in'. He had therefore placed them on a place near Vicksburg, which had recently fallen to the trust, two-thirds of the crop they were then making for his own account and then balance for the account of the trust. The Bacon Trust and the institution of slavery were hopelessly locked up with each other.[318]

Many letters passed between Roberts and his junior agents in Vicksburg, Jackson, Woodville, and Columbus on the subject of slave property. Some debtors abandoned their land and 'ran off' their slaves to Louisiana and the Republic of Texas. The extent of these illegal removals to defeat the jurisdiction of Mississippi's courts was enough to justify retaining the services of the Texas statesman and lawyer, J. Pinckney Henderson, to assist in making the Trust's

Mississippi judgments executory and levying on the property of absconding debtors. About one such debtor he advised Henderson:

> Tomlinson is a great scamp - at the time of his second note coming due he attempted to make way with the Negroes, but was prevented by his securities - I then took steps for foreclosure of his Mortgage in the ordinary way, his securities for their own sakes determined to watch him - by illness of one of our Lawyers & neglect on the part of his young partner on the other we did not get a decree until some time last spring & just before the Decree was obtained this Tomlinson came forward to propose a compromise - it was merely a sham, for at that very moment his Negroes were being run off by his son in Law Wylie B. Collins.

Roberts himself traveled to Texas to bring back the Tomlinson slaves, preferring to hazard the journey rather than selling them there and taking a bill on New Orleans which might not be paid at maturity.[319]

Roberts also caused a great many slaves to be seized and sold, often buying them himself at sheriff's sale for the account of the trust. To J. C. Passmore, his agent at Vicksburg, he wrote: 'Can't take Mr. Reading's offer - must have the Negroes sold at once-bid low yourself at first - & only advance $10 a bid, & buy them in my name Individually until you get the amount of the debt & Interest'. Roberts, however, preferred to preserve units of production rather than stripping a plantation of its slaves and causing them to be sold. He was only too willing to extend reasonable terms for paying debts to those who negotiated with him in good faith.[320]

The trust's dealings in slave property appear to have attracted little attention from those creditors with abolitionist sympathies at the North, but the sale of the Springfield Plantation to Joseph Roberts was criticized as self-dealing by their agent. His subsequent offers to purchase other trust property were all politely rejected. Roberts clothed his economic ambitions with the mantle of paternalism. Michael Tadman has shown that such a rationalization was typical: highlighting the prior abuses of those whose slaves he had seized and sold also was consistent with the pattern of excuses which seemed to soften the rough edges of what was at heart an economic institution. Roberts' expression of concern for the slaves who came under his control rarely went beyond the adequacy of their food, clothing, and shelter. No one would question the importance of those for human subsistence, but all can be subsumed under the rubric, 'enlightened self-interest', insofar as they reveal anything about the master's character and motives. Beyond buying supplies for the plantations under his control, Roberts had little or no day to day contact with their operation, relying exclusively on reports regularly sent to him by overseers.[321]

By 1848 the notes of the late United States Bank commanded 90 cents in the dollar, and during the autumn and winter season even higher quotations ruled in the Philadelphia and New Orleans money markets. That astounding

recovery is attributable to a number of factors: purchases by speculators anticipating even higher prices, a demand from southern money markets for notes
suitable for tenders by debtors as well as income from the plantations. However
retrograde slavery may have been as a labor system, there can be little doubt
that it could produce sustained and reliable income streams which reinvigor-
ated the most moribund debts.

Taking Control of the Vicksburg to Jackson Railroad

As early as 1839 out-of-state interests had attempted to gain control of the management of the Commercial and Railroad Bank of Vicksburg to curb alleged
excesses of its directors and officers. The bank's president was none other than
Alexander McNeill, the man so deeply involved with Joseph H. Moore and
Bogart, Hoopes & Co. Many of the stockholders were Philadelphians, and to
safeguard their interest in the wake of the bank's second suspension only weeks
after the commencement of resumption in Mississippi, they dispatched Reuben
M. Whitney to Vicksburg with instructions to the directors to install him as
the new president. His mission accomplished nothing; his offer to assume the
presidency met with an unequivocal rebuff from the directors.[322]

Whitney subsequently wrote an account of his visit to Mississippi that
was published in the newspapers of Philadelphia. Among his complaints was
an accusation that 'many of the debtors to the Bank ... [were] undoubtedly
receiving indulgences at the expence of the stockholders' and, he might have
added, at the expense of creditors as well, particularly the United States Bank
of Pennsylvania. The United States Bank's large claim against the Commercial
and Railroad Bank stemmed from at least two failed ventures; the former institution's cotton operations in 1838 and 1839 which left it with a large claim
against the latter bank and a loan to the Republic of Texas, a portion of which
was arranged and guaranteed through the agency of the Mississippi bank.[323]

The Commercial and Railroad Bank incurred huge costs building the railroad from Vicksburg to Jackson, and the line was not fully in operation when
the second suspension occurred. Joseph Cowperthwaite, the cashier of the
United States Bank, visited Mississippi in January and February 1840 to assess
for himself the condition of the banks and the likelihood of their discharging
their debts to the United States Bank in the foreseeable future. It is remarkable
that what he saw at Vicksburg convinced him of the necessity of his institution advancing an additional $250,000 to the Commercial and Railroad Bank
in order to complete the line. One might say that his action rather justifies
the adage that bankers have a nearly limitless capacity to throw good money
after bad, but perhaps he saw in the railroad's completion an income source
which over time would permit the Commercial and Railroad Bank to liqui-

date its liabilities. The new advance, however, was imprudent to the extent that Cowperthwaite's own institution was in a state of suspension, its credit deeply impaired. But in 1840 no one reckoned that the depression that had descended on the country would last well into the coming decade. The advance was secured by a pledge of all the railroad's tangible assets; i.e., rail lines, cars, locomotives, stations and equipment. That security was the basis for the action that Roberts commenced when he could obtain payment in no other way.[324]

Anticipating the legislature's adoption of what would come to be known as the 'Act of 1840', the Commercial and Railroad Bank had made an assignment of most of its assets to three of its directors and officers who had then commenced collecting the assigned claims for the benefit of the bank's creditors. By 1843 the liquidators had reduced the bank's liabilities by 27 percent, but only $30,000 had been paid on the bonds to the United States Bank, which totaled in excess of $1 million, to say nothing of 4 years of accrued interest. In 1842 the Commercial and Railroad Bank's notes were at a 40 percent discount in the New Orleans money market and in 1844 they commanded only 15 cents in the dollar. Their rapid depreciation in 1843 and afterwards may in part be attributable to the political turmoil over the course to be pursued by the legislature respecting the banks which reached a fever pitch that year with the introduction of the so-called 'Briscoe Bill' or Quo Warranto Law.[325]

Prior to 1843 assignments of bank assets for the benefit of creditors had been voluntary; thereafter, it will be remembered, the district attorneys were empowered to proceed directly against the banks and have trustees appointed to forcibly liquidate them. Critics claimed that the Act of 1843 was the principal device for aiding and abetting debt repudiation. Subsequent legislation required an immediate sale of all bank assets, a provision which insured that bank debtors would be able to buy their claims for pennies in the dollar. This last measure, the Act of 1846, represents the most extreme manifestation of the debt repudiators' agenda. The High Court of Errors and Appeals ultimately declared much of the Act of 1846 unconstitutional. While the rhetoric of repudiation dominated politics in Mississippi during the 1840s, the instances of implementation were rather ineffectual except to the extent that they helped to depress the price of bank money. Measures like the Act of 1843 were rather subtle instrumentalities, and the most that can be said is that they shifted some of the burden of bank failures from debtors to creditors for those institutions. Such legislation was comparatively mild compared to the overt debt repudiation schemes that prevailed in southern legislatures after the Civil War.[326]

When the quo warranto proceeding against the Commercial and Railroad Bank was tried in 1844 the Chancellor sustained the voluntary assignment made in 1840. Roberts, however, thought it doubtful that the High Court of Errors and Appeals would confirm the decision. 'Since the assignment has been sustained by the Chancellor', he wrote to the trustees, 'to my great astonishment, I have observed the quotation of the stock of the Commercial and Railroad Bank of Vicksburg, formerly 2.50 to 3. Drs. in Philadelphia and New York now 10 to 12 Drs'. Roberts expected a comparable rise in the value of the claims against the bank then held by the Trust because 'creditors ought to be paid before stockholders-but in this country they do every thing to cut off foreign creditors & security holders & divide the wreck of assets of property here among themselves'. Roberts was speaking specifically of the state of Mississippi's exertions to wrest control of the assets of the Planters Bank from the assignees and reverse the transfer of the bills receivable to the Bacon Trust which had taken place in 1842.[327]

It should be remembered that at the very time Roberts was formulating a strategy with his lawyers about the best way to proceed to collect on the claims against the Commercial and Railroad Bank, the issue of the bar to the transfer of the bills receivable from the banks was then before Mississippi's highest court. Also pending was a decision by Louisiana's supreme court on the validity of the United States Bank's assignments to the Bacon Trustees. Roberts had occasion to relay invaluable intelligence on the latter matter to the trustees on 11 May 1844.

> I have had the pleasure to meet an old acquaintance, the Honble T. J. Lacy, Judge of the Supreme Court of Arkansas-he has been spending some time in New Orleans - just came up here on some private business & returns to N. O. tomorrow - He is familiar with all our matters there having decided in favor of the assignment of the Real Estate Bank of Arkansas, he has been a good deal sought by the Judges of the Supreme Court [of Louisiana] for his opinions & his references in confidential interchange of impressions & views without committing any of his N. O. friends (the Judges & c or their impressions or opinions) he has stated to me *confidentially* (on my questioning him about *my* purchase of the Springfield property) that *his* inclination is that the assignment will be sustained - but that it may not be so-there is a great uncertainty & great excitement about it & it may be delayed until November - if decided against, the assignment, all done & past even by the [Bacon] Trustees would be considered as having been done without authority, & consequently fraudulent & could not stand & if I became a purchaser & paid for the Springfield plantation upon any occasion that I went to Louisiana, or any cotton or slave, or any of my property there, could be attached on account of any debt or creditors of the Bk. U. States & I be divested of it-& it would have the effect of hundreds of our debtors going there [to Louisiana] & also from Alabama & Arkansas, having connivance with some friend, after putting themselves in the way to be garnisheed or attached to have their own debts bought for ¼ perhaps 1/10th of the amount & so bring about the most ruinous consequences.

Fortunately for the Bacon trustees the assignment made at Philadelphia in 1841 was sustained by Louisiana's supreme court which more-or-less brought an end to the efforts of the government of the United States to pursue the assets of the failed bank.[328]

Roberts proceeded to foreclose the mortgage that had been granted in 1840 to secure the United States Bank's advance of $250,000. The assignees were desperate to retain control of the line and offered him various proposals for settling the claims amicably. The only terms he was prepared to accept by way of a compromise was their agreement to allow a consent judgment to be taken recognizing the trust's claim for the bonded debt of $1,100,000. He again relented, however, and agreed to stay the proceeding provided payments of current funds were made on some of the claims. The assignees subsequently failed to make the payments as agreed and Roberts ordered his lawyer to recommence the foreclosure proceeding.[329]

The extravagance of the assignees in the conduct of the railroad and their collection of bills receivable owed to the bank, as well as their tardiness and negligence, to Roberts was symptomatic of the condition of most of the banks in the state then in *de facto* liquidation. He confided to the trust's agent at New Orleans that there was 'a party high in power endeavoring to bring about in influence to annihilate all the Banks in the state as a public nuisance & its not to be wondered at the way the Banks have acted in tampering with the people, handing out to them different kinds of Notes, & giving such long credits, which was & will continue to destroy the Creditors & the debtors both'. Virtually everyone of consequence in the state was a debtor of the trust; the Chancellor, the Chief Justice of the High Court of Errors and Appeals, numerous lawyers and judges, and all refused to pay. Roberts was not altogether unsympathetic to the criticisms heaped on the banks by the repudiators, noting that the banks did not pay their debts to the local citizens which of course set a bad example for their own debtors.[330]

The assignees of the Commercial and Railroad Bank tried various schemes to preserve their control over the rail line. Thomas E. Robins traveled to New York and Philadelphia, meeting with stockholders and creditors, ostensibly for the purpose of reorganizing the whole enterprise. His meeting with the Bacon trustees appears to have gone well, the trustees apparently finding the scheme interesting enough to write to Roberts about it. Robins's basic proposition was for an 'amalgamation' of all creditor interests, including the bank's shareholders, in a new enterprise whose chief asset would be the railroad. Banking privileges would be forfeited and the remaining bills receivable collected and the proceeds applied to liquidating debts *pro rata*. Roberts strongly advised against any arrangement that would cost the trust its priority claim on the railroad's physical assets. 'Mr. Robins & his particular friends', he wrote to the Bacon trustees, were 'very busy ... electioneering among his Loco foco party to have Briscoe's bill [the Act of 1843] nullified at the next session of the Legislature, & to have some act of the Legislature to permit the Commercial & Railroad Bank' to continue operating without the threat of the quo warranto proceeding already instituted against it. He reminded the trustees that the affairs of the Bacon Trust would one day have to conclude and venturing into a new arrangement and a reshuffling of their priority claims might be beyond their authority. Their primary charge was to liquidate the assigned assets for the benefit of those holding the notes of the late United States Bank.[331]

Roberts concluded his advisory letter to the Bacon trustees with a strong recommendation that they and the Robertson trustees sell all of their claims against the Commercial and Railroad Bank, except the debt secured by mortgage on the railroad's physical assets which then amounted to $300,000, to speculators in New York who Robins had claimed were prepared to buy them. Roberts recommended that a sale be made of a three year credit with interest and security, and that the bonds and claim certificates be disposed of 'at 33 1/3 cents in the dollar & if those New York Gentlemen make 66 2/3 cents in the dollar let them do it-I think there is 15 chances out of 20 against them'. He then advised the Robertson trustees: '[t]he interest which you have in the Commercial & Railroad Bank of Vicksburg by the claim certificates which I hold for your Trust, I would not advise an amalgamation with stockholders on any terms, but a disposal of yours & the Bacon Trustees claims to some of the New York capitalists & Speculators who may agree to amalgamate on being able to purchase your claims at a very low rate'.[332]

There were other claims affecting the property of the bank as well - a judgment in favor of Jackson, Todd & Co. for $100,000 and a judgment pending for $600,000 to the Girard Bank of Philadelphia. Roberts warned his principals when the Girard Bank commenced its action that they 'were very anxious to get Judgment before us'. The president of the Girard Bank in his relations with the trust evidenced only the most cooperative spirit, but his actions seemed to indicate that his solicitude was ambiguous. '[T]he Girard Bank, or Mr. Boker [the President] may talk such nonsense & sane slick in Philada., but out here in Miss. their <u>endeavor</u> had been & their <u>intentions</u> now are to get Judgment in advance of us'. Moreover, Robins had once again succeeded in postponing a sale of the railroad by urging the Chancery Court to stay a sale pending a decision by the High Court of Errors and Appeals respecting the validity of the assignment of 1840. '[T]his is [Roberts wrote] another example of Mr. T. E. R's <u>'smartness'</u>-Mr [George] Yerger is employed in ... behalf [of the assignees] to protect their assignment'.[333]

Roberts was especially unhappy that Yerger was not available to represent the trust in the foreclosure of the mortgage, Yerger having been previously retained by the assignees of the Commercial and Railroad Bank to represent them in the quo warranto proceeding. Quitman & McMurran represented the trust, and Roberts blamed them for all the delays. 'We ought to have had Judgment 6 months ago', he wrote, '& the default had been owing to Messrs.

Quitman & McMurran-first he [Quitman] was too late in bringing suit one term by mistaking the week & at another term when the demurrers were to be argued at Vicksburg, instead of bringing these the evening of the day before, put it off 'til the very day & then missed the cars from Jackson to Vicksburg at 6 o'clock in the Morning by being 10 Minutes too late'.[334]

Talk of amalgamating all the creditor interest continued to surface during the fall of 1846 and winter of 1847. Thereafter matters were quiet until January 1848 when the High Court of Errors and Appeals finally declared the assignment made in 1840 void. Whereupon, Jackson, Todd & Co. proceeded to execute on their judgment and levied on the railroad itself. At this point, George Yerger recommended that the trust and the Girard Bank combine their interests and buy up the judgments of Jackson, Todd & Co. and other small claimants and 'sell the Road under them & buy it for about $250,000'.[335]

On 16 March 1848, Roberts wrote to the trustees enclosing an agreement 'for preserving the Commercial & Railroad Bank of Vicksburg, Rail Road & property to satisfy the Judgment creditors, our special debt, 100 M Drs. to the Girard Bank & for the purpose of paying all other claims ultimately'. Improvements, he reckoned, would make the road more profitable, and in time most of the trust's claims would be paid. But the arrangement was contingent on the Trust advancing money to pay some of the judgments. 'I urge you [he wrote], if your authority & means will permit, to make some advance to prevent this whole property from passing away into the hands of speculators'. Having completed his representation of the now deposed assignees, Yerger felt himself free to represent the trust in the matter of the railroad and Roberts was only too happy to engage his services. He was, according to Roberts, 'of vast importance to us'.[336]

The Bacon Trust, the Robertson Trust, and the Girard Bank finally reached an agreement whereby regardless of which was first in prosecuting a claim to judgment all would have a pro-rata interest in the railroad property 'according to the whole amount of their respective claims'. The Girard Bank's claim was $600,000; the combined claims of the Bacon Trustees and the Robertson Trustees, Roberts alleged, then exceeded $2 million. Their amalgamation was successful in wresting control of the railroad from the assignees and the trustees appointed under the quo warranto law. While the shareholders in theory had a residuary interest, the possibility that they would ever realize anything was indeed remote. Roberts installed George S. Yerger as president of the railroad and he proceeded to reorganize its affairs. Roberts apprized the trustees that under the most optimistic assessment the railroad property could be worth no more than $1 million, a valuation based on a net income stream of from $60,000 to $70,000 a year.[337]

Conclusion

Roberts was not altogether unfavorably disposed to the state of Mississippi's efforts to wind up the banks. There can be little doubt that the 1840 prohibition against the transfer of bills receivable and the later provision which required an immediate sale of bank assets after the appointment of trustees under a quo warranto proceeding greatly retarded his efforts in making collections. Still, he correctly believed that those previously charged to oversee the voluntary assignments of the banks had wasted their resources and were the principal cause for the steep depreciation in the value of bank liabilities such as demand notes and post notes. The trustees appointed under the quo warranto law were strictly prohibited from reissuing any circulation so long as the creditors of the banks remained unsatisfied. Roberts, of course, was then holding hundreds of thousands of dollars of Planters Bank notes, as well as claim certificates against the Commercial and Railroad Bank; so any provision that promised to make his holdings more valuable by stopping note reissues was greatly to the advantage of the trust.

As previously noted, many of those indebted to the Bacon Trust were prepared to gamble in hopes of escaping liability for their debts, if indeed the Act of 1840 contained a penalty clause barring all future collections of the bills receivable transferred in violation of the prohibition. They also gambled that a forced sale of bank assets by the trustees appointed under the quo warranto law would allow the liquidation of their debts for pennies on the dollar. In both instances their speculations were thwarted primarily because the trust never wanted for capable lawyers, but also Mississippi's judiciary demonstrated a degree of dispassion and courage in preventing a wholesale miscarriage of justice. True, the justices of the High Court of Errors and Appeals upheld the constitutionality of the prohibition on the transfer of bills receivable. But their decisions on whether that ban contained a penalty clause were ambiguous.

There can be little doubt that the debts were highly collectible. The efforts of the state legislature to shift some of the burden from debtors to stockholders and bank creditors was partially successful in that the debtors obtained a respite of several years' duration for liquidating their obligations. The shareholders suffered most, but their only hope for salvaging any part of their investment was a resurrection of the banks, something which was politically, and after 1840 economically, impossible. Certainly the actions of the state reduced their chances for making a recovery, but in any even most of their equity stake had already been depleted by the time of the second suspension in Mississippi.

As Tony Freyer has shown the tendency of state judiciaries to be swayed by local considerations in treating with out-of-state creditors in matters dependent on a critical reading of the common law on commercial questions, especially bills and notes, was pervasive in the United States. It would be difficult to say that Mississippi's High Court of Errors and Appeals was captive to debtor interests, even as the rhetoric of repudiation pervaded public discourse in the state. Roberts advised the trustees in 1844 that the 'undecided state of th[e] question' over the transfer of the bills receivable had convinced many of their debtors 'not to pay a dollar in hopes of getting off entirely'. The Whigs were 'very loud against the dishonesty of Repudiation by the State [of the Union Bank bonds, but] in individual & private debts of their own they carry out in practice repudiation beyond the individual acts of the Loco focos'. In December of that year, feeling much discouraged, he cautioned that 'repudiation is the order of the day here, by the Legislature, Courts, Judges, Juries, Lawyers & the community at large & individually in this particular I really think, if any thing, Whigs are worse than the Loco focos'. Still he recognized that the situation was complex and composed of many contradictory elements. For this reason he never abandoned hope. He complained about the 'ravenous disposition of the Lawyers to get [the debtors] … into suits', but noted that the hostility toward the banks was due in part to their failure to pay their own debts and the terrible management of the trustees appointed under the voluntary assignments.[338]

In numerous letters to William J. Minor on the conduct of the Agricultural Bank during the second suspension, Steven Duncan voiced many of the complaints made by Roberts, to wit that the officers and assignees had made overly generous settlements with debtors who were their friends, that the officers were paid their salaries in specie, and that too much paper had passed into circulation over the course of administering the assets. He, too, thought the state Whigs as bad as the Democrats or Loco focos. 'Oh how I wish I were at the head of the bank', he wrote. '[H]ow I would distress the rascals-for I hold, that towards the Agricultural Bank the whigs are as big rascals as the Loco focos'.[339]

Duncan was emphatic about controlling emissions of bank paper. 'I think you ought to burn all your post Notes on hand … & destroy your plates-so that there will be an end to all future issues. If notes are required – let the demand notes be used - … I think you owe this to the shareholders'. Few of those in charge of administering the assigned assets of the failed banks showed much concern for the fate of the shareholders' property. In evaluating the overall progress of their liquidations it is well to remember that the shareholders of the United States Bank lost all in the ruin of that institution.[340]

The banks of Mississippi remained in a state of suspension after 1840 and by the 1850s their corporate identities had for the most part disappeared. The business of exchange, however, quickly revived in the state. It was however concentrated in the hands of dealers, not banks, who were able to mediate the credit needs of their clienteles through the channels of commerce. Local interests predominated in this greatly altered credit system, but some international firms like the Browns carried on extensive commercial agencies in the state. What is evident is the power of an organizational structure based on slave plantations and commercial agencies to command the credit resources requisite for diffusing the risks of producing the great staple for the world market. The business of exchange remained vital after 1840, and by the end of the decade the course of exchange was moving decidedly in favor of southern money markets, especially those in the Lower Mississippi Valley.

CONCLUSION

Most of the nation's economy, even late in the antebellum period, was directly affected in some way by slave agriculture. Much of the livestock employed on slave plantations was raised in places like Kentucky and Ohio, as were a significant amount of foodstuffs as well. Whole manufacturing concerns in New England produced exclusively for slave consumers; whether shoes, clothing, or hats. But the most important contribution of slave agriculture to the nation's economy as a whole were the vast amounts of foreign exchange generated by slave agriculture. Sterling bills drawn at places like New Orleans and made payable in London, often arose from actual consignments of southern staples to agents and buyers abroad. But some portion of those bills were also predicated on more-or-less permanent credit facilities extended by foreign agents as a precondition for obtaining some portion of the consignment business. An agent in New York, London, or Paris, might attract consignments of sugar, cotton , and tobacco from agents at New Orleans or elsewhere in the region, provided he could absorb some portion of the risks inherent in producing those staples. Production costs were very high, considering that labor costs were fixed.

The Second Bank of the United States, by the time its charter expired, had made itself the primary market maker for bills, both domestic and foreign. It's circulation thus obtained a measure of currency which no other institution was remotely prepared to match. The derangement of the domestic exchanges in the aftermath of Andrew Jackson's veto of the Second Bank's re-charter, in 1832, was an inevitable consequence of its operational attempts to wind down and withdraw its capital from disparate locations around the country. When it became obvious that retrieving its capital from many markets across the country would be an impossibility, the bank's managers confected another plan which was to continue operating at least until such time as the reductions at the western branches could finally be realized.

Unfortunately for the United States Bank and the nation, reconstituting a new medium of exchange, a currency which had all the attributes of legal tender, proved to be illusive. It is well to remember that the newly chartered United States Bank continued to emit the demand notes of the old Bank of the United States. Management, in other words, desperately tried to amplify the psychological links between the old bank and the new bank, in hopes of rebuilding a national circulation. But the evidence makes it abundantly clear, that hopes of realizing this pretension were never anything more than just hopes. The new bank simply lacked the machinery, which would have enabled it to press its notes on all sections of the United States, thus gaining time to liquify its investments at distant locations such as Natchez or New Orleans.

The Panic of 1837, then, was simply a consequence of a money market coming to terms with a very painful reality. As the Bank of the United States had contracted its business, especially in the West, credit facilities throughout the country had disappeared and the best efforts of the state banks to restore a smooth operating exchange had come to naught. The pressure on the exchanges was relentless, from 1834 onwards. Increasingly, credit mediators in locales, especially in the West, drew down their credit lines with merchants in the East in order to accommodate clients in need of resources to satisfy curtailments of permanent accommodations and sustain ongoing planting operations.

Somewhere in the midst of this very complex picture of events before and after Andrew Jackson's veto of the Second Bank's re-charter, looms the question of whether the the management of the national bank, in the decade before 1832, had so loosened monetary controls that they had precipitated a credit induced inflationary boom. Rapidly augmenting surpluses in the national treasury certainly seem to suggest as much. And it is rather easy to see how that happened considering the expansive character of the bank's operations in the West. The Second Bank would open credit facilities in places like Natchez, perhaps doubling or even tripling what had previously been available at that place. Local banks found themselves marching lockstep with the national bank's branch. The Bank of the State of Mississippi found it more expedient to liquidate rather than compete with the branch.

The market makers of commercial agriculture, the factorage firms in Natchez, New Orleans, New York, London and Paris, were enabled to expand the facilities they provided their clients. It is shocking that the credit facilities provided by the Natchez branch for even one firm often aggregated to millions of dollars. The branch's permanent accommodations were well within the bounds of prudence, but the huge volume of bills and notes payable at distant locations, which the branch also discounted, often exceeded local discounts by a factor of five. This paper was supported by little else than the credit of the firm and its many endorsers. The loans thus made were only self-liquidating to the extent that another long dated bill would answer for the maturing one. Here is where the complaint, that New Orleans firms and their Natchez affiliates had indulged in check kiting in order to expand their credit facilities beyond permissible limits, had its origins. Certainly there is some truth to the claim, but the practice itself wasn't check kiting because the branches at New

Orleans and Natchez were perfectly aware of what was going on and suffered it to continue.

Supposing that the Second Bank had indeed fostered a credit bubble during the last decade of its life, not only explains the derangement of the exchanges in the years just prior to the general bank suspension in the spring of 1837, but also explains why there was never any possibility of the bank's quietly passing out of existence by turning all the assets in its portfolio into cash. Its circulation was, after all, the only cash equivalent which might have sufficed as an aid or measure in determining whether the winding up of its affairs had been successfully managed. The assets in the new bank's portfolio steadily lost value as the general suspension was followed by a futile attempt to resume in 1839. Biddle probably sacrificed a lot of assets just to raise the needful to meet demands at the agencies in the West. His exertions were especially noteworthy in aiding some of the Mississippi banks to resume, months after the banks of New York City had resumed. But those resumptions proved to be fleeting. And they came at a very high price for the citizens of the state.

The United States Bank obtained the underwriting contract for the sale of Mississippi state bonds to finance the capital of the newly formed Union Bank. So soon as a portion of the funds were realized in state from the sale of the bonds, the proceeds immediately leaked out again in the form of remittance paper. Banks like the Union Bank never obtained a circulation. They were little more than vehicles which permitted the fortunate few to repatriate funds from Mississippi to points East. All too often a similar pattern has been observed when the International Monetary Fund has attempted to restructure a nation's finances. New loans are forthcoming but they have negligible impact on the debtor nation because the new loans effect nothing more than an exchange of one creditor [a bank, perhaps, in New York or London] for another one [the IMF itself].

Mississippi realized little from the sale of the Union Bank bonds. Much of the proceeds from the sale of the bonds, which were paid out in Mississippi, were non-current banknotes from eastern cities. The sale, no doubt, provided some very badly needed relief for the United States bank, because much of the subscription was paid for with tenders of non-current banknotes of the United States Bank. The Mississippi bonds probably prolonged the life of the United States Bank. The bank no doubt received current money, in the form of specie or its equivalent in non-current banknotes, when the bonds were sold. But little specie was ever credited to the Union Bank's account from the sale of the bonds, and the small amounts which arrived in Jackson, immediately migrated back to the East. It is little wonder that the state repudiated the bonds, especially in the aftermath of the collapse of the United States Bank.

In the first hundred years of the nation's life, no bank ever obtained so much influence over the its economic life, as did the Second Bank of the United

States. Andrew Jackson's opposition to the bank, and his unpopular veto of its re-charter, in retrospect seems almost wise. He was right to be suspicious of the institution, not so much because of what it had done, but because of the potential it posed for great mischief in the making and unmaking of the nation's economy. One may certainly argue whether or not the bank had facilitated a credit induced boom in the years before the re-charter crisis, and also whether it had done so in order to influence the politics swirling around the re-charter issue. But the problems always posed by a fiat monetary regime and its management, were there and at least partially understood by contemporaries. The power to print money is far more potent than even the power to tax. And in extreme cases that power even supersedes the power to tax.

There is at least evidence, thanks to the availability of a relatively complete set of Second Bank records for one of its branches, to support a conclusion that the bank's own monetary regime all but guaranteed the impossibility of dismantling the edifice which had been erected during the heyday of its existence. But there is little evidence, at least in the massive collection of Nicholas Biddle's papers at the Library of Congress, to indicate whether he and his subordinates ever saw the difficulty with any clarity.

In this light, Andrew Jackson's pigheaded stubbornness represents the most perspicacious understanding of the dangers posed by the bank to the new nations's constitutional form of government. More so than any of his contemporaries, whether friend or foe of the Leviathan in Chestnut Street, Andrew Jackson seems to have grasped the seriousness of granting a quasi-governmental company a monopoly on printing legal tender. He no doubt believed that the negotiability of fiat money was a matter for private tenders, not a regime to be underwritten by the government. And perhaps he was correct about this, insofar as fiat monetary regimes, managed by either quasi-governmental entities, or governmental agencies, have been problematic, to state the obvious.

Fiat monetary regimes, whose management is entrusted to a central bank, reached their zenith in the twentieth century. Universally, the result has always been the same. Central bank monopolies on the issuance of fiat money have consistently produced currency debasements. The purchasing power of a dollar circulated by the Federal Reserve in 1913, today is degraded ninety-five percent.

One must wonder why fiat monetary regimes, managed by governmentally chartered central banks, have remained so popular in virtually every country in the world today; even after a century of very bad experiences so far as these institutions seeming inability to preserve the purchasing power of the money of account they are charged to preserve. The only answer which comes immediately to mind is that their popularity has persisted because of the rise of the modern totalitarian state. Socialization of risk is a key. Perhaps, too, their persistence helps to explain why we are far more comfortable with terms like 'market economy,' than we are with any term of art which includes the word 'capitalist.' Capitalist' and governmentally sponsored fiat monetary regimes are antithetical to one another.

It was no accident that the economist Peter Temin recognized similarities between the Panic of 1837 and resulting economic depression and the 1929 Crash and its progeny. Both events traced their origins to credit bubbles and dysfunctional financial systems. But Temin concluded that the 1837 collapse had far less impact on the real manufacturing economy of the United States than was the case after 1929. In part he attributed this to the consequent banking suspension and a belief that banks in suspension were free to continue their discount lines without serious curtailments. But this wasn't the case. Banks in suspension had no choice but to relentlessly push themselves into de facto liquidation. More likely, domestic manufacturers received a big boost because of the high cost of purchasing credit instruments suitable for remittance abroad in order to pay for imports.[341]

Still, though, both the 1837 Panic and the 1929 stock market collapse were by-products of credit bubbles. And both events were followed by periods of adjustment which lasted upwards of a decade. It is easy enough to trace the credit bubble which terminated in the 1929 crash back to a quiescent Federal Reserve. The role of the Second Bank of the United States in facilitating a credit bubble is obscure because that bank had already legally ceased to be, more than a year before the general suspension of 1837. But as has been shown, the financial system had already undergone a sea-change in the wake of Andrew Jackson's veto of the Second Bank's re-charter. The general suspension in 1837 merely confirmed that the existing system was in no condition to weather a contraction of credit which had been fostered by the Second Bank.

NOTES

1   The term 'Bank War' probably stems from Thomas Francis Gordon, *The War on the Bank of the United States, Or, A Review of the Measures of the Administration Against That Institution and the Prosperity of the Country* (Philadelphia: Key and Biddle, 1834). The Bank of the United States has had more than its share of advocates. Bray Hammond, *Banks and Politics In America from the Revolution to the Civil War* (Princeton: Princeton University Press, 1957); Fritz Redlich, *The Molding of American Banking: Men and Ideas* (New York: Jefferson Reprint corporation, 1968); Thomas Payne Govan, *Nicholas Biddle, Nationalist and Public Banker, 1786-1844* (Chicago: The University of Chicago Press, 1959). See also Richard E. Ellis, *The Union at Risk: Jacksonian Democracy, States' Rights and the Nullification Crisis* (New York: Oxford University Press, 1987). However, the Papers of Nicholas Biddle at the Library of Congress contain a wealth of information on the bank's extensive loans to highly placed politicians, including Daniel Webster and Henry Clay. In addition, those papers indicate that Biddle acted decisively to bring the whole power of the bank to bear in favor of those opposed to Andrew Jackson in the 1832 elections. His policies are manifest in the chaos that reigned in the domestic and foreign exchanges. See generally, The Papers of Nicholas Biddle, Library of Congress, hereafter cited NBP, LC.

2   Henry Clay to Nicholas Biddle. No. 6035. 15 December 1831. NBP, LC. Clay writes: 'Have you come to any decision about an application to Congress at this session for the renewal of your charter? The friends of the bank here, with whom I have conversed, seem to expect the application to be made. The course of the President, in the event of the passage of a bill, seems to be a matter of doubt and speculation-My own belief is that, if <u>now</u> called upon he would not negative the bill; but that if he should be reelected the event might and probably would be different'. Daniel Webber to Nicholas Biddle, No. 6051. 18 December 1831. NBP, LC. 'I have seen a great number of persons, & conversed with them, among other things, respecting the Bank-The result of all these conversations has been a strong confirmation of the opinion which I expressed at Philadelphia that it is expedient for the Bank to apply for the renewal of its charter without delay. I do not meet a Gentleman, hardly of another opinion, & the little incidents & anecdotes, that occur & circulate among us, all tend to strengthen the impression. Indeed, I am now a good deal inclined to think, that after Genl. Jackson's reelection there would be a poor chance for the Bank'. But Thomas Cadwalader writes Biddle that 'Mr.

McLane … says <u>positively</u> that the President will reject the Bill <u>if the matter is agitated at this session</u>-He (the Prest.) & those about him would regard the movement, before the election, as an act of hostility'. Thomas Cadwalader to Nicholas Biddle, No. 6065. 21 December 1831. NBP, LC. And Cadwalader advised Biddle again on 23 December1831 that 'as far as my consultations with our friends have gone, the Jackson portion of them argue against starting the question at this session-and the Clay portion are especially anxious for its present agitation-The former are clear that we have no chance <u>now</u>, but a good one next year, & the latter are clear that if we let this session go by we have no chance at all'. No. 6071. NBP, LC.

3   William J. Cooper, Jr., *Liberty And Slavery, Southern Politics to 1860* (New York: Alfred A. Knopf, 1983), p. 171.

4   Nicholas Biddle to Thomas H. Perkins, 7 January 1833. Letterbooks, p. 365. NBP, LC. He writes: '[s]ince I have been in the Bank we have added one to our Boston Directors, so as to have two members of the Parent Board from your States. But for several years their attendance has been very rare-and moreover the proportion of Stock owned by Massachusetts has been greatly changed-for while New York owns 40,000 shares-S. Carolina, 39,000-Pennsa. 44-Massachusetts has only 9,000'.

5   Gales & Seaton's Reports of Debates in Congress. 22nd Congress, 4 March 1831 to 3 March 1833. Senate, 11 June 1832, p. 1073. House of Representatives, 3 July 1832, p. 3851.

6   'An Act to incorporate the subscribers of the Bank of the United States', Session, 1815-1816. Stock subscriptions were paid in quarterly installments over a period of twelve months. Twenty percent of each installment has to be paid in coin, either foreign or domestic, and the balance in coin or the funded debt of the United States. All of the funded debt was receivable at par except the 3 percent bonds, which could only be tendered at the rate of 65 cents for each dollar of face value. This point is obscure in Peter Temin's *The Jacksonian Economy* (New York: W. W. Norton, 1969), p. 40. The only acceptable tenders for stock subscriptions were, then, coin and government debt. If subscribers afterwards borrowed against their stock, this was a perfectly acceptable course given the Bank's constitution as a discounter of business paper. It brought the business of the nation's rich capitalists to the Bank. For more on the history of the U.S. national debt, see Robert E. Wright, ed., *The U.S. National Debt, 1785-1900* (London: Pickering & Chatto, 2005).

7   Temin, *Jacksonian Economy*, pp. 29-37.

8   L. E. Davis and J. R. T. Hughes, 'A Dollar Sterling Exchange, 1803-1895', *Economic History Review* 13(August 1960), pp. 60-2; Hugh Rockoff, 'Money, Prices, and Banks in the Jacksonian Era', in Robert William Fogel and Stanley L. Engerman, eds. *The Reinterpretation of American Economic History* (New York: Harper & Row, 1971), pp. 456-8; Temin, *Jacksonian Economy*, pp. 29, 65-7; Lawrence Officer, *Between the Dollar-Sterling Gold Points: Exchange Rates, Parity, and Market Behavior* (New York: Cambridge University Press, 1996).

9   But see Howard Bodenhorn and Hugh Rockoff, 'Regional Investment Rates in Antebellum America', in Claudia Goldin and Hugh Rockoff, eds. *Strategic Factors in Nineteenth Century American Economic Development* (Chicago: The University of Chicago Press, 1992), pp. 159-87; Howard Bodenhorn, 'Capital Mobility and

Financial Integration in Antebellum America', *The Journal of Economic History* 52 (Sept. 1992), pp. 585-602.

10   See generally quotations in the *New Orleans Price Current* and *Commercial Intelligencer*. A discussion of the early origins of bank checks will be found in Fritz Redlich and Webster M. Christmas, 'Early American Checks and an Example of their Use'. *Business History Review* 41(Autumn 1967), pp. 285-8; Robert E. Wright, *The Origins of Commercial Banking in America, 1750-1800* (New York: Rowman and Littlefield, 2001), pp. 112, 117, 120-5.

11   But see Harold D. Woodman, *King Cotton and His Retainers: Financing and Marketing the Cotton Crop of the South, 1800-1925* (Columbia: University of South Carolina Press, 1968), pp. 60-71.

12   Ralph D. Hidy, *The House of Baring in American Trade and Finance, English Merchant Bankers At Work, 1763-1861* (Cambridge: Harvard University Press, 1949), pp. 255-9; John R. Killick, 'The Cotton Operations of Alexander Brown and Sons in the Deep South, 1820-60', *The Journal of Southern History* 43 (May 1977), pp. 169-194.

13   Unless otherwise noted, all emphases in quotations appear in the original.

14   May Humphreys to Edward C. Biddle, No. 15,129. 15 December 1837. NBP, LC. See also, Commercial Bank of Natchez Collection, , Louisiana and Lower Mississippi Valley Collections, hereafter referred to as LLMVC, Louisiana State University Libraries, Louisiana State University, hereafter cited CBNC, LLMVC. 'Cotton Ledger', 'Accounts with Dealers', 'Account Sales of Cotton'.

15   Gavin Wright, 'Capitalism and Slaver on the Islands: A Lesson from the Mainland', *The Journal of Interdisciplinary History* 17 (Spring 1987), pp. 851-70; Gavin Wright, 'Cotton Competition and the Post-bellum Recovery of the American South', *Journal of Economic History* 34 (September 1974), pp. 610-35; Robert William Fogel and Stanley L. Engerman, *Time On The Cross, The Economics of American Negro Slavery* (New York: W. W. Norton & Co., 1974), pp. 89-94.

16   Bank of the United States, Natchez Branch, Collection, hereafter cited BUSN, LLMVC. 'Individual Depositors Ledger'. For other years, see John J. McCusker, 'Comparing the Purchasing Power of Money in the United States (or Colonies) from 1665 to Any Other Year Including the Present', Economic History Services, 2005, URL: http://www.eh.net/hmit/ppowerusd/.

17   'Hoopes & Moore', Individual Depositors Ledger, folios 293, 311, 334, 343, 169. BUSN, LLMVC. Financial historians have for generations attempted to distinguish promissory notes and bills of exchange, the principal assumption being that the former instrument generally evidenced an accommodation loan and the latter a self-liquidating 'commercial' transaction. This distinction is not particularly appropriate insofar as it reflects contemporary commercial usage. A better distinction is between loans that were local in character and those which were to be paid at some distant point. Promissory notes or bills of exchange could be used to facilitate either kind of loan. It was all accommodation paper. Financial historians have relied principally on legal distinctions that often embodied after-the-fact characterizations that distorted the actualities of commercial transactions. An excellent analysis of the history of the distinction between promissory notes and bills of exchange in commercial law is James Steven Rogers, *The Early History Of The Law*

Of Bills and Notes: A Study Of The Origins Of Anglo-American Commercial Law (Cambridge: Cambridge University Press, 1995).

18 Steven Duncan to William J. Minor, 5 August 1839, Box 2, Folder 12, William J. Minor and Family Papers, hereafter cited WJMFP, LLMVC. Steven Duncan to William J. Minor, 27 August 1839, Box 2, Folder 12. Steven Duncan to William J. Minor, 16 September 1839, Box 2, Folder 12. WJMFP, LLMVC.

19 Steven Duncan to William J. Minor, 7 January 1840, Box 2, Folder 13; William J. Minor to Dr. Samuel Gustin, 11 January 1840, Letterbooks. WJMFP, LLMVC.

20 Steven Duncan to William J. Minor. ? August 1842. Box 2, Folder 14, WJMFP, LLMVC.

21 Joseph L. Roberts to Fielding Davis, 5 April 1842. Letterpress Book No. I. John Bacon et. al. Trustees Papers, hereafter cited BTP, LLMVC.

22 Thomas Henderson to Herman Cope, 20 November 1838, Cashier's Letterbook, BUSN, LLMVC.

23 *Shiff vs. Shiff,* No. 17,346, Second District Court, Orleans Parish, Louisiana division, New Orleans Public Library.

24 Steven Duncan to William J. Minor, n.d., Box 2, Folder 13, WJMFP, LLMVC.

25 John Perkins to Jackson, Todd & Co., 9 July 1839. Jackson, Riddle, and Company Papers. Records of Ante-Bellum Southern Plantations from the Revolution through the Civil War. Kenneth M. Stampp, General Editor. Series J. Selections from the Southern Historical Collection, Manuscript Department, Library of the University of North Carolina at Chapel Hill. Part 5: Louisiana, Reel 19. Microfilm copy in the possession of LLMVC.

26 'Reynolds, Marshall & Co.', Individual Depositors Ledger. Folios 544-546. BUSN, LLMVC. That ledger covers the period from March 1831 to August 1833. Unfortunately the Individual Depositors Ledger[s] for the remaining years of the branch's life appear not to have survived.

27 But see Temin, *Jacksonian Economy.*

28 'B. Hughes', Individual Depositors Ledger. Folios 287. 337. BUSN, LLMVC.

29 One of the most recent treatments of the subject of antebellum patriarchal families and wealth accumulation strategies is Christopher Morris, *Becoming Southern, The Evolution of a Way of Life, Warren County and Vicksburg, Mississippi, 1770-1860* (Oxford: Oxford University Press, 1995), pp. 84-102. The financial relationships outlined in this study include some from the Vicksburg area, and they antedate by decades the date Morris identifies as the point at which a frontier society became imbued with what is assumed to be the prevailing ethos of an antebellum southern community.

30 For another recent treatment of the lacuna created by the destruction of the Second Bank, see Robert E. Wright, *America's First Wall Street: Chestnut Street, Philadelphia* (Chicago: University of Chicago Press, 2005). For a more theoretical depiction of the early U.S. financial system as a network, see Richard E. Sylla and Robert E. Wright, "Networks and History's Stylized Facts: Comparing the Financial Systems of Germany, Japan, Great Britain, and the U.S.A.', *Business and Economic History On-Line* (2004). Available at: <http://www.thebhc.org/BEH/04/syllaandwright.pdf>.

31 Bank of the State of Mississippi Collection, Department of Archives and History, Jackson, Mississippi, hereafter cited as BSMC, MDAH. See also Robert C. Weems, Jr., 'The Bank of the Mississippi, A Pioneer Bank of the Old Southwest, 1809-1844', (Ph.D. diss., Columbia University, 1951). Microfilm copy at the Mississippi Department of Archives and History; Robert C. Weems, Jr., 'Mississippi's First Banking System', *The Journal of Mississippi History* 29 (November 1967), pp. 386-408; Marvin Bentley, 'The State Bank of Mississippi: Monopoly Bank on the Frontier (1809-1830)', *The Journal of Mississippi History* 40 (August 1978), pp. 297-318; Larry Schweikart, *Banking In the American South from the Age of Jackson to Reconstruction* (Baton Rouge: Louisiana State University Press, 1987), pp. 202-5; George Tichnor to James Duncan, 5 April 1831, Letterbook, p. 11, BSMC, MDAH.

32 Thomas Wilson to James Duncan, 23 June1827, folder 22. Stephen Duncan to R. L. Booker, 27 June 1831, Letterbook, p. 80, BSMC, MDAH.

33 George Tichnor to Thomas McDonnold, 22 April 1831, Letterbook, p. 27, BSMC, MDAH.

34 General Ledger M, 'Exchange on Orleans', folio 140-145, 385-395, 527-533, and 'Exchange on Philadelphia', folio 155, 613-617, 524-525. Thomas Wilson to James Duncan, 9 June 1827, folder 22, BSMC, MDAH.

35 Samuel Jaudon to James Duncan, 15 June 1827. Samuel Jaudon to James Duncan, 20 July 1827, folder 20, and General Ledger M, 'Farmers & Merchants Bank, Philadelphia', folios 170-181, 453-459, 594-599, BSMC, MDAH.

36 George Tichnor to John Fleming, 24 June 1831, Letterbook, page 77, BSMC, MDAH.

37 Samuel Jaudon to James Duncan, 15 June 1827, folder 20, BSMC, MDAH. The subject of domestic exchanges is considered in Howard Bodenhorn, 'Capital Mobility and Financial Integration in Antebellum America', *Journal of Economic History* 52 (September 1992), pp. 585-610. Foreign exchanges are dealt with in L. E. Davis and J. R. T. Hughes, 'A Dollar-Sterling Exchange, 1803-1895', *The Economic History Review* 13 (August 1960), pp. 52-78. The components of exchange quotations are discussed in John J. McCusker, *Money and Exchange in Europe and America, 1600-1775, A Handbook* (Chapel Hill: The University of North Carolina Press, 1978), pp. 3-26.

38 William McIlvaine to Stephen Duncan, 7 January 1828, Folder 35, BSMC, MDAH.

39 BUSN, LLMVC. The qualitative failures, alleged and otherwise, of the antebellum South's economic development are treated in a host of works. See for example Eugene D. Genovese, *The Political Economy of Slavery* (New York: Vintage Books, 1967). A more sophisticated interpretation of the problems affecting the slave South's qualitative development is Gavin Wright's *Old South, New South: Revolutions In the Southern Economy Since The Civil War* (New York: Basic Books, Inc., 1986).

40 George Tichnor to Jamor W. Downing, 25 March 1831, p. 1; George Tichnor to A. M. Feltus, 2 April 1831, p. 8; George Tichnor to James Duncan, 5 April 1831, p. 11; George Tichnor to F. E. Plummer, 18 April 1831, p. 24. Letterbook. William McIlvaine to Stephen Duncan, 27 February 1827, Folder 35, BSMC, MDAH. The

political climate surrounding the Bank of the United States and the public debate over government deposits are considered in depth in Bray Hammond, *Banks and Politics In America from the Revolution to the Civil War* (Princeton: Princeton University Press, 1957), pp. 326-68.

41 Henry Ewell [?] to Stephen Duncan, 26 September 1826, Folder 35, BSMC, MDAH.

42 General Ledger No. I., 'Notes and Bills Discounted', folios 1-12, 310-321, 479; General Ledger No. II, 'Notes and Bills Discounted', folios 1-15, BUSC, LLMVC.

43 General Ledger No. I, 'Bills of Exchange Domestic', folios 13-24, 470-476. General Ledger No. II, 'Bills of Exchange Domestic', folios 20-37. BUSN, LLMVC.

44 The use of uncovered accounts by Anglo-American firms was widespread in the 1830s. Ralph W. Hidy, *The House Of Baring In American Trade and Finance, 1763-1861* (New York: Russell & Russell, 1949), pp. 140-3.

45 Arthur Fraas, 'The Second Bank of the United States: An Instrument for an Interregional Monetary Union', *The Journal of Economic History* 34 (June 1974), pp. 447-67; *New Orleans Price Current, And Commercial Intelligencer*, issues from 1 October 1833 to 12 July 1834; Peter Temin, *The Jacksonian Economy* (New York: W. W. Norton, 1969) pp. 65-70; Thomas Henderson to H. S. Coxe, 2 September 1835; Thomas Henderson to M. T. Scott, 2 September 1835; Thomas Henderson to J. Robertson, 2 September 1835. Cashier's Letterbook. See also *State of the Bank*. BUSN, LLMVC.

46 George Tichnor to James Duncan, 5 April 1831, p.11; George Tichnor to F. E. Plummer, 18 April 1831, p. 24. Letterbook. BSMC, MDAH.

47 George Tichnor to Thomas McDonnold, 22 April 1831, p. 27. Letterbook. BSMC, MDAH.

48 Stephen Duncan to Horace Binney, 23 May 1831, p, 53; Stephen Duncan to Horace Binney, 25 June 1831, p. 79; Stephen Duncan to Horace Binney, 7 July 1831, p. 89; Stephen Duncan to Horace Binney, 9 July 1831, p. 90. Letterbook. BSMC, MDAH. *Legislative Acts of Mississippi*, 'An Act to Establish a Planters Bank of Mississippi', 13th Session, 1830, pp. 92-93. George Tichnor to John Flemming, 24 June 1831, p. 77. Letterbook. BSMC, MDAH.

49 Stephen Duncan to R. L. Booker, 19 July 1831, p. 99; George Tichnor to W. B. Winston, 20 August 1831, p. 112. George Tichnor to James Duncan, 2 September 1831, p. 115. George Tichnor to James Duncan, 17 September 1831, p. 122; George Tichnor to William McIlvaine, 15 November 1831. Letterbook. BSMC, MDAH.

50 Stephen Duncan to R. L. Booker, 27 June 1831, p. 80; Stephen Duncan to R. L. Booker, 19 July 1831, p. 99; George Tichnor to R. L. Booker, 16 August 1831, p. 110; Stephen Duncan to James Saul, 28 December1831; George Tichnor to Richard L. Booker, 28 December 1831; George Tichnor to L. M. Sargent, 6 July 1831, p. 90. Letterbook. BSMC, MDAH.

51 George Tichnor to A. M. Feltus, 20 August 1831, p. 111. Letterbook. BSMC, MDAH.

52 George Tichnor to W. McIlvaine, 15 November 1831. Letterbook. BSMC, MDAH. General Ledger No. I, 'Bank of the state of Mississippi in Account', folios

286-298, 445-446; General Ledger No. II, 'Bank of the State of Mississippi in Account', folios 401-402. BUSN, LLMVC.

53 George Tichnor to A. M. Feltus, 17 November 1831; George Tichnor to James Duncan, 19 November 1831. Letterbook, BSMC, MDAH.

54 General Ledger No. I, 'Bills of Exchange domestic', folios 17-22. 'Notes and Bills Discounted', folios 5-11. 'Planters Bank of Mississippi in Account', folios 349-55, 363-70, 482. BUSN, LLMVC.

55 Stephen Duncan to Samuel Gustin, 17 November 1831. Letterbook. BSMC, MDAH.

56 George Tichnor to Thomas McDonnold, 17 December 1831. Letterbook. BSMC, MDAH.

57 Stephen Duncan to Thomas McDonnold, 14 November 1831. Letterbook. BSMC, MDAH.

58 George Tichnor to A. M. Feltus, 25 February 1832; Stephen Duncan to Thomas McDonnold, 24 March 1832. Letterbook. BSMC, MDAH.

59 George Tichnor to Samuel Jaudon, 29 December 1831; Stephen Duncan to James Saul, 3 April 1832; Stephen Duncan to James Saul, 5 April 1832; Stephen Duncan to Samuel Jaudon, 26 May 1832. Letterbook. Samuel Jaudon to Stephen Duncan, 11 April 1832. Folder 32. BSMC, MDAH.

60 Samuel Jaudon to William McIlvaine, 21 May 1832. 6840. Papers of Nicholas Biddle, Library of Congress, hereafter cited NBP, LC. Samuel Jaudon to Stephen Duncan, 21 May 1832. Folder 33. BSMC, MDAH.

61 Statistics on the Bank of the United States' expansive discount policy in 1831 and 1832 are available in a variety of places. My primary source has been J. R. McCulloch, *A Dictionary, Practical, Theoretical, and Historical, of Commerce and Commercial Navigation* (Philadelphia: Thomas Wardle, 1843) Vol. I, pp. 158-162. But see also, Walter Buckingham Smith, *Economic Aspects of the Second Bank of the United States* (Cambridge: Harvard University Press, 1953) pp. 82-96; Roy Douglas Womack, *An Analysis of the Credit Controls of the Second Bank of the United States, Including a Brief History of American Currency and Banking Leading Up to the Establishment of that Institution* (New York: Arno Press, 1978). Nicholas Biddle to Daniel Webster, 8 January 1833, p. 370; Nicholas Biddle to George McDuffie, 9 January 1833, p. 372. Letterbooks. NBP, LC.

62 Samuel Jaudon to Stephen Duncan, 21 May 1832. Folder 33. BSMC, MDAH.

63 In the summer of 1832 the Bank of the State's portfolio consisting of local discounts and bills purchased may be conservatively estimated at from $2,000,000 to $2,500,000. The Branch of the Bank of the United States had a combined portfolio of $3,100,000. The Planters Bank portfolio is more difficult to estimate, but it may have ranged up to $2,000,000 and possibly more. Larry Schweikart's 'Reserve Ration Statistics of Southern Banks' shows two Mississippi banks reporting in 1834 with Loans and Discounts of $9,890,000. Schweikart, *Banking In The American South*, p. 66. Loans and discounts of nine reporting banks more than doubled by 1836 to $24,350,000, but a substantial portion of that activity appears to relate to projects commenced by corporations which had been chartered to build railroads. All such companies, however, had banking powers. The state legislature chartered three railroad banks in 1835 and four more in 1836. One

commercial bank was chartered in 1833 and four more incorporated in 1836. It is well to remember that the four improvement banks and four commercial banks incorporated in 1836 were only active for a period of months before the general banking suspension in April and May of 1837. Schewikart's estimates of total loans and discounts appear to agree with J. R. McCulloch, *Dictionary*, Vol. I, p. 156, and Marvin Bentley, 'Incorporated Banks and the Economic Development of Mississippi, 1829-1837', *The Journal Of Mississippi History* 35 (November 1973), pp. 361-380. See especially Table 2, p. 393. See also Julius M. Bentley, 'Financial Institutions and Economic Development in Mississippi, 1809 to 1860', (Ph.D. diss., Tulane University, 1969).

The Bank of the United States always commanded either par funds or a premium for its sight checks which ranged from par to 1 percent premium. Nicholas Biddle to John Cummings, Prest. Off. D. & D., Savannah, 31 March 1835, p. 347, Letterbooks, NBP, LC. 'The Bank never I believe sold its paper at a discount-and it would be extremely reluctant to resort to that course. Nothing therefore but a very urgent necessity should induce the office to make use of that expedient'. New Orleans *Price Current*, 21 April 1827: U. S. Bank checks on western cities were at 1.5 percent premium. On 12 May 1827, U. S. Bank sight checks on the North were at par.

From 1827 to 1831 U. S. Bank sight checks on the North at New Orleans ranged from par to 1 percent premium. In 1833 and 1834 the premium ranged from .25 to .75 percent. But see Bodenhorn, 'Capital Mobility', p. 595. Bodenhorn apparently equates the rates at which the Bank of the United States sold its checks with domestic exchange rates generally. The bank never sold its checks for less than par funds at the location where drawn, and usually it commanded a premium for its checks. At those same locations it generally was possible to purchase sight checks drawn by local banks at par or even a discount. At New Orleans, for example, from the fall of 1829 to the spring of 1830 the local banks sold New York sight checks at a discount, while the Bank of the United States commanded par or even a small premium for its checks. Bodenhorn's Table comparing rates charged by the Bank of the United States for its checks in 1833 and rates charged by New York banks and brokers in 1844 is deficient in another respect. During most of 1844, bills drawn on New Orleans commanded a premium in the New York market. Nevertheless, the yearly average for New Orleans sight bills was 99.87 which indicates that over the course of that year New York sellers still profited if they sold their bills at par. Jurgen Schneider, Oskar Schwarzer, Fredrich Zellfelder, *Wahrungen der Welt I: Europaische und nordamerikanische Devisenkurse 1777-1914* (Stuttgart: Steiner Verlag, 1991) Vol. 3. Exchange on New Orleans at New York.

64 Sight bills on New Orleans in the New York market fell to a discount of 3.5 percent in the fall of 1836. Sixty-day New York bills in the New Orleans market ranged from par to 2.5 percent discount during 1836. Schneider *Wahrungen der Welt*, vol. 3; New Orleans *Price Current*. Out-of-state bank notes, checks, and drafts generally traded at a larger discount, anywhere from 2.5 to 10 percent.

65 Minute Book, 9 February 1831; 2 November 1832. BUSN, LLMVC.

66 Minute Book, 2 March 1831. BUSN, LLMVC.

67 *Ibid.*

68 Minute Book, 16 December 1831. BUSN, LLMVC.
69 Minute Book, 20 December 1831; 20 January 1832. BUSN, LLMVC.
70 Nicholas Biddle to J. C. Wilkins, 16 January 1832, p. 110. Nicholas Biddle to Samuel Jaudon, 16 January 1832, p. 111. Letterbooks. NBP, LC. It is difficult to ascribe political sympathies to a banking institution on the basis of the allegiances of its officers, directors, and shareholders; still there can be little doubt that Stephen Duncan, for example, was a devoted follower of Henry Clay. Duncan certainly was the most influential force in the Bank of the State in the last years of its existence. Robert E. May, *John A. Quitman, Old South Crusader* (Baton Rouge: Louisiana State University Press, 1985), p. 63. The problem of identifying particular banks as 'Whig' or 'Democrat' is shown with great clarity in Harry N. Scheiber, 'The Pet Banks in Jacksonian Politics and Finance, 1833-1841', *The Journal of Economic History* 23 (June 1963), pp. 196-214. See also Robert E. Wright, *The Origins of Commercial Banking in America, 1750-1800* (New York: Rowman and Littlefield, 2001), p. 84.
71 Negative perceptions about banks seem to have been almost universal during the antebellum decades. As Naomi R. Lamoreaux has pointed out, large amounts of 'insider lending' characterized New England banks. That pattern did not hold everywhere, but everywhere banks were rather exclusive institutions, largely because usury laws forced them to ration loans on a non-price basis, i.e. on quantity rather than interest rate. Naomi R. Lamoreaux, *Insider Lending, Banks, Personal Connection, and Economic Development in Industrial New England* (Cambridge: Cambridge University Press, 1994); Wright, *Origins*, p. 166; Robert E. Wright, 'Bank Ownership and Lending Patterns in New York and Pennsylvania, 1781-1831', *Business History Review* 73 (Spring 1999), 40-60. 'Popularity is not always the surest test of the solidity of a Bank - It is certainly desirable that a Bank should possess the confidence of the community, and this office is not without its full share, yet in our peculiar situation, anxious to secure the interest of the Stockholders, it is a question, surrounded as we have been and are yet, by an opposition growing out of Political feeling and the interest of rival State Institutions-whether, we ought not to cultivate and enlarge that kind of popularity, the result of a desire to be a benefit to the community, as far as this object can be attained, consistently with the security and Profit of this Office'. Minute Book. 20 December 1831. Report of Special Committee. BUSN, LLMVC.
72 Nicholas Biddle to William Shipp, 31 July 1832, p. 276. Nicholas Biddle to Edward Shippen, 11 November 1832, p. 315. Nicholas Biddle to Thomas H. Perkins, 26 November 1832, p. 325. Nicholas Biddle to John Rathbone, 21 November 1832, p. 322. Letterbooks. NBP, LC.
73 Nicholas Biddle to Daniel Webster, 8 January 1833, p. 370. Letterbooks. NBP, LC.

1832	LOANS	DOMESTIC BILLS	TOTALS	SPECIE
January	49,602,577. 87	16,691,129.34	66,293,707.21	7,038,823
May	47,375,078.20	23,052,972.52	70,428,070.72	7,890,347
January	43,626,870.32	18,069,043.25	61,695,913.57	8,951,847

74 Samuel Jaudon to Branch Board, 16 November 1832. Resolution, 24 May 1833. Minutebook. BUSN, LLMVC.

75 General Ledger No. I, 'Profit and Loss', folio 65. General Ledger No. II, 'Profit and Loss', folio 120. BUSN, LLMVC.

76 Hammond, *Banks and Politics*, pp. 397-404. General Ledger No. I, 'Off. Louisville', folios 331-336. 'Off. Lexington', folios 340-345. BUSN, LLMVC. On 31 August 1835, the balance in favor of the Louisville Office was $168,806.87. On 30 May 1835, the balance in favor of the Lexington Office was $202,006.46.

77 General Ledger No. I, 'Off. New York', folios 412-413. 'Planters Bank of Mississippi in Acct'., folios 360-370, 481-484. BUSN, LLMVC.

78 But see Bodenhorn, 'Capital Mobility', pp. 595-597.

79 Samuel Jaudon to Nicholas Biddle, 16 May 1832. 6822. NBP, LC.

80 Samuel Jaudon to William McIlvaine, 17 May 1832. 6827. NBP, LC.

81 *Ibid*. William McIlvaine to Nicholas Biddle, 11 June 1832. 6925. NBP, LC.

82 Samuel Jaudon to William McIlvaine, 21 May 1832. 6840. NBP, LC.

83 Hammond, *Banks and Politics*, pp. 397-404.

84 Nicholas Biddle to Thomas Ewing, 24 May 1832. 6852. NBP, LC.

85 Nicholas Biddle to Thomas Cadwalader, 20 June 1832. 7002. NBP, LC.

86 Nicholas Biddle to R. Lenox, 17 January 1834, p. 96. Nicholas Biddle to C. A. Davis, 21 January 1834, p. 100. Letterbooks. NBP, LC.

YEAR	LOANS AND DISCOUNTS ($)	SPECIE ($)	NOTES ($)	DEPOSITS (including Treasury) ($)
1832				
January	66,293,707	7,038,823	21,355,724	20,696,517
July	67,416,081	7,519,083	20,520,068	19,987,472
1833				
January	61,695,913	8,951,847	17,518,217	20,271,220
October	60,094,202	10,663, 441	19,128,189	17,877,296
1834				
January	54,911,461	10,031,237	19,208,379	10,765,374
October	46,006,791	15,561,374	15,637,676	8,952,944
1835				
February	55,524,806	16,369,525	19,733,527	11,514,204
July	65,197,692	13,429,328	25,322,820	11,244,867

Source: J. R. McCulloch, *Dictionary*, Vol. I, p. 159.

The item 'Loans and Discounts' is composed of local discounts and domestic bills purchased. While complete and reliable statistics on the percentage of the portfolio invested in domestic bills are not available, data for the Natchez branch indicate that local discounts were curtailed by one-third from the fall of 1832 to the summer of 1834. The portfolio expanded thereafter to its former level, but purchases of domestic bills accounted for all of the increase. There is reason to suppose that curtailments of local discounts at the western branches were even more drastic.

87 Temin, *Jacksonian Economy*, p. 63.

88 Nicholas Biddle to General S. Smith, 11 January 1833, p. 375. Nicholas Biddle to General S. Smith, 17 January 1833, p. 390. Letterbooks. NBP, LC.

BRANCHES IN	LOANS ($)	BILLS OF EXCHANGE ($)	TOTAL ($)
Ohio, Kentucky, Indiana, Illinois, Missouri, & Tennessee	7,931,000.89	5,245,524.44	13,176,525.38
New Orleans	5,565,473.71	2,894,435.06	8,459,908.77
Natchez	1,443,682.24	2,440,921.28	3,884,603.52
Mobile	1,375,531.19	493,941.73	1,869,472.92
TOTAL SOUTHERN			14,213,985.21

89 Nicholas Biddle to Genl. S. Smith, 11 January 1833, p. 375. Letterbooks NBP, LC.

90 Nicholas Biddle to Manuel Eyre, 13 February 1833, p. 419. Nicholas Biddle to J. G. Watmaugh, 16 February 1833, p. 436. Letterbooks. NBP, LC.

91 Nicholas Biddle to Henry Clay, 20 January 1834, p. 102. Nicholas Biddle to James M. White, 19 June 1834, p. 237. Letterbooks, NBP, LC. Biddle calculated the interest charge and cost of exchange separately; interest at the legal rate, and exchange at the bank's posted rate of the day. This raises the interesting question of whether exchange quotations, as reported in the financial newspapers of the day, even reflect a charge for interest.

92 McCulloch, *Dictionary*, Vol. I., p. 159.

93 Hammond, *Banks and Politics*, pp. 412-34. Thomas Payne Govan, *Nicholas Biddle, Nationalist and Public Banker, 1786-1844* (Chicago: University of Chicago Press, 1959), pp. 223-46. But see Temin, *Jacksonian Economy*, pp. 60-1.

94 In October 1834, specie in the bank was $15,561,374 and notes outstanding stood at $15,637,676. The combined reduction in circulation and increase in specie levels from January 1832 levels was $14,240,595. If the float time from issuance to tender for deposit for the bank's notes and checks matched the volume of maturing 90-day bills, then the impact of the reduction over the course of a year would have been four times the combined reduction in circulation and increase in specie. Biddle himself estimated the bank's exchange operations by direct purchases and agencies performed by it aggregated to $250,000,000 in 1832, so the impact of the reduction in circulation may have been substantially greater than the estimate we have ventured. Nicholas Biddle to J. G. Watmaugh, 16 February 1833, p. 436. Letterbooks. NBP, LC.

95 Nicholas Biddle to Henry Clay, 20 January 1834, p. 102. Letterbooks. NBP, LC.

96 Minutebook. 21 March 1834. L. M. Marshall to Nicholas Biddle, 22 March 1834. President's Letterbook. BUSN, LLMVC.

97 Minutebook. 25 April 1834. BUSN, LLMVC.

98 General Ledger No. I. 'Profit and Loss', folio 60. General Ledger No. II. 'Profit & Loss', folio 120. Journal No. II, 31 May 1833, p. 202; 31 May 1834; 29 November 1834, p. 377; 30 May 1835, p. 586; 30 November 1835, p. 741. BUSN, LLMVC.

99 General Ledger No. I, 'Bills of Exchange, Domestic, Protested', folios 90, 178. General Ledger No. II, 'Bills of Exchange, Domestic, Protested', folio 60. General Ledger No. I, 'Notes and bills Discounted, Protested', folios 25-6, 335-8, 511-13, 506-7; General Ledger No. II, 'Notes and Bills Discounted, Protested', folios 40-50. BUSN, LLMVC.

100 Minutebook, 8 August 1834. BUSN, LLMVC.

101 Temin, *Jacksonian Economy*, p. 53.

102 Smith, *Economic Aspects*, p. 181. McCulloch, *Dictionary*, Vol. I, pp. 160-1. 'Bills discounted on other securities', were $18,914,952 on 31 March 1836. On 4 July 1836 those discounts stood at $29,404,921, or 51 percent of the entire portfolio. Biddle seems to have believed that because there were extremely well-developed markets for stocks and bonds in New York and Philadelphia, those securities could be safely and readily turned into cash. For the development of those securities markets, see Robert E. Wright, *The Wealth of Nations Rediscovered: Integration and Expansion in American Financial Markets, 1780-1850* (New York: Cambridge University Press, 2002); Robert E. Wright, *Hamilton Unbound: Finance and the Creation of the American Republic* (New York: Praeger, 2002), pp. 89-126.

103 Nicholas Biddle to C. A. Davis, 5 June 1835, p. 371. Letterbooks. NBP, LC.

104 Smith. *Economic Aspects*, p. 174. Smith estimates that the sales on long credits of the remains of the portfolios at Mobile, New Orleans, and Natchez aggregated to $5 million dollars, but the actual figure appears to be closer to $4 million dollars. However, by the summer of 1836 the large volume of bills returned under protest to the Bank's agencies in those cities could easily have increased the claims to be collected to something in excess of $5 million dollars. The sale to the Planters Bank at Natchez consisted of three items: Local loans, $877,149.97; Notes and bills discounted, protested, $129,728.03; and protested exchange, $53,393. L. R. Marshall to Samuel Jaudon, 13 November 1835. Cashier's Letterbook. BUSN, LLMVC.

105 Nicholas Biddle to R. M. Blatchford, 19 August 1835, p. 394. Letterbooks. NBP, LC. McCulloch, *Dictionary*, Vol. I, pp. 160-1.

106 Temin, *Jacksonian Economy*, pp. 75-6. Lamoreaux, *Insider Lending*, Table 3.3, p. 61.

107 General Ledger No. I, 'Profit and Loss', folio 65. General Ledger No. II, 'Profit and Loss', folio 120. BUSN, LLMVC.

108 23 April 1835; Bank Notes Circulating, $1,362,310, Branch Drafts Circulating $638,185. 30 July 1835; Branch Notes, $1,440,560, and Branch Drafts, $1,193,845. *State of the Bank*. Thomas Henderson to J. Andrews, 1st. Asst. Cashier, Philadelphia, 18 December 1835: 'The Branch Drafts of $20 No. 7301 to 7700 filled up and endorsed by J. Foster & No. 7701 to 7800 filled up and endorsed by J. D. Henderson dated 30 June 1834 have been placed in the hands of the Teller for circulation'. Cashier's Letterbook. BUSN, LLMVC.

109 McCulloch, *Dictionary*, Vol. I, pp. 160-161. Smith, *Economic Aspects*, pp. 178-230.

110 But see Temin, *Jacksonian Economy*, pp. 71-82.

111 *Ibid.*, pp. 80-2. Long dated bills in the China trade are discussed by Hugh Rockoff, 'Money, Prices, and Banks In The Jacksonian Era', in *The Reinterpretation Of*

American Economic History, ed. by Robert William Fogel and Stanley L. Engerman (New York: Harper & Row, 1971), pp. 453-4.

112 Hiddy, *House of Baring*, pp. 110-12.

113 General Ledger No. I, 'Cash Account', folios 31-42, 450-458. General Ledger No. II, 'Cash Account', folios 72-90, 300-302. BUSN, LLMVC.

114 Schweikart, *Banking In The American South*, Table I, pp. 65-6.

115 John Sergeant to Nicholas Biddle, 28 April 1838, No. 16,088, NBP, LC.

116 'An Act to repeal the State Tax on Real and Personal Property, and to continue and extend the Improvements of the States, by Railroads and Canals, and to charter a state bank, to be called the 'United States Bank". Secs. 2-15. Act 22, pp. 36-47. 18 February 1836. *Laws of the General Assembly of the Commonwealth of Pennsylvania, Passed at the Session of 1835-36* (Harrisburg: Theo. Fenn, 1836); Hammond, *Banks and Politics*, pp. 440-1. Smith, *Economic Aspects*, pp. 178-80. Thomas Payne Govan, *Nicholas Biddle, Nationalist and Public Banker, 1786-1844* (Chicago: University of Chicago Press, 1959), pp. 293-5.

117 Nicholas Biddle to Joseph McIlvain, ? March 1837, p. 161. Letterbooks. NBP, LC.

118 Memorandum from Nicholas Biddle to Daniel Webster, ? February 1838, p. 354. Nicholas Biddle to John Sergeant, 6, 26 April 1838, pp. 393, 410. Nicholas Biddle to J. R. Poinsett, 11 July 1838, p. 473. Nicholas Biddle to R. M. Blatchford, 31 July 1838, p. 480. Nicholas Biddle to Samuel Jaudon, 3 August 1838, p. 483. Letterbooks. NBP, LC. Charles Macalester to Nicholas Biddle, 2, 3 May 1838, No.16,132, No.16,158. NBP, LC. For a discussion of the litigation in the commercial Court of New Orleans, see Richard Holcombe Kilbourne, Jr., *Louisiana Commercial Law, The Antebellum Period* (Baton Rouge: Paul M. Herbert Law Center Publications Institute, 1980), pp. 157-202. It appears that the last installment owed to the government was in fact paid subsequent to the assignments at great sacrifice. Thus the only claim which the government continued to assert was the damages claimed by the Bank on the dishonored 'French Bill' which had been deducted from the settlement reached in 1837 between the old bank and the Treasury.

119 Joseph L. Roberts to Thomas S. Taylor, Secretary of the Robinson Trustees, 10 July 1846, Letterpress Book No. 4, inserts at the end of the manuscript. John Bacon et. al. Trustees Papers, hereafter cited BTP, LLMVC.

120 Nicholas Biddle to James Erwin, 25 June 1836, p. 46. Nicholas Biddle to Thomas Urquhart, 1 October 1836, p. 71. Nicholas Biddle to John Minturn, 2 January 1837. Letterbooks. NBP, LC. James Erwin to Nicholas Biddle, 23 March 1837, No.13,734. John P. Erwin to Nicholas Biddle, 5 December 1838, No.17,127. Nicholas Biddle to C. A. Davis, 23 December 1841. S. Allen to Nicholas Biddle, 30 December 1841. Nicholas Biddle to Samuel Jaudon, 8 September 1842. A. F. Schwab to Nicholas Biddle, 30 September 1842. Nicholas Biddle to Samuel Jaudon, 3 October 1842. NBP, LC. *Foster & McAllister vs. Bank of New Orleans*, 21 *Louisiana Annual Reports*, 338.

121 W. J. Jones to Nicholas Biddle, 4 May 1837, No.13,979. NBP, LC. 'I suspect very strongly a design on the part of the Van Buren charlatans who have managed or mismanaged the Planters & Merchants and the Mobile Bank which are certainly

insolvent in my opinion, to offer you one or both of the charters of those institutions, and I feel that I owe it to you, as I advised the purchase of the former before I knew its condition, to warn you against touching either'.

122 'Assignment by the President, Directors and Company of the Bank of the United States to John Bacon A. Symington and Thomas Robins, Trustees, at Philadelphia, June 7, 1841', p. 3. BTP, LLMVC. Total stock purchases in the Commercial Bank of Natchez were $446,600. The Bank also had stock in the Planters Bank of Mississippi to the amount of $45,700; the Agricultural Bank, $1,300; the Commercial Bank of Manchester, $6,100; the Commercial Bank of Rodney, $17,400; the Grand Gulf Rail Road and Banking company, $200,506; the Bank of Port Gibson, $21,300; and the West Feliciana Rail Road and Banking Company, $93,200. 'Assignment', BTP, LLMVC.

123 Over the course of the summer of 1841, three trusts were established at Philadelphia and Bank assets transferred to them for the security of various creditors. The Dundas Trust was intended to secure the banks of Philadelphia which were left holding upwards of $5 million of post notes of the late Bank. The Robinson Trust enjoyed a rather nominal existence, being the recipient of the residue of property not transferred to the other two trusts. The highly controversial loans of Nicholas Biddle and Daniel Webster fell to this trust. The Dundas Trust encompassed largely Pennsylvania claims. The Bacon Trust, the most important of the three trusts, was to secure the late Bank's notes and received all of the best claims in jurisdictions outside of Pennsylvania. All of the assets of the Bank's New York agency fell to this trust. Those assets consisted of bills and notes with an assigned value of $435,372.74. Most of that paper had been negotiated by firms involved in the cotton trade that had suspended along with their correspondents at New Orleans elsewhere in the South. The claims at the Merchants Bank of New Orleans aggregated to $2,245,223.76 and consisted principally of bills receivable. 'Assignment', BTP, LLMVC.

On 11 April 1840, discounts of the principal New Orleans banks were as follows: the New Orleans Canal & Banking Company, $3,201,941; the Citizens Bank, $3,984,907; The Gas Light and Banking Company, $2,565,422; the Bank of Louisiana, $4,669,125; the Louisiana State Bank, $2,619,358; and the Union Bank, $6,341,984. *Price Current* 11 April 1840. See also George D. Green, *Finance And Economic Development In The Old South, Louisiana Banking, 1804-1861* (Stanford: Stanford University Press, 1972), Table c.I, pp. 202-204. Clearly the United States Bank had not been a large player in the New Orleans market after the expiration of its federal charter.

124 In January 1837, nine Mississippi banks reported loans and discounts of $24,351,414. This sum includes both local discounts as well as purchases of domestic exchange. McCulloch, *Commercial Dictionary*, Vol. I, p. 156. Marvin Bentley's compilations show ten banks with $26 million dollars of assets in December 1836. Purchases for exchange accounts aggregated to 43 percent of the total assets. It is reasonable to assume that the assets of the three Natchez banks, the Planters, the Agricultural, and the Commercial, account for at least one-half of all the loans and discounts in the state. Bentley, 'Incorporated Banks', Table I, p. 391. Bentley notes that growth in the number of banks in the state, as well as total assets, was

particularly rapid in 1836. 'However, as a percentage of total assets, banking assets did not increase until 1837. Between 1831 and 1836, this ratio remained relatively low with the level of 1836 being the same as the level in 1831. The increase in the ratio from .45 in 1836 to .65 in 1837 was due to the banks having to convert their unpaid bills of exchange to banking assets. Accordingly, this increase in the ratio was not an autonomous change by the banks but followed from a break down in the structure of credit which existed before 1837'. p. 394. Bentley could find little evidence to support the charge of 'irresponsible practices by the banks'. p. 398. See also 'Discounted Notes', folios 95-108, and 'Domestic Exchange', folios 116-24, General Ledger No. I., Commercial Bank of Natchez collection, hereafter cited CBNC, LLMVC.

125 McCulloch, *Commercial Dictionary*, Vol. I, p. 157. Bentley indicates that as of December 1837, 13 banks had total exchange purchases of only $5.19 million, down from $11.33 million of such purchases by 10 banks in December 1836. But the banks were also holding $6.15 million dollars of exchange under protest in December 1837. The banks then had actually contracted their operations over the course of 1837, thus preparing for the resumption of specie payments. Bentley, 'Incorporated Banks', Table I, p. 391.

126 Bentley's calculations seem to confirm this. Exchange purchases nearly doubled from December 1834 to December 1835. The Bank of the United States' exchange purchases reached $4 million in January and February of 1836. Bentley also shows a rise in local discounts over the course of 1836. (Granted, the number of banks reporting also increased that year.) The role of the Bank of the United States in stimulating the growth of local credit facilities would, nevertheless, seem to be observable. Bentley, 'Incorporated Banks', Table I, page 391.

127 The Depreciation of Mississippi Bank Paper In The New Orleans Market

DATE	SPECIE	U. S. BANK NOTES	PLANTERS, AGRICULTURAL, & COMMERCIAL BANKS	
1840			DEMAND NOTES	POST NOTES
7 March	3 ½ to 4 ½% PM.	Par to 1% Disct.	4 to 6% Discount	25 to 30% Disct.
4 April	5 ½ to 6 ½% PM.	Par to 1% Prem.	4 to 6% Disct.	30 to 40% Disct.
10 October	1 ½ to 2 ½% PM.	same	5 to 6% Disct.	*5 to 20% Disct.
12 December	2 to 3% PM.	Par to 1% Disct.	5 to 18% Disct.	same
1841				
6 March	6 to 7%	10 to 15% Disct.		*5 to 22% Disct.
24 December	same	35 to 37 ½% Disct.		*5 to 30% Disct.

*The widening spread indicates that the relative value of Mississippi bank paper varied considerably from bank to bank. The notes of the Commercial Bank were at a discount of 5 percent, whereas the notes of the Planters Bank were quoted at a 30 percent discount. Source: New Orleans *Price Current*.

128 'An Act Authorizing the Banks in this State to issue post notes, and for other purposes'. 12 May 1837. *Laws of The State of Mississippi, Passed at an Adjourned Session of the Legislature Held in the Town of Jackson, In January, 1837* (Jackson: Printed by G. R. & J. S. Fall, 1837), pp. 175-8.

129 Bills of Exchange Domestic', folios 31-35; 'Notes and Bills Discounted', folios 48-50. General Ledger No. II, BUSN, LLMVC.

130 Bentley, 'Incorporated Banks'. Table I, p. 391. Schweikart, *Banking in the American South*, pp. 176-8.

131 Thomas Henderson, to John Sommerville, 23 October 1835. Thomas Henderson to Peter Bacot, 2 January 1836. Cashier's Letterbook. BUSN, LLMVC.

132 Thomas Henderson to James Saul, 3 February 1836. Cashier's Letterbook. BUSN, LLMVC.

133 Thomas Barrett & Co. to Jackson Riddle & Co., 16 March 1836. 'Records of Antebellum Southern Planters from the Revolution through the Civil War'. Kenneth M. Stampp, General Editor. Series J. Selections from the Southern Historical Collection Manuscript Department, Library of the University of North Carolina at Chapel Hill. Part 5: Louisiana. Reel 19. Microfilm copy in the possession of LLMVC. Hereafter cited JRC, UNC. McCulloch, *Commercial Dictionary*, Vol. I, pp. 159-60.

134 Thomas Henderson to Peter Bacot, 31 December 1835. Thomas Henderson to J. Callendar, 4 January 1836. Cashier's Letterbook. BUSN, LLMVC.

135 'Bills of Exchange, Domestic, Protested', General Ledger No. II, folios 64-66. Journal, 31 March 1836, 'Protested Exchange to Sundries', to Domestic Bills for No. 5890 Bogart, Hoopes $2,699. 1 April 1836, 'Protested Exchange to Sundries', to Domestic bills 6091 Bogart, Hoopes $6,000 and 6092 Bogart, Hoopes $6,000. 9 April 1836, 'Protested Exchange to Sundries', to Domestic Bills returned by Gas Bank 5910 Bogart, Hoopes $2,083.33, 5912 Bogart, Hoopes $2,083.33, 6120 Bogart, Hoopes $1,240. BUSN, LLMVC.

136 Journal, 16 January 1836, 'Cash to Sundries', Domestic Exchange Paid Here, $120,253.35. This item is composed of 37 bills drawn at Natchez on Bogart, Hoopes at New Orleans during the summer and fall of 1835 and purchased by the branch. Deposit Scratcher, 16 January 1836. BUSN, LLMVC.

137 Thomas Henderson to James Saul, 19 February 1836. Cashier's Letterbook. BUSN, LLMVC.

138 'Bills of Exchange, Domestic, Protested', folios 65 and 67. 'Protested Notes', folios 372-4. 'Bills of Exchange, Domestic', folio 37. 'Discounted Notes', folio 560. General Ledger No. II. The sum of $700,000 included accrued interest and damages for 5 years, as well as protested exchange purchased from other syndicates in 1835. BUSN, LLMVC.

139 Thomas Henderson to Samuel Jaudon. 27 February 1837. Cashier's Letterbook. BUSN, LLMVC.

140 Thomas Henderson to Samuel Jaudon, 30 December 1836. Thomas Henderson to Samuel Jaudon, 6 March 1837. Proposition to the U. S. Bank by J. H. Moore & Co. 4 March 1837. B. Hughes to Thomas Henderson, 27 March 1837. Cashier's Letterbook. BUSN, LLMVC.

141 Thomas Henderson to Samuel Jaudon, 27 February 1837. Cashier's Letterbook. BUSN, LLMVC. Temin, *Jacksonian Economy*, pp. 120-9, 136-9, 146-7. Sir John Clapham, *The Bank of England, A History* (Cambridge: Cambridge University Press, 1944), Vol. II, pp. 150-61. McCulloch, *Commercial Dictionary*, Vol. I, pp. 159-61.

142 Nicholas Biddle to Lewis Williams, 23 March 1836, p. 15. Nicholas Biddle to John Williams, 23 March 1836, p. 15. Letterbooks. NBP, LC.

143 McCulloch, *Commercial Dictionary*, Vol. I, p. 665. 'Loans in Europe':

Huth & Co.		
Redeemable in 1847	£200,000	$888,888.9
Interest at 5% payable in April & Oct.		
Dennison & Co.		
Redeemable 15 April 1841	£400,000	$1,777,777.78
Redeemable 15 April 1842	£400,000	1,777,777.78
Interest at 6% payable April & Oct.		
Hope & Co.		
Redeemable Jany. 1845	[Guilders]10,000,000	$4,000,000.00
Interest at 5% payable at 5% Jany. & July.		
Rothchild		
Redeemable 15 Oct. 1841	[French Francs]11,385,000	$2,134,687.50
Redeemable Oct. 15, 1842	[French Francs]11,385,000	$2,134,687.50
	22,770,000	$4,469,375.00
Less Debenture purchased by B.U.S.		
	[French Francs]569,250	$4,162,640.63
TOTAL		$12,607,085.09
Bonds in Europe		$775,550.09

Source: Liabilities of the United States Bank, 1 October 1840. John Bacon et. al. Trustees, 1390-A, Fidelity-Philadelphia trust Co. Collection, The Historical Society of Pennsylvania, hereafter cited BT, F-P, HSP.

144 Bray Hammond writes: '[t]he lesser evil, in [Biddle's] … opinion was to have the bank take the risk in the debtor interest, general welfare being more dependent on that course for the moment than of the creditor interest. Posterity, in similar circumstances, seems to have agreed with him'. Hammond, *Banks and Politics*, p. 470. About the cotton speculations, Temin writes that '[t]he motives for this venture are not altogether clear; some historians say that Biddle was trying altruistically to raise the price of cotton, and others, that he was expanding his business to replace the lost business of the Federal Government. In any case, his attempts to purchase cotton helped to raise its price'. Temin, *Jacksonian Economy*, p. 150. He cites W. B. Smith, Bray Hammond, and R. C. O. Matthews, *A Study in Trade-Cycle History*. In the Biddle Papers will be found this intriguing letter from [?] Swift to Nicholas Biddle about the firm of Thomas Biddle & Co. dated 12 April 1841. 'If you have any idea of alluding to the settlement made by the Bank with Thos. Biddle & Co., for one I could say to not, considering the immense amount of the Loans-I think the Committee have passed them by as leniently as they well could, altho' you were not present when it was agreed to take the Stocks, and make an additional advance, still I must think it was understood to be your wish, and that you stated Thos. Biddle & Co. must not think of making an assignment. I had just returned from New Orleans, and was at that time considered but a cipher, as to the management of the house, the loans were very enormous & many of the Stocks of doubtful character.

I cannot think they were ever made through my agency, or on any credit of my poor name, but of this it would be needless to speak, their existence cost me many an anxious hour and at this late date I can not justify to myself the granting of so much to one house. It is therefore I say better to let the matter rest, if it will, as it is'. NBP, LC.

145 'Assignment', BTP, LLMVC. William L. Coker, *Repudiation and Reaction-Tilghman M. Tucker and the Mississippi Bond Question* (Floral Park, New York: Graphicopy, 1969). Dallas C. Dickey, *Seargent S. Prentiss, Whig Orator of the Old South* (Baton Rouge: Louisiana State University Press, 1945) pp. 198-228.

146 'Discounted Notes', General Ledger No. 1, folio 101. 'Domestic Exchange', General Ledger No. 1, folio 120. On 30 June 1838, the balance against the Canton Branch, in favor of the parent bank, was $429,775.38, but the bulk of the balance appears to have accrued from exchange purchases in connection with the bank's advances on cotton. 'Branch at Canton', General Ledger No. 2, folio 154. CBNC, LLMVC.

147 'Exchange Account [for the B. U. S.]', General Ledger No. 1, folio 480. 'Exchange Account', General Ledger No. 1, folio 137. The 'Profit and Loss Account' was composed of the following deposited items: income from exchange, discounts, interest and profits remitted from the branches at Canton, Holmesville, and Shieldsboro. Debits from this account were for expenses, dividends, and allocations to the surplus. 'Profit and Loss Account', General Ledger No. 1, folio 552. General Ledger No. 2, folio 209. CBNC, LLMVC.

148 'Exchange Account [for the Bank of the United States]', General Ledger No. 1, folio 480, 19 November 1836. Journal, 19 November 1836. CBNC, LLMVC. Thomas Henderson to Samuel Jaudon, 2 December 1836, Cashier's Letterbook. BUSN, LLMVC.

149 New Orleans *Price Current*. Schneider, *Wahrungen der Welt I*.

150 Bodenhorn, 'Capital Mobility'. He writes: 'If the interest charge on sight bills was essentially zero - that is, the discount represented only the commission and collections costs - interest rates on 60-day bills can be calculated from the spread between long and short rates'. p. 587. But assuming sixty-day bills were inferior to sight bills, then the 'spread' would be composed of factors besides the time value of money, such as the relative demand for this relatively low risk species of paper.

151 John Stuart Mill, *The Principles of Political Economy* (London, Parker, 1848), Book 3, Chapter 20. <http://socserv2.socsci.mcmaster.ca/~econ/ugcm/3ll3/mill/prin/book3/bk3ch20>

152 A limited series of buy rates for sixty-day bills on the North and sell rates for sight bills on the North for the New Orleans branch of the Bank of the United States will be found in the New Orleans *Price Current* between 1827 and 1834.

DATE	SIGHT BILLS, SELL	SIXTY DAY BILLS, BUY
1827		
March 24	½% Premium	2 ½% Discount
April 28	par	3% Discount
August 18	same	same
1828		
April 12	same	2 ½% Discount
June 28	same	2 to 2 ½% Discount
October 18	½ to 1% Premium	2% Discount
1829		
June 6	par	2 ½% Discount
December 5	½% Premium	same
1830		
April 10	par	2 ½% Discount
July 24	½% Premium	2% Discount
1833		
August 17	¼% Premium	1 ¼% Discount
October 19	par	1 ½% Discount
November 22	same	1 ¾% Discount
1834		
March 15	¾% Premium	2% Discount
April 5	same	2 ½% Discount
July 19	not drawing	1 ½% Discount

The bank's own charge for the difference between the rate it purchased at and the rate it sold at was always 1.5 percent. It would seem that the interest component disappeared altogether in 1833. It would be logical to assume that the Bank of the United States had the pick of the best paper in the market when it purchased and commanded the best prices for its checks when it drew on the North. Because the western branches generally had large balances in their favor at the New Orleans branch, sight checks on western cities drawn by the branch generally commanded a much larger premium than was the case with sight checks on New York and Philadelphia. The premium for checks on Cincinnati for example was 1.5 to 2 percent premium, more than double the premium for checks on New York. It was an inconvenience for the New Orleans branch to create more liabilities with the Cincinnati branch. The New Orleans branch also paid better prices for sixty-day bills on western cities than it paid for sixty-day bills on New York. The differentials are attributable to the course of trade, not changing rates of interest.

153 Byrne, Hermann & Co. to Jackson, Riddle & Co., 24 May 1836. Byrne, Hermann & Co. to Jackson, Riddle & Co., 1 June 1836. JRC, UNC.

154 Nicholas Biddle to Genl. S. Smith, 11 January 1833, p. 375. 'In fact the real loan is what is called the local loans, for the Bills of Exchange are in great measure drawn on persons out of State for produce sent to them'. Nicholas Biddle to Manuel Eyre, 13 February 1832, p. 419. Nicholas Biddle to J. D. Watmaugh, 16 February 1833, p. 436. Letterbooks. NBP, LC.

155 Kilbourne, *Louisiana Commercial Law*, Appendix A, pp. 208-9. The Lizardi group has been mentioned in a number of secondary works. Stanley Chapman, *The*

Rise Of Merchant Banking (London: Unwin Hyman Ltd., 1984), pp. 11, 39, 41, 73; Stanley Chapman, *Merchant Enterprise In Britain* (Cambridge: Cambridge University Press, 1992), pp. 71, 161, 166; Clapham, *The Bank of England*, vol. 2, pp. 152-58l; Hidy, *The House of Baring*, pp. 221-33.

156 New Orleans, *Price Current*, various numbers.

157 Byrne, Hermann & Co. to Jackson, Riddle & Co., 16 June 1836. Byrne, Hermann & Co., to Jackson, Riddle & Co., 14 June 1836. JRC, UNC.

158 Byrne, Hermann & Co. to Jackson, Riddle & Co., 17, 18 February, 3 March 1836. Thomas Barrett & Co. to Jackson, Riddle & Co., 18 March, 1 April, 7, 26 July, 8, 29 August, 15 September, 13 November 1836. JRC, UNC.

159 *Bogart, Hoopes vs. Byrne, Hermann & Co.*, First Judicial District Court, Orleans Parish, Docket No. 15,908, 20 April 1838. Louisiana Division, New Orleans Public Library.

160 Thomas Barrett & Co. to Jackson, Riddle & Co., 29 August 1836. JRC, UNC. New Orleans *Price Current*. Schneider, *Wahrungen der Welt I*.

161 Quotations at New Orleans and New York

DATE	BILLS ON LONDON	SIXTY DAY SIGHT BILLS ON NEW YORK	SIGHT BILLS ON N.O.
NEW ORLEANS			**NEW YORK**
1836			
1 October	8 to 8 ½% Premium	2% Discount	3 ½% Discount
15 October	7 ¼ @ 8 ½% Premium	1 to 2% Discount	same
5 November	7 ½ @ 8 ¾% Premium	same	same
10 December	9 ½ to 9 ¼% Premium	1 to 1 ½% Discount	same
31 December	9 to 9 ¼% Premium	1 ½% Discount	same
1837			
14 January	8 ¾ to 9 ¼% Premium	1 to 1 ½% Discount	same
4 February	10 to 10 ½% Premium	same	same
25 February	10 to 11% Premium	same	same
18 March	same	same	4% Discount
1 April	9 to 9 ½% Premium	same	same
15 April	same	same	same
22 April	same	same	same
29 April	nominal	nominal	same
June			8 % Discount
July			11 ½% Discount
August			10 ½% Discount
September			7 ½% Discount
14 October	17 to 20% Premium		5% Discount
2 December	16 to 18% Premium		2 ½% Discount
1838			
24 February	8 ¼ to 8 ½% Premium	½% Discount	
31 March	9 ½ to 10% Premium	2 ¼ to 3% Premium	5% Discount
21 April	11 % Premium	5 ½ to 6 ½% Premium	
5 May	11 to 14% Premium	6% Premium	8% Discount

Source: New Orleans *Price Current*. Schneider, *Wahrungen der Welt I*.

162 Thomas Barrett & Co. to Jackson, Riddle & Co., 28 September 1836. JRC, UNC.

163 Thomas Henderson to Samuel Jaudon, 14 March 1837, Cashier's Letterbook. BUSN, LLMVC. Roswell L. Colt to Nicholas Biddle, 17 March 1837, No. 13,698. Roswell L. Colt to Nicholas Biddle, 21 March 1837, No 13,713. NBP, LC.

164 This view is expressed by Hammond, *Banks and Politics*, pp. 455-7, and Govan, *Nicholas Biddle*, pp. 300-3.

165 Temin, *Jacksonian Economy*, pp. 123, 125, 128-36.

166 Clapham, *The Bank of England*, Vol. 2, 150-61. Temin, *Jacksonian Economy*, pp. 144-45.

167 Temin, *Jacksonian Economy*, p. 144.

168 Nicholas Biddle to Baring Brothers, ? January 1837, No. 13,461. NBP, LC.

169 Roswell L. Colt to Nicholas Biddle, 5 March 1837, No. 13,629. NBP, LC.

170 Roswell L. Colt to Nicholas Biddle, 25 March 1837, No. 13,736. NBP, LC.

171 Roswell L. Colt to Nicholas Biddle, 25 March 1837, No. 13,761. NBP, LC.

172 Roswell L. Colt to Nicholas Biddle, 27 March 1837, No. 13,797. NBP, LC.

173 Manuel Eyre to Nicholas Biddle, 31 March 1837, No. 13,797. Roswell L. Colt to Nicholas Biddle, 7 April 1837, No. 13,829. NBP, LC.

174 Roswell L. Colt to Nicholas Biddle, ? April 1837, No. 13,841. NBP, LC.

175 Roswell L. Colt to Nicholas Biddle, 18 April 1837, No. 18,893. NBP, LC.

176 Temin, *Jacksonian Economy*, p. 114; *Denton vs. Commercial and Rail Road Bank of Vicksburg*, 13 *Louisiana Reports*, 486 (1839).

177 Stephen Duncan to Jackson, Todd & Co., 8 April 1839. JRC, UNC.

178 Nicholas Biddle to John Minturn, 2 January 1837, p. 99. Letterbooks. NBP, LC.

179 Temin, *Jacksonian Economy*, Table 3.3, 'The Supply of Money and Its determinants, 1820-39', p. 71.

180 New Orleans *Price Current*, 22 April, 14 October 1837, 24 February 1838.

181 Nicholas Biddle to C. B. Penrose, 28 March 1836, p. 18. Nicholas Biddle to N. Allen, 29 July 1836, p. 52. Nicholas Biddle to J. L. Barbour, 30 August 1836, p. 64. Letterbooks. NBP, LC.

182 Nicholas Biddle to John Minturn, 2 January 1837, p. 99. Letterbooks, NBP, LC. The subject of state regulation of interest rates is discussed in Bodenhorn and Rockoff, 'Regional Interest Rates'. Table 5.6 'Legal Interest Rates and Usury Penalties, 1841', p. 179. But see also Wright, *Hamilton Unbound*, pp. 19-26. Whether charges for 'exchange' were effective in circumventing municipal regulations respecting usury was an old subject. John Steven Rogers, *The Early History Of The Law Of Bills And Notes, A Study Of The Origins Of Anglo-American Commercial Law* (Cambridge: Cambridge University Press, 1995) pp. 70-4, 89-90. *Daniel W. Coxe vs. Charles N. Rowley*, 12 *Robinson's Reports* (La.) 276 (1845). 'A loan of depreciated bank notes, payable by the borrower in money, at a rate which, added to the depreciation, will exceed the highest rate of conventional interest, is undoubtedly usurious'. The test devised by the Louisiana Supreme Court in this case was whether the loan of depreciated paper was in fact worth the equivalent of specie to the borrower on the date of the contract in settling a claim or claims against himself. This decision may be extended by analogy to include all commercial paper. However, in the case of Bank of *Louisiana vs. Briscoe*, 3 *Louisiana Annual Reports*, 157 (1848) the Louisiana Supreme court more or less excluded commercial paper from the usury prohibition. 'The provisions of Article 2895 of the Civil Code, establishing the

rate of conventional interest, has always been confined to loans of money, and held not to apply to the purchase and sale of promissory notes, bills of exchange or other negotiable instruments, nor of credits'. Presumably an exchange charge would not be included in any calculation of interest for purposes of establishing a usurious loan.

183 John Gamble to Nicholas Biddle, 22 April 1837, No. 13,914. NBP, LC. 'Assignment', BTP, LLMVC.

184 John Sommerville to Nicholas Biddle, 28 April 1837, No. 13,951, NBP, LC.

185 Stephen Duncan to William J. Minor, 7 August 1839, Box 2, folder 12, William J. Minor and Family Papers, LLMVC, hereafter sited WJMFP, LLMVC.

186 The removal of federal deposits from the Second Bank of the United States provoked much criticism of the Jackson Administration. One alleged pernicious consequence was that the depository banks immediately lent out the deposits they received from the government. That was all but inevitable given the constitution of the monetary and banking systems in antebellum America. The depository banks in the west, for example, received tenders from the government in the form of claims on other banks, often located in eastern commercial cities. Such tenders could only be realized if the depository sold those claims to its customers in need of paper suitable for remittance. Purchasers generally tendered a bank's own notes or 'cashed' a bill of exchange at the same institution in order to purchase checks on New York or Philadelphia. When the Treasury requested the depository to cash a warrant, the depository bank did so by purchasing bills of exchange on the location where the order was to be paid and then tendered a check drawn against the proceeds to the bearer of the Treasury warrant. It would have been nonsensical for a depository bank in the west to simply 'hold' the paper originally tendered to it when the government made a deposit until such time as the government withdrew the deposit. Such a strategy would have left the Bank of the United States as the government's sole depository. It was, then, impossible for the state bank depositories to ever realize those deposits without making loans by cashing bills of exchange drawn by those in need of sight checks on points east. Given the heavy demand in the west in 1834, 1835, and 1836 for remittance paper on points east it is probable that government deposits in the west may have facilitated a more orderly contraction of credit facilities which was well underway after 1834.

187 Nicholas Biddle to P. P. F. Degrand, 20 May 1837, p. 198. Letterbooks, NBP, LC.

188 Temin, *Jacksonian Economy*, p. 116. Roswell L. Colt to Nicholas Biddle, 22 May 1837, No. 14,100, NBP, LC.

189 Thomas Henderson to J. Andrews, 25 June 1838. Thomas Henderson to M. Robinson, 13 September 1838. Cashier's Letterbook. BUSN, LLMVC.

190 Nicholas Biddle to C. A. Davis, 20 September 1837. p. 258. Letterbooks, NBP, LC.

191 Bills of exchange with collateral securities attached to them began to appear in the New Orleans money market in the late 1830s. Whether a holder could retain the bill of lading after acceptance by the drawee was the central issue presented to Louisiana's supreme court in the case of *Lanfear vs. Blossman*, 1 *Louisiana Annual Reports* 148 (1846). This case is discussed at length in Kilbourne, *Louisiana Commercial Law*, pp. 150-6. After 1840 the New Orleans *Price Current* regularly

reported quotations for 'clear bills' and bills with attached shipping documents. Strangely enough, clear bills always commanded a better price than bills with collateral attached to them. That only underscores the importance of market forces in grading bills of exchange. It also tends to reinforce earlier contentions that valuations for sight and sixty-day bills included factors (supply, demand, risk) besides the time value of money.

192 Roswell L. Colt to Nicholas Biddle, 26 June 1837, No. 14,267, NBP, LC.

193 That letter is referred to in a letter from W. H. Shelton to Nicholas Biddle, dated November 8, 1837, No. 15,085. Nicholas Biddle to George D. Blaikie, 2 December 1837, No. 15,086. NBP. LC.

194 John B. Byrne to Washington Jackson, 3 November 1837. JRC, UNC. Thomas Henderson to Samuel Jaudon, 27 February 1837. Cashier's Letterbook. BUSN, LLMVC.

195 May Humphreys to Edward C. Biddle, 15 December 1837, No. 15,129. May Humphreys to Nicholas Biddle, 1 January 1838, No. 15,292. May Humphreys to Nicholas Biddle, 20 July 1838, No. 16,529. Edward C. Biddle to Nicholas Biddle, 5 August 1838, No. 16,589. O. Barber to Nicholas Biddle, 8 October 1838, No. 16,831. May Humphreys to Nicholas Biddle, 14 October 1838, No. 16,867. May Humphreys to Nicholas Biddle, 6, 20, 30 November, 1, 14 December 1838, Nos. 16,973, 17,048, 17,050, 17,163. NBP, LC.

196 Bennett, Ferriday & Co. to Washington Jackson, 21 January 1838. JRC, UNC.

197 James Hagarty to Nicholas Biddle, 15 December 1837, No. 15,131. NBP, LC. 'Advances on Shipments of Cotton', General Ledger No. 1, folio 635; General Ledger No. 2, folio 63. 'Cotton Account', General Ledger No. 1, folio 621; General Ledger No. 2, folios 249-51. 'W. & J. Brown in Account', General Ledger No. 1, folio 627; General Ledger no. 2, folio 257, 'Baring Brothers in Account', General Ledger No. 1, folio 624. CBNC, LLMVC. Nicholas Biddle to Edward C. Biddle, 1 October 1838, p. 511. Letterbooks. NBP, LC. 'He [J. C. Wilkins, Prest. of the Planters Bank] told me his Bank had sent last year 60,000 bales of cotton to Dennisons, on which they lost a very large sum'. William J. Minor to Messrs. W. & J. Brown, 2 November 1837. 'The board of Directors of the [Agricultural] Bank having concluded to consign the cotton shipped to England on A/C of this institution to your House, with the understanding, however, that your house in New York will make no charge for negotiating our bills should we require. Now I have the pleasure of informing you, you will receive about 25,000 bales during the season'. Letterpress book. WJMFP, LLMVC. The Agricultural Bank, the Planters Bank, and the Commercial Bank shipped, then, 110,000 bales of cotton to England. Those shipments accounted for at least one-third of all the cotton sent from the state in the late fall of 1837 and the winter and spring of 1838. Combined with shipments from other banks in the state, it is safe to assume that five or six banks in the state gained controlled at least half of the crop. The banks 'advanced' on the shipments; all the losses sustained by the consignees in England in the spring and summer of 1838 were charged back to the banks in Mississippi, which in turn claimed the difference from their customers. It is easy to see how many in Mississippi came to regard the banks in a less than friendly light. The arrangement certainly left a great potential for overreaching by the banks. Even as

the banks advanced directly on cotton they were attempting to shrink their port-folios. Ultimately their customers were left with an enlargement of their debts and drastically curtailed credit facilities.

198 George Dickey to Washington Jackson, 19, 20, 21, 23, 26 March, 10, 13, 16, 17, 18, 20, 21 April 1838. JRC, UNC.

199 'Advances On Shipments Of Cotton', General Ledger No. 1. folio 635; General Ledger No. 2, folio 62. CBNC, LLMVC. May Humphreys to Nicholas Biddle, 20, 24, 30 November, 1, 14 December 1838, Nos. 17,048, 17,049, 17,050, 17,163. NBP, LC.

200 Stephen Duncan to William J. Minor, 27 August 1839, Box 2, Folder 12, WJMFP, LLMVC. 'I hope you have come to the conclusion, that you ought to be *satisfied* that you did not attempt to '*make 50,000$*' out of your knowledge that the crop was to be a short one. The *attempt* would have lost 3 times 50,000$-Abijah Fisk *wanted* to make 50,000$ & he lost 200,000$. H. P. P. & Co. *wanted* to make 15,000$ & they lost 40,000$. Mr. [J. U.] Payne *wanted* to make 80,000$ and he will lost 180,000$. I thought I would have 38,000$ to draw for, after I reached Philada. I drew for 9000$ and I will have 15,000 to remit. Many bills will come back [under protest]'. May Humphreys to Nicholas Biddle, 25 February 1839, No, 17,726, NBP, LC. '[A]ll the Mississippi Banks, whose interest the House [of Humphreys & Biddle] protected by advancing upwards of L 700,000-and holding their cotton from four to eight months, by which they gained an immense benefit to their Institutions and Planters, are now sending the cotton under their control to other houses, having agents on the spot to advance to them which is not only disgustingly ungrateful, but somewhat mortifying'.

201 May Humphreys to Nicholas Biddle, 2 October, 24 December 1839, Nos. 19,992, 20,155. T. Dunlap, Prest. to Bevan & Humphreys, 5 February 1840, No. 20,365. NBP, LC.

202 'Assignment', BTP, LLMVC.

203 Nicholas Biddle to Samuel Jaudon, 21 August, 2 October 1838, pp. 496, 514. Letterbooks. NBP, LC.

204 Nicholas Biddle to Samuel Jaudon, 31 August 1838, p. 496. Letterbooks. NBP, LC.

205 Nicholas Biddle to Samuel Jaudon, 2 October 1838, p. 514. Letterbooks. NBP, LC.

206 Nicholas Biddle to Samuel Jaudon, 19 October 1838, p. 532. Letterbooks. NBP, LC. See also 'Bond Files', MDAH.

207 Nicholas Biddle to Samuel Jaudon, 19 October 1838, p. 532. Letterbooks. NBP, LC.

208 Nicholas Biddle to W. W. Frazier, 29 September 1838. Letterbooks. NBP, LC.

209 Nicholas Biddle to J. C. Wilkins, 8 October 1838. Letterbooks. NBP, LC.

210 'Assignment', BTP, LLMVC. 'Assets of Bank of the United States, October 1, 1840'. BT, F-P, HSP. Stocks Deposited For Loans in Europe. Mississippi 5 per cents-$3,086,000. Presumably the balance of bonds had been sold to investors. McGrane, *Foreign Bondholders*, p. 198.

211 Nicholas Biddle to John Minturn, 28 December 1838, p. 39. Letterbooks. NBP, LC.

212 Nicholas Biddle to S. S. Prentiss, 18 January 1839, p. 54. Letterbooks, NBP, LC.
213 James Hagarty to Nicholas Biddle, 1 January 1839, No. 17,361. NBP, LC.
214 James Hagarty to Nicholas Biddle, 5 January 1839, No. 17,378. NBP, LC.
215 James Hagarty to Nicholas Biddle, 7 January 1839, No. 17,395. NBP, LC.
216 James Hagarty to Nicholas Biddle, 10 January 1839, No. 17,407. NBP, LC.
217 James Hagarty to Nicholas Biddle, 21 January 1839, No. 17,456. NBP, LC.
218 'Protested Notes Received From The Agricultural Bank', April 10, 1840. General Ledger No. 2, folio 515, $149,195.46. 'Discounted Notes Received From the Agricultural Bank'. General Ledger No. 2, folio 454, $94,175.31. BUSN, LLMVC. 'Bank of the United States in Account', General Ledger No. 1, folios 436-41. General Ledger No. 2, folios 200-02, 323-28. The Commercial Bank's bonds were transferred to the United States Bank on June 19, 1839. Journal, 19 June 1839, folio 6. 'Bank of the United States to Bonds'. 'Bonds', General Ledger No. 2, folio 410. Journal, 11 June 1845, 'Bonds to Morrison & Sons & Co'. 'Morrison & Sons & Co. In Account', General Ledger No. 2, folio 603. CBNC, LLMVC. A few very rare numbers of these bonds, issued by the Planters Bank to cover its debt to Brown Brothers, can be found in the Henry D. Mandeville Papers, Box 8, folder 83, LLMVC. The following is an example:

> NO. 23   ONE THOUSAND DOLLARS   NO. 23
> Know All Men by these Presents, That the Planters Bank of the State of Mississippi, acknowledges itself indebted to Samuel Nicholson in the just and full sum of One thousand Dollars lawful money of the United States, which sum the said Planters Bank of the State of Mississippi promises to pay to the order of the said Samuel Nicholson [the agent in Louisiana and Mississippi for Brown Brothers] in the just and full sum of One Thousand Dollars lawful money of the United States, which sum the said Planters Bank of the State of Mississippi promises to pay to the order of the said Samuel Nicholson, with interest, at the rate of Eight per cent per annum, from the first day of January One Thousand eight hundred and forty, until the payment of the principal of this bond. This bond is given in a settlement of bonds of this bank heretofore issued, in favor of W. & S. Brown & Co., which were payable in sterling money, in London, on said first day of January A. D. 1840.
>
> In Testimony Whereof, the President of said Planters Bank of the State of Mississippi hath signed, and the Cashier hath countersigned these presents; and the Board of Directors has caused the Seal of the Corporation to be affixed thereto, at the said Bank, in Natchez, Mississippi, this twenty-fifth day of February, One Thousand eight hundred and forty-two. J. P. Walworth, Prest.
>
> H. D. Mandeville, Cashier
> Endorsement without Recourse
> Samuel Nicholson

219 Joseph L. Roberts to John Bacon et. al., 23 January 1844, Letterpress Book 2, p. 322. Joseph L. Roberts to T. S. Taylor, 19 February 1844, Letterpress Book 2, p. 351. BTP, LLMVC.
220 James Hagarty to Nicholas Biddle, 25 January 1839, No. 17,490. NBP, LC.
221 Commercial and Rail Road Bank to James Hagarty, 26 January 1839, No. 17,506, NBP, LC.

222 Commercial Bank, Cash Account.

DATE	NET DEBITS ($)	NET CREDITS ($)	TOTAL ($)
1836			
31 October - 30 November	2,931,093.50	2,595,836.90	5,526,930.40
30 November - 31 December	3,357,160.00	3,293,017.30	6,650,177.30
1837			
31 December - 31 January	3,330,644.90	3,538,340.02	6,868,984.90
31 March - 29 April	1,716,352.40	1,557,501.10	3,263,853.50
1 August - 30 August	448,930.29	441,377.52	890,307.81
30 September - 31 October	488,698.10	478,352.22	967,041.30
30 November - 30 December	1,682,902.30	1,639,994.70	3,322,897.00
1838			
28 February - 31 March	2,695,149.50	2,702,682.80	5,397,832.30
30 April - 30 May	1,913,606.30	1,846,890.30	3,760,496.60
30 June - 31 July	581,190.40	571,791.90	1,152,982.30
30 November - 31 December	1,311,250.00	1,380,492.10	2,691,744.20
1839			
1 January - 30 June	7,499,517.20	7,543,927.50	15,043,444.00
30 June - 30 September	728,143.70	728,020.40	1,456,164.10
1840			
31 December - 31 March	2,460,286.80	2,153,969.80	4,614,256.60
30 April - 30 May	333,255.20	320,967.40	654,222.60
31 July - 31 August	63,691.16	73,949.15	137,640.31
31 October - 30 November	201,745.24	185,796.46	387,541.70
1841			
30 January - 27 February	912,343.20	784,581.50	1,696,924.70
27 February - 31 March	975,737.70	906,754.50	1,882,492.20
30 April - 31 May	554,179.70	514,529.00	1,068,708.70
30 June - 31 July	186,393.80	896,291.70	1,082,685.50
30 September - 30 October	348,810.10	269,291.70	618,599.70
30 October - 30 November	527,522.90	563,904.40	1,091,427.30
1841			
30 November - 31 December	807,594.00	774,917.60	$1,582,511.60

Source: 'Cash Account', General Ledger No. 1, folios 1-16; General Ledger No. 2 folios 1-18, 546-57. CBNC, LLMVC.

223 Planters Bank in Account

DATE	NET DEBITS ($)		TOTAL ($)
1836			
Oct. 31 - Nov. 30	177,648.81	255,591.15	403,239.96
Nov. 30 - Dec. 31	479,990.20	381,908.19	861,898.39
1837			
Dec. 31 - Jan. 31	389,675.63	435,472.62	825,148.24
Jan. 31 - Feby. 28	233,487.90	213,530.49	447,018.39
March 31 - April 29	105,018.24	69,612.01	174,630.25
May 31 - June 30	51,289.59	11,911.95	63,201.44
Sept. 30 - Nov. 30	94,198.03	9,389.29	103,587.32
1838			
Dec. 30 - Jan. 31	91,102.67	266,513.36	357,616.03
Jan. 31 - Feby. 28	143,022.53	137,338.14	280,360.67
April 30 - May 31	137,101.53	31,219.76	168,321.19
May 31 - June 30	6,122.84	20,849.59	26,967.43
Sept. 29 - Dec. 31	57,734.47	140,652.71	198,387.18
1839			
Dec. 31 - June 29	33,320.20	182,908.69	216,228.89
June 29 - Dec. 31	0.00	5,022.75	5,022.75
1840			
Dec. 31 - June 30	65,725.46	11,158.97	76,884.43

Source: 'Planters Bank In Account', General Ledger No. 1. folios 22-32. General Ledger No. 2, folios 19-21. CBNC, LLMVC. Thomas Henderson to J. Andrews, 25 January, 28 March 1839. Cashier's Letterbook. BUSN, LLMVC.

224 James Hagarty to Nicholas Biddle, 27 February 1839, No. 17,735. NBP, LC. 'Protested notes', General Ledger No. 1, folios 214-23; General Ledger No. 2, folios 134, 419-22, 466-77, 605-06, 613, 655-62. 'Protested Exchange', General Ledger No. 1, folios 330-39; General Ledger No. 2, folios 142-44. 'Notes and Bills in Suit', General Ledger No. 2, folios 430-33, 592-97, 684-86. 'Domestic Exchange', General Ledger No. 2, folio 80. 'Discounted Notes', General Ledger No. 2, folio, 75.

225 James Hagarty to Nicholas Biddle, 28 March, 2 April 1839, Nos. 17,942, 17,983. NBP, LC.

226 James Hagarty to Nicholas Biddle, 24 February 1839, No. 17,772, NBP, LC.

227 Stephen Duncan to W. J. Minor, 16 September, 6 December 1839, Box 2, folder 12, WJMFP, LLMVC.

228 Stephen Duncan to W. J. Minor, 7 August 1839, Box 2, folder 12. WJMFP, LLMVC.

229 Thomas Henderson to J. Andrews, 13 September 1838. Cashier's Letterbook. BUSN, LLMVC. Thomas Henderson to J. B. Mitchell, 12 March 1839, No. 17,827. James Hagarty to Nicholas Biddle, 25 January 1839, No. 17,490. NBP, LC.

230 Stephen Duncan to W. J. Minor, 7, 13, 28 August 1839. Box 2, Folder 12, WJMFP, LLMVC.

231 New Orleans *Price Current*. Schneider, *Wahrungen der Welt*.

232 Stephen Duncan to Jackson, Todd & Co., 8 April 1839. JRC, UNC.

233 Nicholas Biddle to C. A. Davis, 1, 4 October 1838, pp. 511, 518. Letterbooks. C. A. Davis to Nicholas Biddle, 1, 5 October 1838, Nos. 16,801, 16,816, NBP, LC.

234 Temin, *Jacksonian Economy*, pp. 144-7.

235 Nicholas Biddle to Samuel Jaudon, 3 October 1842. NBP, LC.

236 Samuel Jaudon to Nicholas Biddle, 5 October 1842. NBP, LC.

237 Henry Cary to Nicholas Biddle, 25 October 1842. NBP, LC. The Report is *Report from the Select Committee on Banks of Issue, with Minutes of Evidence Appendix and Index*. Session 16 January-11 August 1840. *Monetary Policy, General*, Vol. IV. Irish University Press Series of British Parliamentary Papers, (Shannon: Ireland: Irish University Press, 1968).

238 Bray Hammond, *Banks And Politics In America from the Revolution to the Civil War*, (Princeton: Princeton University Press, 1957), pp. 315-23; Peter Temin, *The Jacksonian Economy* (New York: W. W. Norton & Company, 1969), pp. 29-58; Fritz Redlich, *The Molding of American Banking: Men and Ideas* (New York: 1951), vol. 1, pp. 124-45; Tony Allan Freyer, *Forums of Order, The Federal Courts and Business in American History* (Greenwich: JAI Press, Inc., 1979), pp. 36-52; Tony Allan Freyer, 'Law and the Antebellum Southern Economy: An Interpretation', in *Ambivalent Legacy, A Legal History of the South*, edited by David J. Bodenhamer and James W. Ely, Jr., (Jackson: University Press of Mississippi, 1984), pp. 49-68; Tony A. Freyer, *Producers versus Capitalists: Constitutional Conflict in Antebellum America* (Charlottesville: University Press of Virginia, 1994), pp. 57-91.

239 Morton J. Horwitz, *The Transformation of American Law, 1780-1860* (Cambridge: Harvard University Press, 1977), p. 212; Freyer, *Producers versus Capitalists*, pp. 57-59; James Steven Rogers, 'The Myth of Negotiability', *Boston College Law Review* (1990), pp. 315-26.

240 'An Act, to render Cotton Receipts, Promissory Notes, Bonds, and Other writings Obligatory, for the payment of money, or other things negotiable: and prescribing the mode of protesting, Foreign and In land Bills of Exchange, and the effects thereof', approved 25 June 1822, pp. 382-5. *Laws of the State of Mississippi Passed by the General Assembly at the Adjourned Session of June 1822* Printed by P. Isler, State Printer; Records of the Bank of the State of Mississippi, 1812-1831, Mississippi Department of Archives and History, Jackson, Mississiappi; John R. Killick, 'The Cotton Operations of Alexander Brown and Sons in the Deep South, 1820-1860', The *Journal of Southern History* 43 (May 1977), pp. 169-94; John R. Killick, 'Risk, Specialization and Profit in the Mercantile Sector of the Nineteenth Century Trade: Alexander Brown and Sons, 1820-1880', *Business History* 41 (January 1974), pp. 1-16. John Hebron Moore, *The Emergence Of The Cotton Kingdom in the Old Southwest, Mississippi 1770-1860* (Baton Rough: Louisiana State University Press, 1988), p. 165.

241 Hammond, *Banks and Politics*, pp. 513-18; *The United States versus The President, Directors, and Company Of The Bank Of The United States* 8 *Robinson's Reports* (Louisiana) pp. 264-416, (June 1844); *United States versus The Bank of the United States*, 11 *Robinson* 418 (July 1845).

242 Assignment, John Bacon et. al. Trustees Papers, hereafter cited BTP, Louisiana and Lower Mississippi Valley Collections, hereafter cited LLMVC, Louisiana State University Libraries, Louisiana State University.

243 Minute Book, 16 November 1841, p. 42, John Bacon et. al. Trustees, 1390-C, Historical Society of Pennsylvania, Philadelphia.

244 Nicholas Biddle to J. C. Wilkins, 8 October 1838, p. 520. NBP, LC. Statement of Liabilities, 1 October 1840, Fidelity-Philadelphia Trust Co. Collection, 1390-A, The Historical Society of Pennsylvania, Philadelphia. Bond Account, General Ledger No. 2, p. 410, Commercial Bank of Natchez Collection, hereafter cited CBNC, LLMVC.

245 Nicholas Biddle to Samuel Jaudon, 31 August, 2 October 1838, pp. 496, 514. Letter Books, NBP, LC.

246 Domestic Exchange Protested, General Ledger, No. 2, page 67; Bills of Exchange Domestic, General Ledger No. 1, pp. 13-24, 470-76; General Ledger No. 2, pp. 20-35, Natchez Branch, Bank of the United States Collection, hereafter cited NB, BUS, LLMVC.

247 Notes and Bills Discounted, General Ledger No. 1, pp. 1-12; 310-21; 479. General Ledger No. 2, p. 1; NB, BUS, LLMVC. 7 November 1835, credit entry Sale to Planters Bank $871,024.47, in Bills and Notes Discounted, General Ledger No. 2, NB, BUS, LLMVC.

248 Joseph L. Roberts to Quitman & McMurran, 2 June 1843, Letterpress Book No. 2, page 117, BTP, LLMVC.

249 Interest Account General Ledger No. 1. pp. 230-34; General Ledger No. 2, pp. 310-19; 580-3; 676-9. Profit & Loss Account, General Ledger No. 1, p. 552; General Ledger No. 2, pp. 236-40, CVNC, LLMVC.

250 May Humphreys to Nicholas Biddle, 15 November 1839, No. 20,092, Vol. 88, NBP, LC. Stephen Duncan to William J. Minor, 5 December 1839; same to same, no date; same to same, no date; Box 2, Folder 12. Stephen Duncan to William J. Minor, 17, 22 February 1840, Box 2, Folder 13, Stephen Duncan to William J. Minor, no date, Box 2, Folder 14, William J. Minor and Family Papers, hereafter cited WJMFP, LLMVC.

251 Joseph L. Roberts to Quitman & McMurran, June 2, 1843, Letter Press Book No. 2, p. 117, BTP, LLMVC.

252 Such legislation helps to curtail the rise of 'zombie banks' like the failed Savings and Loans in the 1980s. Failed banks have a clear incentive to take large risks in the hopes of big gains that will make them solvent again. They literally have nothing to lose. Also, the managers of failed banks have incentives to raid the bank's assets for their own portfolios. For a fuller discussion, see David L. Mason, *From Buildings and Loans to Bail-Outs: A History of the American Savings and Loan Industry, 1831-1995* (New York, Cambridge University Press, 2004).

253 'An Act requiring the several banks of this State to pay in specie, and for other purposes', Chapter One, pp. 13-20, approved 21 February 1840. 'An Act Supplemental to an act, entitled 'An Act requiring the several banks of this state to pay specie, and for other purposes', Chapter Two, pp. 21-2, approved 22 February 1840. *Laws of the State of Mississippi Passed at a Regular Session Of the Legislature Held in the City of Jackson In The Months of January and February AD 1840* (Jackson: C. M. Price. State Printer, 1849).

254 Stephen Duncan to William J. Minor, 20 March 1840, box 2, Folder 13, WJMFP, LLMVC. emphasis added.

255 No. 117. 'An Act to provide Revenue to meet the demands on the Treasury, and for other purposes', sections 18-20, pp. 316-319. No. 118. 'A Supplement To an act entitled 'a supplement to the act entitled an act to incorporate the Trustee of the township and borough of Wilkesbarre, the Trustees of the township of Plymouth, and the Trustees of the Township of Hanover, in the County of Luzerne, passed the fourteenth day of April, one thousand eight hundred and thirty-five and for other purposes', extending the provisions of the act to Providence township, in said county, and to enable the Bank of the United States to close its concerns'. Sections 4-11 pp. 321-3, approved 5 May 1841. *Laws of The General Assembly Of the Commonwealth of Pennsylvania, Passed at The Session of 1841* (Harrisburg: Peacock & McKinley, 1841).

256 Nicholas Biddle to William Ayers, 27 April 1841, Vol. 96, NBP, LC.

257 Nicholas Biddle to D. Sprigg, Cashier of Merchants Bank of Baltimore, 18 September 1841, Vol. 98, NBP, LC. D Sprigg to Nicholas Biddle, 29 September 1841, Vol. 98, NBP, LC.

258 Kilbourne, *Louisiana Commercial Law*, pp. 173-202.

259 Nicholas Biddle to Joseph L. Roberts, 17 January 1837, p. 114; 31 July 1837, p. 229; 9 August 1837, p. 232; 15 September 1837, p. 251; 2, 25, 29 November 1837, pp. 275, 287, 289; 28 January 1838, p. 324; 19 December 1838, p. 31; 9 January

1839, p. 46; 9 April 1839, p. 117. Letter Books, NBP, LC. Joseph L. Roberts to Thomas S. Taylor, 19 July 1845, Letterpress Book No. 4, BTP, LLMVC.

260 Joseph L. Roberts to John Bacon et. al., 17 January 1842, Letterpress Book No. 1, BTP, LLMVC.

261 Joseph L. Roberts to John Bacon et. al., 12 November 1845, Letterpress Book 3, page 53, BTP, LLMVC.

262 Joseph L. Roberts to John Bacon et. al., 5 April 1842, Letterpress Book 1, BTP, LLMVC.

263 S. G. Wood to Nicholas Biddle, 26 June 1843, Vol. 103, NBP, LC.

264 Planters Bank Bond file, Mississippi Department of Archives and History, Jackson.

265 Joseph L. Roberts to John Bacon et. al., 12 November 1845, Letterpress Book No. 3, p. 53, BTP, LLMVC.

266 Joseph L. Roberts to E. Profilet, 23 December 1843, Letterpress Book No. 2, p. 235; Joseph L. Roberts to Fielding Davis, 6 January 1844, Letterpress Book 2, p. 279; Joseph L. Roberts to William Hardeman, 8 January 1844, Letterpress Book 2, p. 283; Joseph L. Roberts to John Bacon et. al., 23 January 1844, Letterpress Book No. 2, p. 322; Joseph L. Roberts to John Bacon et. al., 17 February 1844, Letterpress Book No. 2, p. 347. BTP, LLMVC.

267 Joseph L. Roberts to John Bacon et. al., 10 June 1843, Letterpress Book No. 2, p. 152; Joseph L. Roberts to John Bacon et. al., 24 December 1843, Letterpress Book No. 2, p. 236; Joseph L. Roberts to Fielding Davis, 20 March 1845, Letterpress Book No. 2, p. 694. BTP, LLMVC.

268 Joseph L. Roberts to Samuel L. Lambdin, 7 January 1843, Letterpress Book No. 1. BTP, LLMVC.

269 Chapter 3. 'An Act to prescribe the mode of proceeding against incorporated Banks; for a violation of their corporate franchises, and against persons pretending to exercise corporate privileges under acts of incorporation, and for other purposes'. Approved 26 July 1843. *Laws of the State of Mississippi Passed at a called Session of the Legislature held in the City of Jackson in July, A. D. 1843* (Jackson: C. M. Price & G. R. Fall, State Printers, 1843), pp. 52-7. Joseph L. Roberts to Genl. John A. Quitman, 17 November 1843, Letterpress Book No. 2, p. 206; Joseph L. Roberts to John Bacon et. al., 25 December 1843, Letterpress Book No. 2, p. 236. BTP, LLMVC.

270 Joseph L. Roberts to J. C. Passmore, 26 December 1843, Letterpress Book No. 2, p. 246; Joseph L. Roberts to John Bacon et. al., 17 February 1844, Letterpress Book No. 2, p. 347; Joseph L. Roberts to John Bacon et. al., 14 March 1844, Letterpress Book No. 2, p. 379. BTP, LLMVC.

271 Joseph L. Roberts to John Bacon et. al., 6 January 1844, Letterpress Book No. 2, p. 286. BTP, LLMVC.

272 *Ibid.*

273 *Ibid.*

274 *Payne, Green & Wood v. Baldwin, Vail & Hufty* (November Term, 1844) High Court Of Errors And Appeals, 3 *Smedes & Marshall's Reports* 661.

275 *Ibid.*

276 *The President, Directors & Company Of The Planters Bank Of The State Of Mississippi v. Thomas L. Sharp et. al.* (November Term, 1844), High Court Of Errors And Appeals, 4 *Smedes & Marshall's Reports* 17.

277 *Ibid.*

278 Joseph L. Roberts to George S. Yerger, 20 November 1844, Letterpress Book No. 2, page 561; Joseph L. Roberts to W. W. Frazier, 28 November 1844, Letterpress Book No. 2, p. 568. BTP, LLMVC.

279 Joseph L. Roberts to John Bacon et. al., 6 February 1845, Letterpress Book No. 2, p. 628, BTP, LLMVC.

280 Joseph L. Roberts to Dr. Wm. L. Balfourm, 6 April 1848, Letterpress Book No. 4, p. 109, BTP, LLMVC.

281 *The Planters' Bank Of Mississippi, Plaintiffs In Error* v. *Thomas L. Sharp, Edward Englehard, And Henry Hampton Bridges, Defendants In Error. Matthias W. Baldwin, George Vail, And George Hufty, Merchants And Persons In Trade Under The Name, Style, And Firm Of Baldwin, Vail & Hufty, Plaintiffs In Error* v. *James Payne, Abner E. Green, And Robert Y. Wood, Defendants In Error.* Supreme Court, (January Term, 1848); 6 *Howard's Reports* 301; *Bank Of The United States* v. *The United States*, 43 *U. S.* (2 *Howard*) 711, 735 (1844); *The United States* v. *The Bank Of The United States*, 46 *U. S.* (5 *Howard*) 382, 401 (1847); J. D. Doty to Nicholas Biddle, 29 March 1841, Vol. 95, NBP, LC.

282 *Planters Bank* v. *Sharp*, 6 *Howard's Reports* 301.

283 *John B. Nevitt v. The Bank of Port Gibson*, High Court of Errors & Appeals, (January Term, 1846); 6 *Smedes & Marshall's Reports*, 513.

284 'An Act authorizing the banks in this State to issue post notes, and for other purposes'. May 12, 1837. *Laws of the State of Mississippi, Passed at an Adjourned Session of The Legislature Held in the Town of Jackson, In January, 1837* (Jackson: Printed by G. R. & J. S. Fall, 1837), pp. 175-8.

285 *Planters Bank* v. *Sharp*, 6 *Howard's Reports* 301.

286 *Ibid.*

287 Joseph L. Roberts to Fielding Davis, 30 December 1848, Letterpress Book No. 4, p. 169, to T. S. Swift, 17 January 1849, Letterpress Book No. 4, p. 177, to John L. Goddard, 8 February 1849, Letterpress Book No. 4, p. 194, to Robert Jelks, 13 March 1849, Letterpress Book No. 4, p. 208, to Judge Edward McGehee, 16 June 1849, Letterpress Book No. 4, p. 272. BTP, MLMVC.

288 Joseph L. Roberts to John Bacon et. al., 4 May 1844, Letterpress Book No. 2, p. 441, to Fielding Davis, 20 March 1845, Letterpress Book No. 2, p. 694. BTP, LLMVC.

289 George D. Green, *Finance and Economic Development in the Old South, Louisiana Banking, 1804-1861* (Stanford: Stanford University Press, 1972), pp. 102-35.

290 Freyer, *Forums of Order*, pp. 36-52.

291 Joseph L. Roberts to John Bacon et. al., 18 November 1841. Letterpress Book No. 1. BTP, LLMVC.

292 *Natchez Courier*, 28 March 1853.

293 Hidy, *House of Baring*, pp. 277, 279, 310, 317; John R. Killick, 'The Cotton Operations of Alexander Brown and Sons in the Deep South, 1820-1860', *Journal of Southern History* 43 (May 1977), p. 169; *Pickersgill & Co. vs. Brown*, 7 *Louisiana*

Annual Reports 397 (May 1852). *Phoenix Bank New York vs. Agricultural Bank*, No. 19,041. *Brown Brothers vs. Jos. Hoxie & Co.*, No. 17,642. *The Governor and Company of the Bank of England vs. Samuel Hermann & Son*, No. 19,999. *The Governor and Company of the Bank of England vs. Martineau, Cueger & Co.*, No. 18,276. First District Court, Orleans Parish, Louisiana: Louisiana Division, New Orleans Public Library.

294 See generally Lance E. Davis and Robert J. Cull, *International Capital Markets and American Economic Growth, 1820-1914* (Cambridge: Cambridge University Press, 1994), pp. 1-9; Killick, 'Cotton Operations'.

295 Joseph L. Roberts to Messrs. Pinchard & Henderson, 10 November 1847. Letterpress Book No. 4, p. 39. BTP, LLMVC.

296 Temin, *Jacksonian Economy*, pp. 114-18; Green, *Finance and Economic Development*, pp. 99-101.

297 Joseph L. Roberts to John Bacon et. al., 13 December 1841, Letterpress Book No. 1. BTP, LLMVC.

298 Thomas Henderson to W. R. McAlpin, 7 August 1841, Letterpress Book No. 1, BTP, LLMVC. Thomas Henderson to J. Cowperthwaite, 20 August 1838. Cashier's Letterbook. BUSN, LLMVC.

299 Joseph L. Roberts to T. S. Taylor, 1 January 1844. Letterpress Book No. 2, p. 255. BTP, LLMVC. Parmenas Briscoe was not the bill's primary author. Its primary attribution belongs to a lawyer by the name of Ellett. 'An Act to provide the mode of proceeding against incorporated Banks; for a violation of their corporate franchises, and against persons pretending to exercise corporate privileges under acts of incorporation and for other purposes', Leg. Sess. 1843, Ch. 3. *Laws of the State of Mississippi Passed at a Called Session of the Legislature* (Jackson: C. M. Price and G. R. Fall, State Printers, July 1843), pp. 52-57. Section 8 provided that the loss of corporate powers under the act would not release those indebted to the bank from their liabilities. '[I]t shall be the duty of the court rendering such judgment to appoint one or more trustees to take charge of the books and assets of the same; to sue for and collect all debts due such bank or banks'. This provision was known as Judge Guion's amendment. Guion was the representative from Adams County. On Parmenas Briscoe generally see: J. F. H. Claiborne, *Mississippi, As A Province, Territory and State* (Baton Rouge: Louisiana State University Press, 1964 reprint, originally Jackson: Power and Barksdale, 1880).

300 Joseph L. Roberts to T. S. Taylor, 1 January 1844. Letterpress Book No. 2, p. 255. Joseph L. Roberts to Payne, Harrison, 28 December 1844. Letterpress Book No. 2, p. 582. BTP, LLMVC.

301 Steven Duncan to William J. Minor, N/D, Folder 12. WJMFP, LLMVC.

302 Joseph L. Roberts to W. W. Frazier, 4 January 1845 Letterpress Book No. 2, P. 606. Joseph L. Roberts to John Bacon et. al., 28 April 1843. Letterpress Book No. 2, p. 14. Joseph L. Roberts to W. W. Frazier, 17 January 1844. Letterpress Book No. 2, p. 308. Joseph L. Roberts to T. Davidson, 9 November 1847. Letterpress Book No. 4, p. 25. BTP, LLMVC.

303 Joseph L. Roberts to John Bacon et. al., 11 September 1845. Letterpress Book. No. 3, p. 11. BTP, LLMVC.

304 Joseph L. Roberts to John Bacon et. al., 18 September 1845. Letterpress Book No. 3, p. 15. Joseph L. Roberts to John Bacon et. al., 6 October 1845. Letterpress Book No. 3, p. 25. BTP, LLMVC.

305 Joseph L. Roberts to Alonzo Snyder, 30 January 1846. Letterpress Book No. 3, p. 143. BTP, LLMVC. With regard to James Erwin, see: Joseph L. Roberts to John Bacon et. al., 6 February 1846. Letterpress Book No. 3, p. 155. Thomas Henderson to Messrs. John Bacon et al., 7 August 1841. Letterpress Book No. 1. Joseph L. Roberts to W. W. Frazier, 20 March 1844. Letterpress Book No. 2, p. 385. Joseph L. Roberts to John Bacon et. al., ? May 1844. Letterpress Book No. 2, p. 443. Joseph L. Roberts to John L. Goddard, 1 May 1844. Letterpress Book No. 2, p. 440. BTP, LLMVC.

306 Joseph L. Roberts to John Bacon et. al., 6 February 1846. Letterpress Book No. 3, p. 155. Joseph L. Roberts to Robert Copland, 31 December 1845. Letterpress Book No. 3, p. 105. Joseph L. Roberts to John Bacon et. al., 1 July 1846. Letterpress Book No. 3, p. 282. Joseph L. Roberts to George Morgan, 5 June 1846. Letterpress Book No. 3, p. 267. BTP, LLMVC.

307 Joseph L. Roberts to John Bacon et. al., 28 April 1843. Letterpress Book No. 2, p. 14.

308 On the short-lived Bankruptcy Act of 1841, see Charles Warren, *Bankruptcy In United States History* (Cambridge: Harvard University Press, 1935); Peter J. Coleman, *Debtors and Creditors in America, Insolvency, Imprisonment for Debt, and Bankruptcy, 1607-1900* (Madison: The State Historical Society of Wisconsin, 1974), pp. 22-4; Edward Balleisen, *Navigating Failure: Bankruptcy and Commercial Society in Antebellum America* (Chapel Hill: University of North Carolina Press, 2001).

309 Joseph L. Roberts to John Bacon et. al., 28 April 1843. Letterpress Book No. 2, p. 14. BTP, LLMVC.

310 Joseph L. Roberts to John Bacon et. al., 23 December 1851. Letterpress Book No. 5, p. 192. George S. Yerger to L. M. Day, December 30, 1852. Letterpress Book No. 5. BTP, LLMVC; Moore, *Emergence Of The Cotton Kingdom*, p. 239; Joseph L. Roberts to John Bacon et. al., 4 May 1844. Letterpress Book No. 2, p. 441. BTP, LLMVC.

311 *Ibid.*

312 *Ibid.*

313 Joseph L. Roberts to G. C. Gwathney, 11 May 1844. Letterpress Book No. 2. BTP, LLMVC.

314 Joseph L. Roberts to Thomas Robbins & A. Symington, 4 May 1844. Letterpress Book No. 2, p. 441. BTP, LLMVC.

315 Joseph L. Roberts to John Bacon et. al., 13 December 1841. Letterpress Book No. 1. Joseph L. Roberts to Fielding Davis, 20 March 1845. Letterpress Book No. 2, p. 694. BTP, LLMVC.

316 Joseph L. Roberts to George S. Yerger, 28 February, 14 April 1845. Letterpress Book No. 2, pp. 677, 715. Joseph L. Roberts to G. S. Swift, 17 January 1849. Letterpress Book No. 4, p. 177. BTP, LLMVC.

317 Joseph L. Roberts to David Stanton, 25 January 1845. Letterpress Book No. 2, p. 622. BTP, LLMVC.

318 Joseph L. Roberts to John Bacon et. al., 28 December 1844. Letterpress Book No. 2, p. 589. BTP, LLMVC.

319 Joseph L. Roberts to J. J. Person, 10 May, 4 June 1844. Letterpress Book No. 2, pp. 450, 487. Joseph L. Roberts to J. Pinckney Henderson, 28 November 1844. Letterpress Book No. 2, p. 565.

320 Joseph L. Roberts to J. C. Passmore, May 10, 1844. Letterpress Book No. 2. p. 456.

321 Michael Tadman, *Speculators and Slaves, Masters, Traders, and Slaves in the Old South* (Madison: The University of Wisconsin Press, 1989), pp. 211-224; Joseph L. Roberts to J. L. Farmer, 20 May 1846. Letterpress Book No. 3, p. 252; Joseph L. Roberts to Messrs. John Bacon et. al., 5 August 1846. Letterpress Book. No. 3, p. 300.

322 Item 18,299-A, July 11, 1839. NBP, LC.

323 James Hagarty to Nicholas Biddle, 16, 18, 23 March 1839. Nos., 17,866, 17,874, 17,898. NBP, LC. Kilbourne, *Louisiana Commercial Law*, pp. 190-6.

324 'Assignment', BTP, LLMVC.

325 Thomas E. Robins to Nicholas Biddle, 25 July 1843. NBP, LC. 'An Act to amend an act entitled an act to prescribe the mode of proceeding against incorporated banks for a violation of their corporate franchises, and against persons pretending to exercise corporate privileges under acts of incorporation, and for other purposes, approved July 26, 1843'. Leg. 1846, Session January. *Laws Of The State Of Mississippi Passed at a Regular Biennial Session of the Legislature Held In The City of Jackson in January, February and March, A. D. 1846.* (Jackson: C. M. Price & G. R. Fall, 1846), Ch. 9, p. 118; *John B. Nevitt vs. The Bank of Port Gibson*, 6 *Smedes & Marshall's Reports* 513. (1846). *The Commercial Bank of Natchez vs. John M. Chambers et. al.*, 8 *Smedes & Marshall's Reports* 9. (1847). On debt repudiation schemes after the Civil War see John P. Dawson and Frank E. Cooper, 'The Effects of Inflation on Private Contracts: United States, 1861-1879: The Confederate Inflation', 33 *Michigan Law Review* (1935), pp. 422-46; Richard H. Kilbourne, Jr., *Debt, Investment, Slaves; Credit Relations In East Feliciana Parish, Louisiana* (Tuscaloosa: The University Of Alabama Press, 1995), pp. 92-9.

327 Joseph L. Roberts to T. S. Taylor, 18 April 1844. Letterpress Book No. 2, p. 424. BTP, LLMVC.

328 Joseph L. Roberts to John Bacon et. al., 11 May 1844. Letterpress Book No. 2, p. 454. *The United States vs. The President, Directors, and Company Of The Bank Of The United States*, 8 *Robinson's Reports* 262. (1844). Kilbourne, *Louisiana Commercial Law*, pp. 167-200.

329 Joseph L. Roberts. to John Bacon et. al., 28 December 1844. Letterpress Book No. 2, p. 589.

330 Joseph L. Roberts to W. W. Frazier, 4 January 1845. Letterpress Book No. 2, p. 606. Joseph L Roberts to John Bacon et. al., 6 February 1845. Letterpress Book No. 2, p. 628. BTP, LLMVC.

331 Joseph L. Roberts to John Bacon et. al., 17 July 1845. Letterpress Book No. 2, p. 805. BTP, LLMVC.

332 Joseph L. Roberts to Thomas S. Taylor, 8 August 1845. Letterpress Book No. 3, p. 5. BTP, LLMVC.

333 Joseph L. Roberts to Messrs. John Bacon et. al., 10 June 1846. Letterpress Book 3, p. 271. Same to Same, 18 June 1846. Letterpress Book 3. BTP, LLMVC.

334 *Ibid.*

335 Joseph L. Roberts to John Bacon et. al., 22 January 1847. Letterpress Book No. 3. Joseph L. Roberts to John Bacon et. al., 15 January 1848. Letterpress Book No. 4, p. 76. Joseph L. Roberts to T. S. Taylor, 1 February 1848. Letterpress Book No. 4, p. 86. BTP, LLMVC.

336 Joseph L. Roberts to Messrs. John Bacon et. al., 10, 13 March 1848. Letterpress Book No. 4, p. 95. BTP, LLMVC.

337 Joseph L. Roberts to John L. Goddard, 3 December 1848. Letterpress Book No. 4, p. 148. BTP, LLMVC.

338 Freyer, *Producers Versus Capitalists*, pp. 9-12, 15-25. Joseph L. Roberts to John Bacon et. al., 3 May 1844. Letterpress Book No. 2, p. 443. Joseph L. Roberts to H. Cope, 28 December 1844. Letterpress Book No. 2, p. 584. Joseph L. Roberts to John Bacon et. al., 6 February 1845. Letterpress Book No. 2, p. 628. BTP, LLMVC.

339 Steven Duncan to William J. Minor, Folder 14, N/D. WJMFP, LLMVC.

340 Steven Duncan to William J. Minor, Folder 14, July 27, 1842. WJMFP, LLMVC.

341 See Temin, *The Jacksonian Economy.*

BIBLIOGRAPHY

Secondary Sources

Balleisen, Edward. *Navigating Failure: Bankruptcy and Commerical Society in Antebellum America*. Chapel Hill: University of North Carolina Press. 2001

Bentley, Marvin. 'The State Bank of Mississippi: Monopoly Bank on the Frontier (1809-1830)'. *The Journal of Mississippi History* 40 (August 1978), pp. 297-318.

Bentley, Marvin . 'Incorporated Banks and the Economic Development of Mississippi, 1829-1837'. *The Journal Of Mississippi History* 35 (November, 1973), pp. 361-380.

Bentley, Julius M. 'Financial Institutions and Economic Development in Mississippi, 1809-1860'. Ph.D. diss., Tulane University, 1969.

Bodenhorn, Howard and Hugh Rockoff. 'Regional Investment Rates in Antebellum America', in Claudia Golding and Hugh Rockoff, eds., *Strategic Factors in Nineteenth Century American Economic Development*. Chicago: The University of Chicago Press, 1992.

Bodenhorn, Howard. 'Capital Mobility and Financial Integration in Antebellum America'. *The Journal of Economic History* 52 (Sept. 1992) pp. 585-602.

Chapman, Stanley. *The Rise Of Merchant Banking*. London: Unwin Hyman Ltd., 1984.

Chapman, Stanley. *Merchant Enterprise In Britain*. Cambridge: Cambridge University Press, 1992.

Claiborne, J.F.H. *Mississippi, As A Province, Territory and State*. Baton Rouge: Louisiana State University Press. 1964.

Clapham, *Sir John. The Bank of England, A History*. Cambridge: University Press. 1944.

Coker, William L. *Repudiation and Reaction-Tilghman M. Tucker and the Mississippi Bond question*. Floral Park, N.Y: Graphicopy, 1969.

Coleman, Peter J. *Debtors and Creditors in America, Insolvency, Imprisonment for Debt, and Bankruptcy, 1607-1900*. Madison: The State Historical Society of Wisconsin. 1974.

Cooper, William J., Jr. *Liberty And Slavery, Southern Politics to 1860*. New York. Alfred A. Knopf, 1983.

Davis, L.E. & J. R. T. Hughes. 'A Dollar Sterling Exchange, 1803-1895'. *Economic History Review* 13(August 1960).

Davis, Lance E. and Robert J. Cull. *International Capital Markets and American Economic History, 1820-1914*. Cambridge: Cambridge University Press. 1994.

Dawson, John P. and Frank E. Cooper. 'The Effects of Inflation on Private Contracts: United States, 1861-1879. The Confederate Inflation'. 33 *Michigan Law Review* (1935). Pp. 422-46.

Dickey, Dallas C. Seargent S. Prentiss, *Whig Orator of the Old South*. Baton Rouge: Louisiana State University Press, 1945.

Ellis, Richard E. *The Union at Risk: Jacksonian Democracy, States' Rights And the Nullification Crisis*. New York: Oxford University Press, 1987.

Fogel, Robert William and Stanley L. Engerman. *Time On The Cross, The Economics of American Negro Slavery*. New York: W. W. Norton & Co., 1974, pp. 89-94.

Frass, Arthur. 'The Second Bank of the United States: An Instrument of An Interregional Monetary Union'. *The Journal of Economic History* 34 (June 1974), pp. 447-67.

Freyer, Tony Alan. *Forums of Order, The Federal Courts and Business in American History*. Greenwich: JAI Press, Inc., 1979.

Freyer, Tony Alan. 'Law and the Antebellum Southern Economy: An Interpretation'. David J. Bodenhamer and James W. Ely, Jr.eds. *Ambivalent Legacy, A Legal History of the South*. Jackson: University Press of Mississippi, 1984.

Freyer, Tony Alan. *Producers versus Capitalists: Constitutional Conflict in Antebellum America*. Charlottesville: University Press of Virginia, 1994.

Genovese, Eugene D. *The Political Economy of Slavery*. New York: Vintage Books, 1967.

Gordon, Thomas Francis. *The War on the Bank of the United States, Or, A Review of the Measures of the Administration Against That Institution and the Prosperity of the Country*. Philadelphia: Key and Biddle, 1834.

Govan, Thomas Payne. *Nicholas Biddle, Nationalist and Public Banker, 1786 -1844*. Chicago: The University of Chicago Press, 1959.

Green, George D. *Finance And Economic Development In The Old South, Louisiana Banking, 1804-1861*. Stanford: Stanford University Press,

Hammond, Bray. *Banks and Politics In America from the Revolution to the Civil War*. Princeton: Princeton University Press, 1957.

Hidy, Ralph. *The House of Baring in American Trade and Finance, English Merchant Bankers at Work, 1763-1861*. Cambridge: Harvard University Press, 1949.

Horwitz, Morton J. *The Transformation of American Law, 1780-1860*. Cambridge: Harvard University Press, 1977.

Kilbourne, Richard Holcombe, Jr. *Louisiana Commercial Law, The Antebellum Period.* Baton Rouge: Paul M. Hebert Law Center Publications Institute, 1980.

Killick, John R. 'The Cotton Operations of Alexander Brown and Sons in The Deep South, 1820-60'. *The Journal of Southern History* 43(May 1977) pp. 169-94.

Killick, John R. 'Risk, Specialization and Profit in the Mercantile Sector of The Nineteenth Century Trade: Alexander Brown and Sons, 1820-1880'. *Business History* 41 (January 1974) pp. 1-16.

Lamoreaux, Naomi R. *Insider Lending, Banks, Personal Connection, and Economic Development in Industrial New England.* Cambridge: Cambridge University Press, 1994.

Mason, David L. *From Buildings and Loans to Bail-Outs: A History of The American Savings and Loan Industry, 1831-1995.* New York: Cambridge University Press, 2004.

May, Robert E. *John A. Quitman, Old South Crusader.* Baton Rouge: Louisiana State University Press, 1985.

McCulloch, J. R. *A Dictionary, Practical, Theoretical, and Historical, Of Commerce and Commercial Navigation.* Philadelphia: Thomas Wardle 1843.

McCusker, John J. *Comparing the Purchasing Power of Money in the United States (or Colonies) from 1665 to Any Other Year Including The Present, Economic History Services, 2005,* URL: http://www.eh.net/hmit/ppowerusd/.

McCusker, John J. *Money and Exchange in Europe and America, 1600-1775 A Handbook.* Chapel Hill: The University of North Carolina Press, 1978.

Mill, John Stuart. *The Principles of Political Economy.* London: Parker, 1848.

Moore, John Hebron. *The Emergence of the Cotton Kingdom in the Old Southwest, Mississippi 1770-1860.* Baton Rouge: Louisiana State University Press, 1988.

Morris, Christopher. *Becoming Southern, The Evolution of a Way of Life, Waren County and Vicksburg, Mississippi, 1770-1860.* Oxford: Oxford University Press, 1995.

Officer, Lawrence. *Between the Dollar-Sterling Gold Points: Exchange Rates, Parity, and Market Behavior.* New York: Cambridge University Press, 1996.

Redlich, Fritz. *The Molding of American Banking: Men and Ideas.* New York: Jefferson Reprint Corporation, 1968.

Redlich, Fritz and Webster M. Christmas. 'Early American Checks and an Example of their Use'. Business History Review. 41(Autumn 1967) pp. 285-8.

Rockoff, Hugh. 'Money, Prices and Banks in the Jacksonian Era'. Robert Fogel and Stanley L. Engerman, eds. *The Reinterpretation of American Economic History.* New York: Harper & Row, 1971.

Rogers, James Steven. 'The Myth of Negotiability'. *Boston College Law Review* (1990), pp. 315-26.

Rogers, James Steven. *The Early History Of The Law Of Bills and Notes: A Study Of The Origins Of Anglo-American Commercial Law.* Cambridge: Cambridge University Press, 1995.

Scheiber, Harry N. 'The Pet Banks in Jacksonian Politics and Finance, 1833-1841'. *The Journal of Economic History* 23 (June 1963), pp. 196-214.

Schneider, Jrugen, Oskar Schwarzer, Fredrich Zellfelder. 'Wahrungen der Welt I: Europaische und nordamerikanische Devisenkurse 1777-1914'. Stuttgart: Steiner Verlag, 1991.

Schweikart, Larry. *Banking In the Amerian South from the Age of Jackson to Reconstruction.* Baton Rouge: Louisiana State University Press. 1987.

Smith, Walter Buckingham. *Economic Aspects of the Second Bank of the United States.* Cambridge: Harvard University Press, 1953.

Sylla, Richard E., and Robert E. Wright. 'Networks and History's Stylized Facts: Comparing the Financial Systems of Germany, Japan, Great Britain, and the U.S.A.' *Business and Economic History On-Line 2004.* http://www.thebhc.org/BEH/04/syllaandwright.pdf.

Tadman, Michael. *Speculators and Slaves, Masters, Traders and Slaves in the Old South.* Madison: The University of Wisconsin Press. 1989.

Temin, Peter. *The Jacksonian Economy.* New York: W. W. Norton, 1969.

Warren, Charles. *Bankruptcy In United States History.* Cambridge: Harvard University Press. 1935.

Weems, Robert C., Jr. 'The Bank of the Mississippi, A Pioneer Bank of the Old Southwest, 1809-1844'. Ph.D. diss., Columbia University, 1951. Microfilm copy at the Mississippi Department of Archives and History.

Weems, Robert C., Jr. 'Mississippi's First Banking System'. *The Journal of Mississippi History.* 29 (November 1967), pp. 386-408.

Woodman, Harold D. *King Cotton and His Retainers: Financing and Marketing the Cotton Crop of the south, 1800-1925.* Columbia: University of South Carolina Press, 1968.

Womack, Douglas. *An Analysis of the Credit Controls of the Second Bank Of the United States, Including a Brief History of American Currency And Banking Leading Up to the Establishment of that Institution.* New York: Arno Press, 1978.

Wright, Gavin. 'Cotton Competition and the Post-bellum Recovery of the American South'. *Journal of Economic History* 34 (September 1974),pp. 610-35.

Wright, Gavin. 'Capitalism and Slaver on the Islands: A Lesson from the Mainland'. *The Journal of Interdisciplinary History* 17 (Spring 1987), pp.851-70.

Wright, Gavin. *Old South, New South: Revolutions In The Southern Economy Since The Civil War.* New York. Basic Books, Inc., 1986.

Wright, Robert E. *America's First Wall Street: Chestnut Street, Philadelphia.* Chicago: University of Chicago Press, 2005.

Wright, Robert E., ed. *The U.S. National Debt, 1785-1900.* London: Pickering & Chatto, 2005.

Wright, Robert E. 'Bank Ownership and Lending Patterns in New York and Pennsylvania, 1781-1831'. *Business History Review* 73 (Spring 1999), pp. 40-60.

Wright, Robert E. *The Wealth of Nations Rediscovered: Integration and Expansion in American Financial Markets, 1780-1850*. New York: Cambridge University Press, 2002.

Wright, Robert E. *Hamilton Unbound: Finance and the Creation of the American Republic*. New York: Praeger, 2002.

Wright, Robert E. *The Origins of Commercial Baning in America, 1750-1800*. New York: Rowmann and Littlefield, 2001.

Primary Sources

Manuscript and Manuscript Collections

The Papers of Nicholas Biddle. Library of Congress. Washington, D.C.

Commercial Bank of Natchez Collection, Louisiana and Lower Mississippi Valley Collections. Baton Rouge, Louisiana.

Bank of the United States, Natchez Branch Collection, Louisiana and Lower Mississippi Valley Collections. Baton Rouge, Louisiana.

William J. Minor & Family Papers, Louisiana and Lower Mississippi Valley Collections. Baton Rouge, Louisiana.

John Bacon et. Al., Trustees Papers, Louisiana and Lower Mississippi Valley Collections. Baton Rouge, Louisiana.

Henry D. Mandeville Papers. Louisiana and Lower Mississippi Valley Collections. Baton Rouge, Louisiana.

Jackson, Riddle, and Company Papers. Records of Ante-Bellum Southern Plantations from the Revolution through the Civil War. Kenneth M. Stampp, General Editor. Series J. Selections from the Southern Historical Collection, Manuscript Department, Library of the University of North Carolina at Chapel Hil. Part 5: Louisiana, Reel 19. Microfilm copy. Louisiana and Lower Mississippi Valley Collections. Baton Rouge, Louisiana.

Bank of the State of Mississippi Collection. Department of Archives and History. Jackson, Mississippi.

Planters Bank Bond file, Mississippi Department of Archives and History. Jackson, Mississippi. Jackson, Mississippi.

Fidelity-Philadelphia Trust Co. Collection. The Historical Society of Pennsylvania. Philadelphia, Pennsylvania

John Bacon et. Al. Trustees. 1390-C. Historical Society of Pennsylvania. Philadelphia, Pennsylvania.

Shiff vs. Shiff, No. 17,346, Second District Court, Louisiana Division, New Orleans Public Library. New Orleans, Louisiana.

Bogart, Hoopes vs. Byrne, Hermann & Co., First District Court, Orleans Parish, Docket No. 15,908, 20 April 1838. Louisiana Division, New Orleans Public Library. New Orleans, Louisiana.

Phoenix Bank New York vs. Agricultural Bank, No. 19401. *Brown Brothers vs. Jos. Hoxie & Co.*, No. 17,642. *The Governor and Company of the Bank of England v. Martineau, Cueger & Co.*, No. 18,376. First District Court. Orleans Parish, Louisiana. Louisiana Division, New Orleans Public Library. New Orleans, Louisiana.

Public Records (Printed) Federal Government

Gales & Seaton's Reports of Debates in Congress. 22nd Congress.

An Act to incorporate the subscribers of the Bank of the United States. Session, 1815-1816.

Bank Of The United States v. The United States. 43 U.S. (2 Howard) 711, 735. 1844.

The United States v. The Bank Of The United States. 46 U.S. (5 Howard) 401. 1847.

The Planters' Bank Of Mississippi, Plaintiffs In Error v. Thomas L. Sharp, Edward Englehard, And Henry Hampton Bridges, Defendants In Error. Matthias W. Baldwin, George Vail, And George Hufty, Merchants And Persons In Trade Under The Name, Style, And Firm Of Baldwin, Vail & Hufty, Plaintiffs In Error v. James Payne, Abner E.   Green, And Robert Y. Wood, Defendants In Error. Supreme Court of The United States. 6 Howard's Reports 301. 1848.

Public Records (Printed) State Of Pennsylvania

Laws of the General Assembly of the Commonwealth of Pennsylvania, Passed at the Session of 1835-36. Harrisburg: Theo. Fenn, 1836.

Laws of The General Assembly Of the Commonwealth of Pennsylvania, Passed at the Session of 1841. Harrisburg: Peacock & McKinley. 1841.

Public Records (Printed) State of Mississippi

'An Act to render Cotton Receipts, Promissory Notes, Bonds, and Other Writings Obligatory, for the payment of money, or other things Negotiable: and prescribing the mode of protesting, Foreign and In Land Bills of Exchange, and the effects thereof.' 25 June 1822, pp. 382-5.

Laws of the State of Mississippi Passed by the General Assembly at The Adjouned Session of June 1822. Printed by P. Isler, State Printer.

Legislative Acts of Mississippi. "An Act to Establish a Planters Bank of Mississippi. 13th Session, 1830, pp. 92-3.

'An Act Authorizing the Banks in the State to issue post notes, and for other purposes.' 12 May, 1837. *Laws of The State of Mississippi, Passed at an Adjourned Session of the Legislature Held in the Town of Jackson, In January, 1837.* Jackson: Printed by G. R. & J. S. Fall, 1837, pp. 175-8.

Laws of the State of Mississippi Passed at a Regular Session Of the Legislature Held in the City of Jackson In The Months of January and February AD 1840. Jackson: C. M. Price, State Printer. 1840.

Laws of the State of Mississippi Passed at a called Session of the Legislature Held in the City of Jackson in July, A.D. 1843. Jackson: C. M. Price & G. R. Fall, State Printers, 1843.

Laws Of The State Of Mississippi Passed at a Regular Biennial Session of the Legislature Held In The City of Jackson in January, February and March, A.D. 1846. Jackson: C.M. Price & G. R. Fall. 1846.

Payne, Green & Wood vs. Baldwin, Vail & Hufty. Mississippi High Court Of Errors And Appeals. 3 Smedes & Marshall's Reports 661. 1844.

The President, Directors & Company Of The Planters Bank Of The State of Mississippi v. Thomas L. Sharp et. Al. High Court of Errors and Appeals 4 Smedes & Marshall's Reports 17. 1844.

John B. Nevitt vs. The Bank of Port Gibson. 6 Smedes & Marshall's Reports 513. 1846.

The Commercial Bank of Natchez vs. John M. Chambers et. Al. 8 Smedes & Marshall's Reports 9. 1847.

Public Records (Printed) United Kingdom

'Report from the Select Committee on Banks of Issue, with Minutes of Evidence Appendix and Index'. Monetary Policy, General, Vol. IV. *Irish University Press Series of British Parliamentary Papers.* Shannon: Ireland: Irish University Press. 1968.

Public Records (Printed) Louisiana

Denton vs. Commercial and Rail Road Bank of Vicksburg, 13 Louisiana Reports, 486. 1839.

The United States versus The President, Directors, and Company Of The Bank Of The United States. 8 Robinson's Reports (Louisiana), pp. 264-416, (June 1844).

Daniel W. Coxe vs. Charles N. Rowley, 12 Robinson's Reports (La.) 276. 1845.

United States versus The Bank of the United States. 11 Robinson 418. (July, 1845).

Lanfear vs. Blossman, 1 Louisiana Annual Reports 148. 1846.

Bank of Louisiana vs. Briscoe, 3 Louisiana Annual Reports, 157. 1848.

Pickersgill & Co. vs. Brown. 7 Louisiana Annual Reports 397. 1852.

Foster & McAllister vs. Bank of New Orleans. 21 Louisiana Annual Reports, 338.

Newspapers

New Orleans *Price Current and Commercial Intelligencer*

INDEX